Oliver Optic

Palace and Cottage; or, Young America in France and Switzerland

A Story of Travel and Adventure

Oliver Optic

Palace and Cottage; or, Young America in France and Switzerland
A Story of Travel and Adventure

ISBN/EAN: 9783337173302

Printed in Europe, USA, Canada, Australia, Japan

Cover: Foto ©Andreas Hilbeck / pixelio.de

More available books at **www.hansebooks.com**

The Burning Steamer. — Page 41.

PALACE AND COTTAGE;

OR,

YOUNG AMERICA IN FRANCE AND SWITZERLAND.

A Story of Travel and Adventure.

BY

OLIVER OPTIC.

BOSTON:
LEE AND SHEPARD, PUBLISHERS.
NEW YORK:
LEE, SHEPARD AND DILLINGHAM.
1874.

Entered according to Act of Congress, in the year 1868, by
WILLIAM T. ADAMS,
In the Clerk's Office of the District Court of the District of Massachusetts.

ELECTROTYPED AT THE
Boston Stereotype Foundry,
No. 19 Spring Lane.

TO MY YOUNG FRIEND,

WALTER L. PALMER

THIS VOLUME

IS

AFFECTIONATELY DEDICATED.

YOUNG AMERICA ABROAD.

BY OLIVER OPTIC.

A Library of Travel and Adventure in Foreign Lands. First and Second Series; six volumes in each Series. 16mo. Illustrated.

First Series.

I. *OUTWARD BOUND;* OR, YOUNG AMERICA AFLOAT.
II. *SHAMROCK AND THISTLE;* OR, YOUNG AMERICA IN IRELAND AND SCOTLAND.
III. *RED CROSS;* OR, YOUNG AMERICA IN ENGLAND AND WALES.
IV. *DIKES AND DITCHES;* OR, YOUNG AMERICA IN HOLLAND AND BELGIUM.
V. *PALACE AND COTTAGE;* OR, YOUNG AMERICA IN FRANCE AND SWITZERLAND.
VI. *DOWN THE RHINE;* OR, YOUNG AMERICA IN GERMANY.

Second Series.

I. *UP THE BALTIC;* OR, YOUNG AMERICA IN DENMARK AND SWEDEN.
II. *NORTHERN LANDS;* OR, YOUNG AMERICA IN PRUSSIA AND RUSSIA.
III. *VINE AND OLIVE;* OR, YOUNG AMERICA IN SPAIN AND PORTUGAL.
IV. *SUNNY SHORES;* OR, YOUNG AMERICA IN ITALY AND AUSTRIA.
V. *CROSS AND CRESCENT;* OR, YOUNG AMERICA IN GREECE AND TURKEY.
VI. *ISLES OF THE SEA;* OR, YOUNG AMERICA HOMEWARD BOUND.

PREFACE.

PALACE AND COTTAGE, the fifth of the "YOUNG AMERICA ABROAD" series, is a further continuation of the history of the Academy Squadron in the waters of France, with the journey of the students to Paris, and through a portion of Switzerland. Like the volumes of the series which have preceded it, the book contains an outline-sketch of the history of each of the countries visited, a brief statement of its principal geographical features, a description of its form of government, and the note-worthy peculiarities of its manners and customs. As "Paris is France," the greater portion of the time of the young tourists was devoted to sight-seeing in the gay capital, though Havre, Rouen, Dijon, Mâcon, Lyons, Strasbourg, Chamouni, and Mont Blanc were visited. The tour in Switzerland included several of the lakes — Geneva, Lausanne, Montreux, Martigny, Sion, the Simplon, Altorf, Luzerne, Interlaken, Thun, Berne, and Basle. None of these places are minutely described, only their peculiar features being mentioned. So far as the work claims to be descriptive and historical, the greatest care has been taken to secure entire accuracy.

The story of the runaway cruise of the Josephine occupies a considerable portion of the volume; and if it inculcates in another form the trite but never worn-out moral, that "the way of the transgressor is hard," and the moral episode that it is unsafe to "fight the devil with his own weapons," it will only accomplish what the writer intended.

The first series of YOUNG AMERICA ABROAD, of which the present volume is the last but one, has been received with a degree of favor so far beyond the author's expectations that he is encouraged to persevere in his original purpose of including all the countries of Europe in his plan; though for the present it is more than ever incumbent upon him to acknowledge his sense of grateful obligation for the kindness of his young friends, as well as of their parents and guardians, and the conductors of the press, for the generous welcome and the unexpected favor accorded to these volumes.

HARRISON SQUARE, MASS.,
November 23, 1868.

CONTENTS.

CHAPTER		PAGE
I.	WHISTLING FOR A BREEZE.	11
II.	THE BURNING STEAMER.	27
III.	THE RESCUED PASSENGERS.	43
IV.	LANDING THE SURVIVORS.	59
V.	THE BAG OF GOLD.	75
VI.	THE LITTLE VILLAIN.	92
VII.	CABIN AND CROSSTREES.	108
VIII.	SOMETHING ABOUT THE GEOGRAPHY AND INSTITUTIONS OF FRANCE.	125
IX.	AN EPITOME OF THE HISTORY OF FRANCE.	142
X.	THE KNIGHTS OF THE GOLDEN FLEECE AT WORK.	166
XI.	THE CAPTURE OF THE JOSEPHINE.	183
XII.	A FEW HOURS IN ROUEN.	200
XIII.	THE KNIGHTS AT SEA.	217
XIV.	PALACES IN PARIS.	235

CONTENTS.

CHAPTER		PAGE
XV.	Rides and Walks about Paris.	252
XVI.	The Exchequer of the Runaways.	270
XVII.	The Presentation at Court.	288
XVIII.	The Way of the Transgressors.	308
XIX.	A Visit to Chamouni and Mont Blanc.	319
XX.	A Run through Switzerland.	334

PALACE AND COTTAGE.

PALACE AND COTTAGE;

OR,

YOUNG AMERICA IN FRANCE AND SWITZERLAND.

CHAPTER I.

WHISTLING FOR A BREEZE.

"THIS is lazy work," said Captain Paul Kendall, of the Josephine, to the vice-principal, as he paced the deck rather impatiently for a young man in his dignified position.

"Yes; but it will be lazier than this before it is any livelier," replied Mr. Fluxion.

"I'm afraid we shall not see Havre to-morrow," added the young commander.

"Probably not; for if I am not mistaken in the indications, we shall have a head wind before night."

"Well, I would rather beat dead to windward all night than roll about in one of these stupid calms," added the captain. "I hate calms."

"So does every genuine salt-water sailor; but we have no influence with the clerk of the weather, and we must take things as they come — calm as well as storm."

"I suppose we must," yawned Captain Kendall, as the topsails began to shake for the want of a breeze to fill them.

"By the way, captain, don't you think it's rather undignified for a commander to complain or grumble at the weather?"

"I know it is; but I never grumble at anything but calms."

"Do you expect to grumble up a breeze, Paul?"

"Of course not. The rule is, to whistle for a breeze."

"Then follow the rule."

"But I don't believe in it."

"Don't believe in whistling for a breeze!" exclaimed the vice-principal, laughing, and with apparent astonishment.

"I certainly do not," replied Paul; "though J remember being out with an ancient skipper at Brockway, who, when the wind died out, as we were going through a narrow place against the tide, began to whistle as though the safety of his venera ble craft depended upon the vigor of his piping."

"Didn't the wind come?" asked Mr. Fluxion.

"I believe it did, after we had drifted back half a mile," laughed Paul.

"Exactly so. The breeze came; that is all I want to prove. If you only whistle long enough, 'tis sure to bring the wind."

"But what has the whistling to do with it?" demanded Paul.

"I don't know; I can't explain the meteorological process by which the wind is started; I only know that, if you keep whistling, a breeze is sure to come, sooner or later. I never knew it to fail," added Mr. Fluxion, seriously.

"Shall I set the watch on deck to whistling, sir?" asked Paul.

"If you please. You command this vessel," answered the vice-principal, gravely.

"Do you really think, sir, that we can whistle up a breeze?"

"Do you really think you can grumble up a breeze?"

"No, sir; I do not pretend that I can."

"I only mean to say that if you whistle long enough, a breeze will come; and it is a great deal better to spend the time in whistling than in grumbling."

"I think I will not grumble any more, sir," said Paul, accepting the good-natured rebuke as kindly as it was given.

"Better whistle."

"But sailors are proverbial grumblers, Mr. Fluxion."

"Old sailors before the mast have a constitutional right to grumble; but it does not become an officer," replied the vice-principal, as he went back to the steerage to attend to his classes, which he had left for a few moments at recess.

Paul Kendall was full of life and spirit. He was impatient of delay, and had the American anxiety ever to be going ahead, even when he was in no hurry to reach his destination. The breeze certainly did not come for his grumbling; on the contrary, it died out entirely, and the Josephine rose and fell idly on the long swells, her sails flapping and beating as if they too were growling at the inactivity to which the vessel was doomed.

The Young America and her consort had sailed from Rotterdam that morning, and the squadron was bound to Havre, where the students were to be introduced to French life and manners. As boys, they were naturally impatient for something new. Paris, "the city of luxury," had a thousand attractions to them, and the libraries of the two vessels had been thoroughly ransacked for information, and especially for pictures, relating to France and its gay capital. Mr. Lowington, the principal, had always kept the students well supplied with newspapers, and especially with the pictorials, the latter of which, instructing through the eye, he deemed exceedingly valuable as educational agencies. In the bound volumes of the magazines and weekly illustrated papers were pictures of the streets, public buildings, parks, and people of Paris and other cities of Europe. These volumes had been in great demand since the ship sailed from Brockway, and some of the students declared, when they visited Paris, that its palaces and parks seemed as familiar as though they had often seen them before.

Paul was impatient, and though he was able to refrain from manifesting his feeling, it was not so easy to banish it from his mind. He walked the deck uneasily; but the vessel was making no progress, and it was impossible for him to be satisfied. He went below, sat for a while in his state-room, reading the letters he had last received. This occupation consoled him for half an hour, especially as he had a letter from Miss Grace Arbuckle, who was still with her friends in the vicinity of London, but who wrote that the family would soon start for the continent, and would be in Paris early in September. The young commander read the letter several times, but even its perusal did not seem wholly to satisfy him. The Josephine lay idly upon the waters of the German Ocean. Possibly he was afraid the delay would prevent him from reaching Paris in time to see his fair friend.

He went on deck. The Young America, as helpless as her consort, lay rolling on the long billows, less than half a mile distant. Paul voted that the calm was intensely stupid; and at last he found it so difficult to restrain the expression of his impatience, that he ordered the officer of the deck to call the watch, and set them to whistling for a breeze. Of course it was regarded as a merry joke on the part of the commander, and all hands gathered in the waist to execute the order. There was a noted whistler among the crew, who led them in Yankee Doodle.

"Do you expect to raise a breeze in this way, Captain Kendall?" asked Henry Martyn, the second lieutenant, who was on duty.

"Mr. Fluxion says it is better to whistle than to grumble," replied Paul; "and I have adopted his suggestion. He is sure that if we only whistle long enough, the breeze will come."

"No doubt of it," laughed Henry. "But I suppose the same result would follow if we grumbled long enough, and would be just as effectual as the other in stirring up the elements."

"Whether the whistling brings a breeze or not, it has a tendency to keep us good-natured," added Paul.

"That music is not so bad. I'm not sure that we can't beat the Young America's band."

The effect was, as the captain declared, quite pleasing. The boys whistled well, and there was no little music in their piping. It certainly soothed the restlessness of the impatient tars, and actually proved to be a new sensation. It was voted that Ben Duncan, who led the exercise, should be the "chief whistler" of the ship's company. At eight bells in the afternoon, the watch was changed; but the whistling was diligently kept up, though not with such a pleasing effect, on account of the absence from the deck of the "chief whistler." Unfortunately the breeze was very obstinate, and would not come even for all the industrious wooing which was bestowed upon it. The starboard watch whistled, and the port watch whistled. The sun went down; the exercises of the school-room were ended, and both watches whistled in concert, till such a whistling was never heard before; but the wind heeded it not yet.

"Whistling seems to do no good," said Terrill, the first lieutenant.

"We have not whistled long enough," replied Captain Kendall, laughing.

"We have kept it up for about four hours, I believe," added the first lieutenant.

"We may have to keep it up four hours more; but Mr. Fluxion says the wind is sure to come, if we whistle long enough."

Ben Duncan had changed the tune from "Yankee Doodle" to "Hail, Columbia;" which, however, did not seem to produce any better effect upon Old Boreas, for he still held out against all these earnest adjurations. But the boys enjoyed the exercise, and Ben led his piping orchestra through several of the popular airs of the day. Mr. Fluxion and Mr. Stoute listened to the concert with genuine pleasure.

"As playing cards may lead to gambling, I am afraid this sport will lead to pernicious practices," said Professor Stoute. "When I hear a boy whistling in the house, or in a public conveyance, I always conclude that his education has been neglected."

"I agree with you; but as a boy is taught to take off his hat when he enters a parlor, so should he be required to leave his whistle out doors. We will have no whistling in the cabin or steerage."

"It's coming!" exclaimed Captain Kendall, who, as a prudent seaman, cast frequent glances at the sea and the sky. "There's a ripple at the southward."

"I knew it would come, if you only whistled long enough," replied the vice-principal. "I never knew it to fail."

"It's coming from the south-west — dead ahead," added the captain. "Mr. Terrill, brace her sharp up, with her starboard tacks aboard."

"Man the sheets and braces!" shouted the first lieutenant.

"All ready, sir," called the officers of the watch from their stations.

"Haul on the jib-sheet! Haul on the main-sheet! Port the helm, quartermaster!"

"Port, sir," replied the petty officer in charge of the wheel.

"That will do. Belay, all!" added Terrill, when

the jib and mainsail had been hauled as flat as the course required.

These two sails caught the gentle breeze, and the Josephine began to ripple slowly through the water.

"Slack the weather-braces, and haul on the lee-braces!" continued the executive officer. "Haul in the fore-sheet! A pull on the flying-jib-sheet!"

The officers at their stations repeated the orders, each to the hands in his charge, as it related to his duty.

"Belay, all!" called Terrill, when the sails indicated were flat enough to draw.

"So much for whistling," said Paul, gayly, for the breeze seemed to bring a new vitality to his frame.

"I am glad you acknowledge the efficiency of the means, Captain Kendall."

"I am willing to grant that it is better to whistle than to grumble, especially when the fellows whistle as well as ours do."

"But I am afraid you have overdone the matter," added the vice-principal, as a smart flaw suddenly careened the vessel till the water bubbled up through her scupper-holes.

"I hope not," replied Paul. "The night is clear."

"These south-west winds are very unsteady; and you may have whistled up more wind than we want."

"We can take care of it, if we have," laughed Paul. "The Josephine is good against almost any south-west flaw, after she gets her bearings. I don't see any signs of bad weather, sir," added Paul, more anxiously.

"No; I don't think we shall see any very heavy weather to-night; but it may blow pretty hard before morning," replied Mr. Fluxion.

The wind freshened very rapidly, and the whistling appeared to have done its perfect work. As the vice-principal suggested, the wooing of the breeze appeared to have been overdone, for it was soon necessary to take in the foretop gallant-sail, and a little later the main-gaff-topsail, for the Josephine almost buried herself in the billows. Thus relieved, she sped through the water at the rate of ten knots an hour. Then to avoid running away from the Young America, whose best point in sailing was not upon the wind, it became necessary to lower the foresail, and take in the flying-jib. Under this easy sail she went along very comfortably. At ten o'clock, Paul went below, and turned in. Having a good conscience, and no immediate hope of seeing Miss Grace Arbuckle, he dropped asleep without any needless delay.

At eight bells, or midnight, the starboard watch was relieved, and the first lieutenant reported to the captain that the Young America was three miles ahead.

"Direct Mr. Humphreys to set the foresail," said he, turning over, and going to sleep again; for these interruptions were so frequent that they hardly disturbed him.

The wind was still fresh and flawy, and under the additional sail, the Josephine often reeled over until one unaccustomed to such accommodations might have found a good excuse for rolling out of the berth on the floor. Of course Captain Paul Kendall was too dignified to do such an absurd thing; and the uneasy motion of the schooner, as she rolled and pitched, head to the sea, did not even awake him from his peaceful slumbers.

At six bells in the morning there was a lively excitement among the quarter watch in charge of the vessel. Martyn, the second lieutenant, and Pelham, the second master, who had the deck, held a consultation together, while the hands on duty climbed upon the bulwarks, and gazed eagerly at the object which had attracted their attention. It was a bright light to the north-west of the vessel, which had just flamed up with startling brilliancy.

"What is it?" asked Pelham, anxiously.

"I don't know. Would you report it to the captain?" replied Martyn.

"I should do so, if I were in your place. I think it must be a vessel on fire. I can't think of anything else which would make such a light."

"You may inform the captain, if you please," added Martyn, as he raised his spy-glass to examine more carefully the bright light.

Pelham went down into the cabin, and knocked at the door of the captain's state-room.

"Come in!" replied Paul; and Pelham entered.

"We have just discovered a bright light bearing north-west; and Mr. Martyn directed me to report to you, sir," said Pelham.

"What is it?"

"I don't know, sir; but I think it is a vessel on fire."

Paul jumped out of his berth.

"Where is the ship?" he asked.

"She is about two miles to the leeward of us. We have been beating her two to one for the last three hours."

"I will be on deck in a moment," replied Paul, as he began very hastily to dress himself.

"Shall we change her course?"

"No; but call the first part of the port watch."

Pelham went on deck, where Paul soon appeared.

"How long since you discovered the light, Mr. Martyn?" he asked of the officer of the deck.

"Only a minute or two before I reported to you."

"Put her head for the light."

"Stand by sheets and braces!" called the second lieutenant.

"All ready, sir."

"Ease off the fore and main-sheets! Let out the jib-sheet!" continued the officer of the deck.

"Set the foretop-sail!" added the captain, after he had examined the light, which was at least ten miles distant.

Having the wind free now, the Josephine began to tear through the water at a rate highly creditable to her reputation as a fast sailer. The fore-topsail was shaken out, sheeted home, and hoisted up. But even then, Paul was not satisfied, and ordered the fore-topgallant-sail and main-gaff-topsail to be set. He felt that he was justified in crowding on all her spars would bear, and even in risking the lighter ones, for a fire at sea is one of the most terrible of calamities. At that moment, scores of men, women, and children might be struggling for life with the rude waves, and the existence of a score who could endure for another hour might depend upon the brief moments he should gain by pressing the vessel.

For half an hour the Josephine sped furiously on her errand of mercy. The Young America had also crowded on all sail, and was bearing down upon the burning vessel. The consort outstripped her in speed under her heavy press of canvas. Hardly ten minutes had elapsed since the light was discovered, and from a little flame, "no bigger than a man's hand," it had now become a broad sheet of glaring fire. The waters were illuminated for miles around, and the scene, terrible as it was, had an element of sublimity which filled the ship's company with awe. In half an hour, the Josephine had approached near enough to enable the young commander to make out the burning vessel. She was a large steamer. Her smokestack was still standing, and from it poured forth a dense volume of smoke and flame. A closer scrutiny assured him that her wheels were still working. The fire had apparently broken out near the stern, and her head had been turned up to the wind, so the flames could be confined to that part of the vessel. It was evident that she was in the hands of a brave and skilful man, who was doing all that human arm could for the preservation of her passengers.

"There will be a terrible loss of life, I fear," said Paul, with a shudder, to the first lieutenant.

"I saw a small vessel near her just now," replied Terrill.

"So did I; but she cannot do much. She is only a fishing-boat. Where is Mr. Fluxion?" asked Paul, who had been so little accustomed to rely upon others, that it had not yet occurred to him he had a superior on board.

"He has not been on deck," replied Terrill. "I suppose he does not know anything about it."

"Keep her steady as she is," added Paul, as he hastened below to the apartment of the professors, where he knocked at the door.

"Who's there?" called Mr. Fluxion.

"Captain Kendall, sir," replied Paul. "I wish to see you, sir."

"I will be out in a moment."

The captain sat down in the cabin to await the appearance of the vice-principal, who soon opened the door of his room.

"What's the matter, Paul?" demanded Mr. Fuxion, assured, by this unseasonable summons, that some unusual event had occurred.

"There's a steamer on fire within three miles of us," replied Paul.

"On fire!" exclaimed Mr. Fuxion, startled by the intelligence, for his long experience at sea enabled him fully to appreciate the nature of the calamity.

"Yes, sir; I was called more than half an hour ago."

"Why didn't you call me?"

"I was so busy, sir, that I did not think of you," replied Paul, honestly; "but I have done everything I could, and I hope I have done it right."

"No doubt you have. Do you make out the steamer?" inquired the vice-principal, as he hurried on the rest of his clothing.

"She is a large steamer, and seems to be very well

handled. The fire is aft, and they keep her head up to the wind."

"Is there any other vessel at hand?"

"The Young America is a couple of miles astern of us, and I made out a small fishing-boat near the burning vessel."

"What's the matter?" demanded Professor Stoute.

"A steamer afire," replied Mr. Fluxion, as he hastened to the deck with Paul.

"I have crowded on all sail, and we were making twelve knots just now, sir," said the captain. "Can I do anything more?"

"Nothing more can be done till we come up with the burning vessel," replied the vice-principal, as he anxiously surveyed the exciting scene.

A booming gun now broke upon the ears of the appalled beholders, and it was followed, at intervals, by others; and its dull, heavy sound seemed to be in harmony with the catastrophe it proclaimed to all within hearing. Miles away, on the fire-lighted ocean, were other vessels hastening to the scene of peril, guided by the noble instinct of the seaman, who heeds no danger in the service of the suffering and dying upon his chosen element.

Only a mile of white-capped billows, glaring with the reflection of the fiendish destroyer, lay between the Josephine and the burning steamer; and still the gallant bark leaped fiercely over, or impatiently cut her way through, the angry waves, towards the arena of peril. In the angry waters, without the aid of the glass, could now be seen men and women, clinging to various objects for support. Shrieks and groans could be heard above the dashing waves, and the crew of the Josephine were horrified by the scene which a closer inspection revealed. Paul felt that his blood was almost frozen in his veins, and he prayed that God would spare the poor wretches who were struggling with the fire and the waters before him. Though the schooner almost flew on her course, her pace was all too tardy for him. He was impatient to have the work of mercy begin.

"Call all hands, Mr. Terrill!" said he. "Pipe to muster, and see that the boats' crews are ready for duty, with officers detailed for each!"

"All hands on deck, ahoy!" piped the boatswain, who had been expecting the order for some time.

Strange as it may seem, nearly the whole of the starboard watch were asleep below. The regulations forbade any one on duty to go below without permission, and the startling news of the hour had not been communicated to the slumberers. Even the officer of the watch below had not been disturbed. There had been no unusual noise on deck. The manœuvre of tacking, reefing, or setting sail, with whatever of trampling feet and rattling ropes on the deck attended them, had become too familiar to rouse the sleepers. There was many a cry of terror, and many a shout of astonishment when the starboard watch tumbled up the hatchway, and discovered the appalling display.

The crew were piped to muster, and every one took his station, ready to do his duty to the sufferers in the water and on the burning hulk. Paul, in the loudest tones he could command, addressed a few stirring words to the ship's company, admonishing them to obey orders promptly and strictly, and not to expose themselves needlessly to the perils of the fire or the water.

"There is a high sea running, and the service upon which you go is dangerous," he added. "You have distinguished yourselves before by brave and noble conduct, and I hope you will do it again. Remember that the honor of your ship is in your keeping. Be firm and steady, but don't be rash. Clear away the boats, Mr. Terrill."

One after another all the boats' crews were called away, and the four officers who had been detailed to go with them took their stations near the davits, to superintend the preparations for lowering. The adult boatswain and carpenter inspected the boats and rigging, and reported to the first lieutenant that they were ready for use.

The flames were now making fearful progress upon the devoted steamer. Her smoke-stack suddenly went by the board, and her wheels ceased to turn. Two boats, which had been slung inboard abaft the paddle-boxes on one side, could not be reached on account of the fires. When her headway was stopped, she came about, and the fire made quick work of her then. The passengers and crew dropped into the water, and the waves were alive with them, as the Josephine came up into the wind to lower her boats. The gig and the three cutters were lowered, one after another, into the water, and the gallant young tars pulled for the scene of danger.

CHAPTER II.

THE BURNING STEAMER.

DURING the stay of the Academy Squadron at Rotterdam, two twelve-oar boats had been added to the former complement of the Young America. Though the four boats with which she crossed the ocean would accommodate all hands on an emergency, several considerations induced the principal to increase the number. A collision, or any other calamity at sea, which would render it necessary to resort to the boats, might destroy or carry away one or more of them. But, independent of the perils of the sea, exercise at the oars was good for the students; and, in some instances, the tourists could ascend rivers, or visit points, where the depth of water did not permit the passage of the ship, more conveniently in the boats than by public conveyances.

The two barges had been built in Liverpool to the order of Mr. Lowington. They were light for their size, but very strong, and were provided with air-tanks, which made them life-boats. After the ship was clear of the Hock of Holland, the first business of the officers was to re-arrange the boats' crews. In order to test the efficiency of the new details, and to prepare for any emergency, an hour had been taken from the studies, during the calm, and devoted to practice at the oars. Unlike the other boats, these barges were double-banked; that is, the two hands who pulled opposite oars sat on the same thwart — an arrangement admitted by their greater width.

The addition of these two barges required that the boats should receive new names. Thus far the flag-officer had been merely an ornamental personage. He had occasionally been called the "commodore;" but his position was one of honor rather than usefulness. In order to add to the glory of his office, one of the new boats was appropriated to his use, and styled the commodore's barge. He was to go on shore, or visit other vessels, in state, and a twelve-oar barge was necessary to support his dignity. The other of the new boats was called the first cutter; the captain's gig remained the same as before; the professors' barge was the second cutter, and the two four-oar boats were the third and fourth cutters.

The order of the Knights of the Golden Fleece was still in active existence on board of the ship. It was a rebellious band, whose only object was to do a "big thing" in the way of mischief. Its affairs, with the experience of several failures and disasters, were singularly well managed. All the clap-trap of signs, dialogues, and other mystical machinery, had been abandoned as dangerous; and no member was permitted to speak of the affairs of the order in the presence of those who did not belong to it. Wilton and Perth were the prime movers in the enterprise. They had already planned a voyage from Havre to Marseilles, which would occupy about ten days, during which period the knights were promised the best time that ever was known, or could even be imagined.

The members of the order had not much confidence in their leaders. Wilton was a bungler, and had always contrived to be in trouble half his time. They could not depend upon his management; for, however unscrupulous and bold he was, he had no talent for mischief. He was clumsy in his plans. Monroe was positively stupid, and did not pretend to do anything more than follow the lead of others. Perth was relied upon as a navigator, but he was not the fellow they needed for such a tremendous operation as the capture of the Josephine, in the face of all the difficulties which surrounded it. Those who had been members of the old Chain League, which had boldly planned the capture of the ship herself during her passage across the Atlantic, sighed for such a leader as Shuffles or Pelham; but both of these worthies now seemed to be beyond their reach. The former was one of the "chaplain's lambs," and the latter was second master of the Josephine.

Almost every member of the order thought he could manage its affairs better than any other one; and this is very apt to be the case in such organizations. They deferred to such geniuses as Pelham and Shuffles, but not to each other. However, Perth and Wilton had the affair in their own hands, and it was not easy to wrest the power from their grasp without breaking up the order and defeating the end in view.

Among the later additions to the organization was the young man who had volunteered to "serve out" Mr. Hamblin by dropping from the fore-yard of the ship upon the head of the dignified professor. He had done this trick so well, and played his part so cleverly in escaping detection, that he had won the admiration of his companions in mischief. He was a little fellow, and his name was Little, but he was a shrewd one. It was reported on board the ship that, small as he was, he had been so big in mischief his father could do nothing with him, and he had been sent over to the Academy Ship as a last resort. As soon as he was initiated as a Knight of the Golden Fleece, he began to take a prominent part in the affairs of the order. He was cunning and prudent, but he was bold and skilful. Physically he was but a pygmy; but his little body seemed to be composed wholly of muscles, and he was as limber as an eel. He could bend himself into all conceivable shapes, was as quick as lightning, and as nimble as a monkey. Indeed, his queer tricks had won for him the nickname of "Monkey," which, as it was a tribute to his agility, he did not resent.

At four bells in the morning, just before the burning steamer was discerned, the quarter watch on board of the Young America was changed. Little and Greenway were sent into the foretop to keep a lookout ahead. It was in this top, and on this duty, that Little had been inducted into the mysteries of the Knights of the Golden Fleece, on the passage from Antwerp to Rotterdam. He was now familiar enough with the machinery of the order to be greatly dissatisfied with it, and to growl at the tardiness of its movements.

"If you are going to do anything, why don't you

do it?" said he, fretfully, after Greenway had expatiated for a time upon the grand scheme of the knights.

"If we only had such a fellow as Shuffles, or Pelham, we would do it up brown in a few days," replied Greenway.

"Well, why don't you have such a fellow as Shuffles, or Pelham, or both of them, if you want them?"

"We can't get them. They belong to the lambs now."

"That's all in your eye. Bob Shuffles is no more a saint than I am. He has hitched a ten-pound weight to his chin so as to keep on the right side of the chaplain and the professors," added Little. "If you want him, I can ring him in just as easy as Wilton can make a blunder; and every fellow knows that is easy enough."

"It can't be done; Shuffles is a lamb, and if you open your mouth, he would blow on you."

"I can fetch him."

"No, you can't. He has done so well this quarter that he will be an officer next term. I shouldn't be surprised if he were first lieutenant, or even captain, of the ship or the consort."

"Bob Shuffles!"

"Yes, Bob Shuffles. They say he hasn't had a bad mark this term; and Lowington points to him as one of the good results of his system of discipline. You might as well approach the captain himself."

"Well, I shouldn't be much afraid to approach the captain himself," said the confident Little.

"O, get out! If you do things in that way, you will blow the whole affair," protested Greenway.

"The fellows here don't know me. When I spill the fat into the fire, you may burn up the German Ocean."

"What's the use of talking about ringing in the captain?" sneered Greenway. "Be reasonable."

"I tell you a fellow is a fellow, wherever you find him. Do you suppose any of them like this strict discipline? Why, a fellow can't sneeze without asking permission."

"It is different with the officers."

"I know it is, but the officers would like to have a good time as well as any of the rest of us. If we only had this ship to ourselves, what a jolly good thing we could make of it!"

"That's so."

"Do the fellows want Shuffles?" demanded Little.

"That's what they all say; that is, all but Perth and Wilton, who want to boss the job themselves."

"Are you sure?"

"Certainly, I am. Bob Shuffles got up the Chain League that I told you about, and if he and Pelham had not quarrelled, we should have had the ship — at least, I think we should. The plan was all arranged, and I don't see how it could have failed."

"We'll have him, then," replied Little.

"I'll tell you what it is, Monkey; you will make a mess of this business."

"No, I won't make a mess of it. I can crawl through a smaller hole than any of the rest of you, and I'll bet my life I can ring in Bob Shuffles with the lambskin on his back. I know just where to take him, and I can fetch him without telling him a single item of the plan till we have him bound hand and foot."

"I think, if we only had Shuffles, we could make the thing go first rate; but you can't get him."

"Bet your life on it I will!" persisted Little.

Neither of these conspirators deemed it absolutely necessary to the success of the enterprise that Shuffles should be introduced into the order as its leader and commander. Each of them deemed himself abundantly competent to manage the affair. Especially did Little take this view, for he had a high opinion of his own powers. But both of them were willing to grant that they were not available candidates. The popularity of Shuffles, who in ability and personal bearing was the equal of the commodore, or of either of the captains in the squadron, would secure obedience on the part of the knights. He could control them, for he had an influence which none of the present members of the order possessed. He was a genius.

Little did not condescend to explain to his fellow-conspirator the means by which he expected to induce such an important personage as Shuffles to join the order. He only talked mysteriously of certain resources he had which would accomplish the purpose without any danger of exposure. He had a hearty contempt for what he called the pretensions of the "lambs," though, in fact, they made no pretensions at all. He did not understand or appreciate simple goodness. He was of that class who believe that if a person joins the church, or otherwise assumes to be a good man, he does it from some sinister motive.

He could not see how goodness was its own reward, and how religion repays its followers by its very possession. If he could offer sufficient inducement to Shuffles, or even to the most upright of the officers, he was confident he would sell out to the powers of evil without a blush. A boy has reached a very dangerous state of mind when he can wilfully cherish a feeling of contempt for good people, and for goodness itself. It is one of the worst phases of boy character.

"What is that light?" demanded Little, suddenly, as the fire of the burning steamer flashed across the waters. "It's a vessel on fire! On deck, ahoy!" he shouted.

"In the foretop!" replied one of the crew.

"Vessel on fire off on the lee bow!" added Little, so sharp and prompt that he did not afford his companion in the top an opportunity to say a word.

The intelligence was communicated to the officer of the deck, who, after examining the light, sent the midshipman on duty to report to Captain Haven. When the commander of the ship came on deck, he ordered her to be headed for the burning vessel. Mr. Lowington was apprised of the fact; all sail was crowded on, and the ship flew through the water only less rapidly than the Josephine, which, however, was nearer to the steamer when the alarm was given. The principal approved of all that had been done when he came on deck, and manifested the liveliest interest in the fate of the unfortunate people on board the burning vessel.

For an hour the Young America continued on her

course. All hands had been called, the boats' crews piped away, and the officers detailed to command them. As she approached the scene of the disaster, the courses were hauled up, the main-topsail backed, and the ship was hove to. One after another, the boats were lowered, with the crews on board of them. Shuffles was coxswain of the commodore's barge, in which also Little pulled the stroke oar. It was in command of Mr. Ellis, the second lieutenant, who was a better scholar than officer.

The Josephine's boats had for some time been engaged in the humane labor of rescuing the survivors of the burning steamer; but there was still more labor of the same kind to be performed. The devoted vessel was now completely wrapped in flames, and there was no longer standing room for a single person on her decks. All her passengers and crew had taken to the waves for safety. The ship hove to on the weather side of the wreck, while the Josephine had gone to the leeward of it. The fishing vessel — for such it proved to be — was cruising about, picking up here and there a person. No other craft was near enough to render any assistance, though the light of the fire revealed several in the distance, which were bearing down upon the wreck. The ten boats of the squadron, therefore, were, with the exception of the fishing smack, the only ones engaged in the benevolent labor.

The commodore's barge pulled directly for the wreck, the oarsmen cheered on and steadied in their work by the voice of Shuffles. They pulled a splendid stroke, and were kept well in hand by their skilful coxswain.

Mr. Ellis stood up in the stern sheets, as well as ne could in the high sea which was running, on the lookout for persons in the water. They could hear shouts and cries coming up from the angry billows.

"Steady, as she is!" said the officer of the boat. "There is a man on a spar ahead of us."

"Steady," repeated Shuffles.

"Way enough!" added the officer, as the barge approached the unfortunate person.

"In, bows! stand by to help the man!" said Shuffles; and the two bowmen placed themselves in the fore sheets.

"You are running wide of him. Back water!" continued Ellis, as he saw that the boat would shoot ahead of its object.

Shuffles stood up in his place, and examined the situation of the sufferer. The barge was darting past him, the starboard oars were just over his head, and to back water at that moment would be to knock the man from his support.

"Starboard bank, toss oars!" shouted the coxswain, sharply. "Port oars, back water — steady, but strong!"

The effect of this manœuvre was to swing the barge round so that her stern came up to the spar to which the man in the water was clinging.

"Save me!" gasped the drowning man, over whom the waters occasionally swept with all their fury, and he was almost exhausted.

"Stand by here, and help pull him in," said Ellis to the oarsmen.

Little was one of the first to obey this order. He

sprang nimbly to the gunwale, and seized the man by one arm, while Shuffles had the other. At that instant the barge lurched heavily, and instead of pulling the sufferer in, Little was thrown out. The coxswain let go in season to save himself. A gust of wind carried the boat away the instant the hold upon the man was released.

"Let fall, starboard bank!" shouted Shuffles, promptly. "Back on the starboard, pull on the port oars!"

This action turned the barge, so that her head came round to the spar to which Little was clinging. As the bow came up to him, he seized it, and leaped into the fore sheets before any one could render him any assistance. At the same time a huge billow tossed the boat forward, so that it struck heavily against the spar. The fainting, dying sufferer had not strength enough left to resist the shock; he lost his grasp upon the slippery timber, and sank down into the stormy waves, never again to rise.

"Where is the man?" called Shuffles to Little, who had sat down upon the grating in the fore sheets.

"I don't know. I had enough to do to take care of myself," replied Little, puffing with the exertion to which he had been subjected. "He was there a minute ago."

Little glanced behind him into the water, and gave something like a shudder. Perhaps both the cold and the fate of his late companion on the spar were enough to make him shudder.

"He is gone!" said Ellis, coming forward, and glancing at the spar, as it rolled on the waves. "He was nearly dead when we reached him. Give way again, Shuffles. There are others who need our help more than he does, poor man!"

"Stern, all!" shouted Shuffles; and his tones were rather unsteady, for he was thinking of the unfortunate person who had just disappeared beneath the waves. "Hold water! Give way!" he added, when the barge was clear of the log.

These movements did not take place in the quiet of a room on shore, but upon the bosom of the heaving ocean. The sea itself splashed and roared; the oars made much noise; and the officers shouted their orders in the loudest tones, so as to be heard above the din. The scene was intensely exciting, and those in the barge could neither see nor hear what transpired on the spar a moment before the unfortunate man went down. Little himself did not know in precisely what manner he had been thrown out of the boat. Being short in stature, he had reached down so far that only his legs remained in the boat. The sufferer had grasped his arm with the tenacity of a drowning man, and it was no fault of the agile lad that he could not recover his balance when the boat lurched.

He clung to the spar as he went over; indeed, with anything at hand capable of floating a boy, it would have been quite impossible to drown him; for however his support rolled over, he was nimble enough to keep on the right side of it.

"Save me!" whispered the exhausted sufferer, as he saw the barge borne away from him.

"Hold on tight, and you are safe," replied Little. "Get hold of the boat when it comes up again."

"I can't," groaned the man, in broken English. "I have the gold in one hand."

"The gold! Give it to me, and I will throw it into the boat as it comes up."

The wretch clung to his money, even while he seemed to have but a moment's lease of life. He had one arm over the spar, and with that hand clutched a bag of gold, which he had brought with him from the burning vessel. Shuffles had seized his arm, but, instead of making an effort to assist in saving himself, the man had clung to the gold. In clinging to that, his arm encircled the spar, so that the coxswain could not lift him out of the water, as he would have done if the object of his labors had not been thus encumbered.

The sufferer gave the bag of gold to Little, who had placed himself astride of the spar, just as the barge came up. Dropping the treasure upon the bow grating, he leaped into the boat, much exhausted by the labor and excitement through which he had passed. At the same time the bowmen came forward again, but Little was sitting on the bag of gold. When the barge struck the spar, the latter rolled over. Deprived of his support, the poor man had no power to make another effort, and went down.

Little remained in the bow, getting his wind again, as the boat went on her way in search of others who needed assistance. The bag was heavy, and it had cost him no little effort to save it. We must do him the justice to say that he had no evil intentions either in regard to the man or the treasure. He had done his best to save both, and his shudder was occasioned by the thought that a human being had at that instant gone from life to eternity. The wretch had perilled his life for his gold. The gold had been saved, but the life had been lost.

"Are you hurt, Little?" called the officer in charge to him.

"No, sir; I am only tired out."

But he had recovered his breath, and was shivering with cold. He had regained his strength, and he felt that the exercise at the oar would do him good. He was about to rise, and go aft to take his place, when he thought of the bag. At such a time, and in the midst of such a scene, the gold for which men sell their souls seemed to be of little value. What should he do with it? It was no time to talk about it then. He dropped the heavy bag in the pocket of his pea-jacket. It weighed eight or nine pounds, and he was obliged to hold up the side of his coat with one hand, as he crept between the rowers to his seat.

Ellis stood up on the stern sheets, looking all around in search of those who needed help. Though the ocean was lighted up by the flames of the burning steamer, it was not easy to find them, for the boat sank down into the trough of each succeeding billow, and they could only be discovered as they were lifted on the crests of the waves.

"I see one!" shouted he, furiously.

"Where away?" asked Shuffles, standing up in his place.

"Broad on the port bow. He has sunk down into the trough of the sea now. Be more careful this time. Don't run into him. Obey my orders as I give them," replied Ellis, sharply.

"Help, help!" came, in the tones of a female, from the direction the officer had indicated.

"It's a woman!" exclaimed Shuffles.

"Don't run into her, then," repeated Ellis.

"Way enough! Hold water!" added Shuffles.

"You are not within five rods of her yet. Give way again, and steer a little wide of her."

"Take the tiller lines, Mr. Ellis," continued Shuffles. "I will go forward myself, and use the boat-hook!"

Shuffles went forward, the officer making no objection, thinking, perhaps, that he was more likely to make a mistake than the coxswain.

"Way enough! Hold water!" cried Ellis, when the barge which he had steered wide of the object was coming up alongside of the woman.

He intended, when abreast of her, to pull the port oars so as to throw the boat up without the danger of hitting the woman with the bow, for he believed that the man had been lost in this manner. But he was too late. The bow of the barge struck a long spar, to which the person was clinging, at least ten feet from her, repeating the very thing which the coxswain had done. The keel of the boat slid upwards on the spar, lifting the bow so that the water poured in over the stern. Shuffles was quick, and, striking the point of the boat-hook into the stick, he pushed the barge clear of it. But the mischief had been done. The collusion threw the woman from the spar, and she was struggling unaided in the waves, while the boat was receding from her.

The sight filled the gallant coxswain with dismay. It seemed as though another life was about to be sacrificed to the blundering mismanagement of the boat. Kicking off his shoes, and throwing off his pea-jacket and coat, he leaped into the surging tide, as he saw the struggling female rise shrieking upon the crest of a wave, not twenty feet from him, but apparently in the act of sinking beneath the remorseless waters. It was rash, but it was noble.

CHAPTER III.

THE RESCUED PASSENGERS.

BY the time the Young America reached the scene of disaster, the boats of the Josephine had returned to the schooner, loaded with persons from the burning steamer, who had taken to the water to escape the fire. Captain Kendall gave them a hearty welcome, and used every effort to make them comfortable. The boats were sent away a second time just as the ship came up to take part in the humane work. The steamer was from London, bound for Rotterdam. All the passengers knew of the fire was, that an explosion had taken place in the hold, which was immediately followed by the bursting out of the flames so fiercely as to defy all efforts to subdue them.

The consort's four boats again pulled towards the steamer, separating as they left the vessel, so as to give to each a wider field of labor. Some of the surviving passengers were floating on life-preservers, or clinging to barrels, doors, timbers, and other articles, which had been thrown overboard to sustain them. It was painfully evident that many of them had gone down never to rise again, and, in spite of the excitement of the occasion to the young tars, there was a terrible sadness about it which they could not escape.

It was awful to feel that they were in the midst of the harvest of death, and that many were sinking to their last sleep in spite of all their exertions to save them.

Pelham, in the gig, pulled close up to the ill-fated steamer, whose decks were now in a light blaze from stem to stern. No person could be seen on any part of the wreck,—and, indeed, it would have been impossible for a person to live there a single instant,—but several were clinging to the paddles, and other available portions of the hull. They were taken into the gig, which soon had as many as she could safely carry in the heavy sea.

"Pull for the schooner," said Pelham to his coxswain, when he had taken in the last person he could find on the wreck.

"Help, help!" came up from the uneasy billows ahead of them.

"Steady! Way enough!" shouted the active Pelham, as he sprang into the bow of the gig, for, unlike Ellis in the barge, he placed himself where he could see the person he was to save; and of the two boat loads he had picked up, he had drawn in nearly every one with his own hands, assisted by the stout bowmen.

"Way enough!" repeated the coxswain.

"Hold water!" called Pelham. "Steady! Now one stroke ahead!"

Thus carefully he avoided running into the objects of his exertions, or striking with the bow of the boat the supports to which they were clinging. There was no bungling in the gig, as in the commodore's barge, where poor Shuffles had been driven to desperation by the inefficiency of his officer.

"Help!" gasped a man in the water, who was holding on to a plank, and supporting a woman.

"Stand by here, bowmen!" said Pelham, as he grasped the arm of the helpless woman.

"Give me a hand at it," interposed a stout man, who had just been taken in from the rudder of the steamer.

The poor woman was quickly hauled into the gig. She was completely exhausted, and utterly unable to help herself. Her companion was then taken in, and Pelham ordered the coxswain to give way again for the Josephine.

"My daughter! My daughter!" exclaimed the man, who had just been saved, as he gazed eagerly around him on the fire-lighted waves.

"Where is she?" asked Pelham.

"I do not know. She cannot be far from this spot."

"Mr. Arbuckle!" ejaculated the stout man, who had aided in the rescue of the man and woman.

"O, Captain Millbrook! I have lost my daughter!" groaned the unfortunate gentleman.

"Is this Mr. Arbuckle, of Belfast?" asked Pelham.

"Yes; save my daughter!" cried the unhappy father.

"It will not be prudent for me to take in another person," replied Pelham. "The boat is crowded now."

"Do not abandon her!" pleaded Mr. Arbuckle.

"There are nine other boats besides that fishing vessel, picking up the people. Probably she had been saved by some of them."

"I thought your daughter was with you," said Captain Millbrook, who was the commander of the unfortunate steamer.

"She was with me, but a heavy wave broke up the raft I had made, and separated us," replied Mr. Arbuckle. "I drew the plank across a couple of spars I found in the water, and we floated a short distance from the fire. A wave washed the plank from the spars, and my wife lost her hold. I succeeded in drawing her to the plank, but by the time I had done so, one of the spars, with my daughter upon it, had been driven beyond my reach. I am afraid she is lost."

"It's a terrible night," replied the stout captain, with a shudder, as he thought of those who had been hurried from their sleep to the sleep of death.

The gig pulled to the Josephine, and the passengers were assisted on board. By this time Mrs. Arbuckle had partially recovered her strength, and wailed bitterly for her daughter.

"Captain Kendall, Mr. and Mrs. Arbuckle are here!" called Pelham from his place in the stern sheets of the gig.

"Is Grace with them?" demanded Paul, the blood in his veins almost frozen by the intelligence.

"She was with them, but we have not found her yet."

The young commander heard the agonizing story from the lips of the father and mother as the gig departed a third time on her errand of mercy. The ten boats of the squadron pulled around the steamer several times, till not another person could be found. The Josephine's boats had picked up nearly all the survivors before the ship came to the scene of action, and not more than a dozen passengers had been conveyed to the latter. The gig repaired at once to the locality where Mr. and Mrs. Arbuckle had been saved, and searched eagerly to the leeward of it for the lost daughter. Pelham found several spars, planks, doors, and other articles which had supported the passengers, but he could not find Grace. She had gone down in the waves, or been rescued by some other boat.

Diligently and faithfully the squadron's boats cruised the ground over till not another person could be found. The wind was increasing in violence, and there were indications of bad weather. The crews were all wet to the skin by the flying spray, which now enveloped the boats, and it was no longer prudent to continue the search, even if there were hope of saving another individual. The signal for the return was hoisted on board the ship, and the weary oarsmen pulled for their respective vessels.

Though the boats of the squadron had frequently come within hail of each other, no communication had passed between them, for each avoided the others the more effectually to perform its appointed work. Where one boat was, another was not needed. Just as the gig of the Josephine had picked up Mr. Arbuckle and his wife, the commodore's barge came up to leeward of her, and struck the spar to which the woman was clinging.

Instead of going into the fore sheets, where he could intelligently direct the movements of the barge, Ellis remained in the stern. Shuffles was too good a seaman to prompt an officer in regard to his duty; but he had gone forward himself to do what the lieutenant neglected. Without knowing the true reason why the man upon the spar had been lost, he believed that he had been sacrificed to the mismanagement of the boat. It was mortifying to have the blunder repeated.

Shuffles saw the woman on the spar, and saw her fall struggling from her support when the boat struck it. The sight was too much for his nerves. He was made desperate by it, and leaped into the angry waves, as has before been related, to save her. He was an expert and powerful swimmer — one of the best in the squadron. He could not see the woman perish before his eyes, as the man had, for he realized that she had no power to do anything for herself. Breasting the huge waves with iron muscles, he reached the unfortunate lady, and grasping her with a strong arm, he struck for the floating spar, which was almost within his grasp. Without this friendly support, he would have been almost as helpless as his frail burden. Throwing his disengaged arm over the spar, he clung to it, skilfully counteracting, as far as he was able, the struggles of the female and the violent action of the waves. A less resolute and powerful person than himself must have been sacrificed in that fierce struggle for life.

Shuffles was more afraid of being struck and rendered helpless by the barge, under the awkward management of the lieutenant, than of being swept away by the waves. The boat, after sliding off the spar, had drifted away broadside to the leeward. Ellis was confused and uncertain; but the two bowmen, who had gone to the fore sheets to assist Shuffles, kept their gaze fixed upon him while he was in the water.

"Pull, port!" shouted one of them; and the crew, in the fierce excitement of the moment, obeyed the order, without considering that it was not given by an officer.

This threw the barge round, so that she was again headed towards the spar.

"Give way!" shouted Ellis, as he caught a glance of the coxswain.

"Way enough!" called one of the bowmen, after the crew had given a few vigorous strokes.

The other struck his boat-hook into the spar, and thus prevented a collision, while both of them seized hold of the lady. She was drawn into the boat without difficulty, and the coxswain followed her. The two bowmen resumed their oars, and the barge, with Ellis still at the tiller ropes, pulled away in search of other sufferers.

Shuffles found that the person he had saved was a young lady. Taking the handkerchief from the pocket of his pea-jacket, he tenderly wiped the water from her face, and smoothed back the long hair from her brow. She was not unconscious, but her strength was exhausted by the fearful struggle through which she had passed. She shivered with the cold, and the coxswain wrapped her up in his pea-jacket, placing her in a reclining posture in the bottom of the boat. Having done this kindness to the poor girl, he went aft, and took his place at the tiller ropes.

"Is she dead?" asked Ellis.

"No; she will do very well, I think," replied Shuffles, his teeth chattering with the cold.

"It was very rash for you to do what you did," added the officer of the boat.

"The girl would have been drowned if I had not done it. She was the second person we had knocked off a spar by our clumsiness, and I was ashamed of it."

"You did not obey my orders," answered Ellis.

"I intended to do my duty."

"So did I," replied Ellis, rather sharply.

There might have been a dispute, if another sufferer had not been discovered at that moment. He was picked up, and proved to be a fireman of the steamer, who had clung to a tub for support. This was the last person saved by the barge, and when the signal appeared, the boats returned to the ship, not a moment too soon, for the wind was now blowing a gale, and it was with the greatest difficulty that the boats were hoisted up to the davits. Those from the ship had saved only twelve persons, while those from the Josephine had brought in nearly sixty.

The young lady rescued by the barge was borne to the main cabin, where a good fire had been made in the stove, in anticipation of the sufferings of the survivors. Dr. Winstock, the surgeon, immediately attended to her case, and she was made as comfortable as the resources of the ship would permit.

"Where are my father and mother?" asked she, as soon as she was carried into the cabin.

"I hope they are saved," replied the doctor, tenderly.

"We were separated by a great wave, and I am afraid they are lost," she added with a wail of agony.

"Hope for the best. Have I not seen you before?" inquired Dr. Winstock, as he gazed earnestly into the face of the patient.

"Yes. I am Miss Arbuckle; but my father and mother!"

"I have no doubt they are saved."

"Where are they?"

"They are not on board of this ship, certainly," replied the doctor, much embarrassed by the grief and terror of the poor girl.

It was the fair Grace Arbuckle whom Shuffles had rescued from certain death; but it is not surprising that her deliverers had not at first recognized her, so changed was her appearance under the pressure of this terrible calamity. She did not seem to realize that she was in the company of friends. She looked bewildered, and hardly noticed anything around her.

"My father! My mother!" was her oft-repeated cry.

"Do not despair, Miss Grace," said the kind doctor. "I feel almost certain that your father and mother were saved."

"I fear they are lost! Poor mother!"

"The Josephine is close by the ship, and they may be on board of her," added the doctor.

"Can't you ascertain? O, find them if you can!" pleaded the poor girl.

"The wind is blowing a gale now, and the boats were only recalled to keep them from being swamped," answered Dr. Winstock. "It would be impossible to send a boat to the Josephine now."

"Where is Captain Kendall?" asked she, perhaps with a feeling that so devoted a friend could aid her in this extremity.

"He is still in the Josephine. She was nearer to the steamer when the fire was discovered, and, sailing faster than the ship, had her boats out half an hour before us. I feel confident that your parents were saved either by her or by the fishing vessel."

"O, if I only knew it, how happy I should be!" cried Grace, clasping her hands.

A state-room was prepared for the forlorn girl, and the doctor insisted that she should remove her wet clothing, and go to bed. She cared not for herself, and it required a great deal of persuasion to induce her to do so. The doctor buried her in blankets after she had retired, and physically she was soon made comfortable; but for her agonizing suspense in regard to her father and mother there was no present remedy.

The day dawned cold and stormy upon the little squadron, still lying to near the scene of disaster. Other vessels had come up; but the work was all done, and they went on their way. The steamer had burned to the water's edge, and, foundering in the heavy sea, had gone down. The little fishing vessel was still rolling and pitching on the angry waves; but as soon as it was light enough to see, a signal of distress was discovered at her mast-head. Under reefed topsails and courses, with all hands at their stations, the ship wore round, and stood for the vessel. Peaks, the adult boastswain, who had a voice like a bull, was sent into the weather main rigging to hail her as the Young America passed to leeward.

"Stand by tacks and sheets!" shouted the first lieutenant, as the ship approached the fisherman. "All ready to clew up the courses!"

"All ready, sir," reported officers.

"Let go tacks and sheets! Clew up!"

"Sloop, ahoy!" shouted Peaks, through a speaking trumpet.

"On board the ship!" came hoarsely back.

"What's the matter?"

"I have more than I can carry," responded the skipper of the sloop, as the Young America swept on out of hearing.

"That's bad," said Mr. Lowington, anxiously, as he glanced at the raging sea, which was rapidly increasing in fury.

"She is very much crowded, sir," added the boatswain; "and she will lose some of her people overboard in this gale."

"It will blow heavier before it is over; and what we do must be done quickly," continued the principal.

"I think the barge will make tolerably good weather of it, sir."

"Who is coxswain of the barge?"

"Shuffles, sir."

"Pass the word for Shuffles."

The coxswain of the commodore's barge touched his cap to the principal, who simply made some inquiries in regard to his boat's crew.

"Send the barge to the relief of the fisherman," said Mr. Lowington to the captain.

The order was given in due form through the first lieutenant, and the barge's crew were piped away at once, taking their places in the boat at the davits.

"Mr. Ellis made some complaint against Shuffles for not obeying his orders," added Captain Haven to the principal.

"I heard Shuffles's story, and I am satisfied, though he did not say so, that Ellis was inefficient," replied Mr. Lowington. "All the space in the boat will be required for the passengers, and no other officer than the coxswain need be sent."

The ship wore round again, and hove to under the lee of the fisherman. Taking advantage of a favorable moment, the barge was dropped into the water, and the twelve oarsmen gave way with a will. The oars bent under their vigorous strokes, and when the boat came up under the lee of the sloop, she was half full of water. Shuffles handled the barge skilfully, and the crew had so much confidence in him, that all orders were promptly obeyed. The boat was quickly baled out by the boys, who used their caps for the purpose in the absence of a sufficient number of tin dishes.

A rope from the fisherman had been made fast to the fore thwart of the barge, which was swayed round under the main boom of the vessel. Twelve men, most of them seamen from the steamer, dropped from this spar, assisted by the foot-rope, into the boat. The skipper declared that he could stow away the rest of his passengers, and the barge was cast off.

"Are you all boys?" asked one of the passengers, who sat near the coxswain.

"Yes, sir; we belong to the Academy ship Young America," replied Shuffles.

"I saw her at Rotterdam. I was the mate of the steamer. We can relieve your crew at the oars if you like. This is no boys' play," added the man, wiping the spray from his face.

"We are used to it. If you will let two or three of your men bale out the boat, I will be obliged to you," said Shuffles, as a combing sea broke over the quarter, and left the water six inches deep in the bottom of the barge.

The mate complied, and the men kept her tolerably free of water during the rest of the passage. The boat came up under the lee of the ship, and the twelve men were hoisted on deck in slings. The falls were hooked on to the barge, and she was hauled up with the crew still in her. Shuffles was congratulated by the principal and the first lieutenant upon the able manner in which he had discharged his difficult task, and the mate was warm in his praise of the good conduct of the crew of the commodore's barge.

"Are there any ladies on board of that fishing vessel?" asked the doctor, when the mate was invited to the main cabin.

"Half a dozen of them, sir," replied he.

"Do you know Mrs. Arbuckle?"

"I do, sir; but she is not on board of the sloop."

The doctor shook his head. One of the chances of the safety of Grace's parents was gone. They might be on board of the Josephine; but there was no opportunity to communicate with her while the gale lasted.

"Do you know anything in regard to the fate of Mr. or Mrs. Arbuckle?" inquired Dr. Winstock.

"I do not. I left them on board the steamer," replied the man.

"Did you, indeed?" said the doctor, rather sharply.

"It was not my fault that I left before the passengers," interposed the mate. "I'll tell you how it was. The firemen, before we had given up all hope of putting out the fire, attempted to escape in one of the boats. They stove it in the heavy sea. They then attempted to lower another, and the captain sent me to drive them back. I leaped into the boat among the cowards, and had kicked one of them out when the beggars let go the falls, and down we went. The boat was swamped, and, clinging to it, bottom up, we were carried away from the ship by the waves. So, you see, it was not my fault that I left so soon."

"I see it was not."

"One of the men, who was brought to the fisherman after I was, says he saw the captain rigging a raft, and letting Mr. Arbuckle and his wife down upon it."

"Had you only two boats?"

"We had four; but the other two were hauled in board, and the fire finished them before we could get them out. It was the sorriest night I ever saw. I hope I never shall see the like again."

"How many passengers were saved by the sloop?" inquired Mr. Lowington, who had just entered the cabin.

"About thirty, I should say."

"How many persons had you on board of the steamer?"

"I don't exactly know. There were forty-two belonging to the ship, and I think we had as many as eighty passengers."

"One hundred and twenty-two persons!" added the principal, with a heavy sigh; "and only about forty of them accounted for. I don't know how many the Josephine has saved."

"Do you mean the topsail schooner?" asked the mate.

"I do — the consort of this ship."

"Well, sir, she had out four boats, and her people worked hard. She has picked up a great many of them."

"I am glad to hear it."

"Where is the ship bound, sir?" inquired the mate.

"To Havre; but I will make a port as soon as possible, and land these unfortunate people," replied the principal.

"You can make Harwich easiest, sir."

"But it is a dangerous harbor to enter without a pilot."

"I know the way in, sir, as well as I know my own name. I used to run on a steamer from Harwich to Rotterdam, and I know every foot of bottom in these waters."

"Very well; we will run for Harwich, then."

The ship was headed for the port indicated, and a signal made to the Josephine to follow. As soon as the course was laid, one watch was piped to breakfast, at seven bells. Half an hour later the watch was changed, and the other half of the crew went below. There was no study or recitation that forenoon, and the students had nothing to do but to talk over the perils of the night. The ship went along very well over the high sea, under close-reefed topsails and fore course; only a quarter watch was needed on deck, and most of the boys were willing to take a nap after the severe exertions of the early morning. The dashing spray, which had wet them to the skin, and the raw September air, enabled them to appreciate the luxury of a dry place with plenty of blankets in the messrooms.

"I say, Greenway, I shall have the pleasure of finding the rocks for our cruise in the Josephine," said Little, in a whisper, as he afforded his companion a single glance at the bag of gold, which he had concealed in his berth sack.

"Where did you get that?" asked Greenway, opening his eyes.

"No matter now. I'll tell you by and by."

"How much is there?"

"I don't know. I haven't counted it. Dry up; not another word;" and Little stretched himself on his bed as innocently as any of the "lambs."

CHAPTER IV.

LANDING THE SURVIVORS.

THE Josephine, obedient to the signal from the ship, kept in the wake of the Young America, carrying only a storm jib and reefed mainsail. In Captain Millbrook she had a pilot for the port of Harwich, though not only the commander and the sailing masters watched his course very closely, but the vice-principal studied the chart and observed the bearings when the vessel had passed the Galloper Light.

The between-decks and the cabin of the Josephine were filled with strangers, all of whom had been roused from their sleep on board the steamer by the fearful cry of fire. Some of them had lost or been separated from their nearest friends, and none of them had been able to save their baggage, so that they had not the means to make themselves comfortable. The stoves, which had just been put up, as the cold nights came on and storms were expected, kept the cabin and steerage very warm and dry, so that none of them suffered. It was an occasion to open and warm the hearts of the students, and all of them had opportunities to make sacrifices for the comfort of their shipwrecked guests. Women and children in the steerage wore pea-jackets which the owners absolutely needed, while attending to their duty, in the gale that raged on deck; but the consciousness that they were doing good service to the sufferers appeared to warm their bodies as well as their hearts.

In the cabin Mr. and Mrs. Arbuckle suffered the most intense anxiety on account of Grace; and Paul was more nervous and gloomy than ever before. He would have sent a boat to the ship and the fishing vessel for information, if Mr. Fluxion had not dissuaded him from doing so. The passage of the barge from the ship to the sloop and back seemed to be an argument in favor of such a step; but the vice-principal declared that no commander would be justified in sending off a boat, in that dangerous sea, except to save life. The signal of distress which the fisherman had hoisted explained and justified the act of the ship.

At seven bells in the afternoon, the ship let go her anchor in the smooth, sheltered waters of Harwich harbor. The Josephine, a few minutes later, moored a cable's length from her.

"Clear away the gig, and pipe down the crew, Mr. Terrill," said the captain of the schooner, as soon as the anchor had touched the bottom.

The first lieutenant gave the order, and then gazed, with pitying interest, at the young commander, who, in spite of his struggles to do so, was unable to conceal his intense solicitude in regard to the fate of Grace. Mr. Arbuckle soon joined him on deck, and cast anxious glances at the ship, as if to fathom the secret she only could reveal.

"I am going on board of the Young America, to report to the principal," said Paul, gloomily; "will you go with me, sir?"

"I dare not leave my wife. She is exceedingly nervous; but I want to hear from you instantly."

"If Grace is on board, I will wave my handkerchief from the main rigging of the ship," added Paul, as he went over the side into the gig.

All hands were on deck, and many of the passengers had come up in their anxiety to learn the fate of friends, who might or might not be on board of the ship. It was a thrilling time to many of those poor shipwrecked ones, for a few moments more would tel' who were widows, who were orphans, who had lost brothers, sisters, friends. They watched the gig as the oarsmen pulled their measured stroke, and every eye followed Paul as he sprang up the accommodation ladder.

"How many have you on board, Captain Kendall?" asked Mr. Lowington, taking his hand, as he stepped down upon the deck.

"Fifty-eight, sir," replied Paul.

"Is Mr. Arbuckle of the number?" inquired Dr. Winstock, pressing forward, and seizing the hand of his young friend.

"He is, and Mrs. Arbuckle also," answered Paul, whose face lighted up as he realized the significance of this question. "Is Grace Arbuckle on board of the ship?"

"She is!" cried the doctor, vehemently. "Thank God, they are all saved!"

"Excuse me a moment, sir," added Paul, rushing forward, and springing into the main rigging.

He waved his handkerchief vigorously for a moment. A heavy load had been removed from his soul, and the movements of his arm indicated the buoyancy of his spirits. Three rousing cheers came from the crew of the Josephine, for those who had heard Paul describe the signal which would indicate that Grace was saved, had communicated it to the others, and when it was made all of them understood it. Miss Grace had been on board the consort so much that she was a universal favorite; and not only the young commander, but all the ship's company, were deeply interested in her fate. Paul waited in the shrouds only long enough to see Mr. Arbuckle rush down the companion way, and he was satisfied with the joy he had telegraphed to those anxious hearts.

Dr. Winstock had also hastened below to gladden his patient with the tidings of her parents' safety. In anticipation of his visit to the ship, Paul had required the acting pursers of the consort to make out a list of all the passengers saved by that vessel. He gave the paper on which the names were written to Mr. Lowington, who handed it to the chaplain, directing him to read it to the unfortunate passengers.

Captain Kendall reported in full to the principal, and was warmly commended for the conduct of himself and his crew during the exciting scenes of the morning. The gig was immediately sent back to the Josephine with a list of the passengers saved by the ship. To some these lists carried joy, to others woe and bitterness of spirit, though no complete report of those on board of the fisherman had yet been received. Some names had been reported on board of the ship by the sailors brought off in the barge, and these were added to the list sent to the Josephine.

Mr. Lowington had ordered the second cutter, intending to go on shore and give information of the disaster, which would be immediately telegraphed to London; and to induce the authorities to send a steamer to the assistance of the fishing sloop. As soon as he had gone, Paul was invited to the main cabin by Dr. Winstock.

"O, Captain Kendall," exclaimed Grace, as he entered, "I am so glad to see you!"

"I am just as glad to see you," said Paul, taking her offered hand.

She was wrapped up in a great-coat belonging to the doctor; and Paul was so light-hearted in view of her safety, that he could not help laughing. And now, for the first time since she had been brought on board, she thought what a singular figure she presented to the tidy young officer. Her father and mother were safe, and she could now think of herself. She blushed as she glanced at the great shaggy coat which enveloped her delicate frame.

"Your father and mother have suffered most terribly in their anxiety about you," added Paul, as he pressed the fair hand he held — pressed it as he had never dared to do before.

"O, how anxious I have been for them!" she replied, smiling. "May I not see them?"

"Very soon, Miss Grace, I hope. Your mother is exceedingly nervous; but I trust the good news will make her better."

"She will be well now, I know. What a terrible night it was!"

"It must have been awful to you in the midst of the fire and the waters."

"I shall never forget it as long as I live; and I shall thank my heavenly Father every day, that he saved us all."

"But how happened you to be on board of this steamer?" asked Paul, who knew that first-class passengers seldom went to Rotterdam by this conveyance.

"My father was acquainted with Captain Millbrook — poor man! I wonder whether he was saved."

"He is on board of the Josephine."

"I am very glad, for no man could have been more kind to us than he was. He invited us to go with him, and as my mother wanted to see something of Holland, we accepted the invitation. I really think that what you wrote in your letters about Holland made my mother desire to see something of the country. We were going to Rotterdam and Amsterdam, and then to Cologne and up the Rhine, expecting to be in Paris in about ten days. But I suppose that plan is all spoiled now, for we have lost our baggage, though we have more clothing at our friends' near London. How thankful we ought to be that our lives were spared! And how strange it was that you should be sailing so near us when the fire broke out!"

"I hope you will still go to Paris," said Paul.

"I don't know that my mother will dare to go upon the water again."

"You can cross the Straits of Dover in less than two hours. And you can choose a pleasant day for the passage. I really hope we shall see you in Paris."

"Perhaps you will. But you don't ask me, Captain Kendall, how I was saved. Do you know that I came very near being lost?"

"I think all did."

"But I came nearer to it than others, I believe. It was awful, Captain Kendall."

"I am ready to believe that, for I saw enough of it to convince me, though I did not go out in the boats to pick up the survivors."

"Captain Millbrook and father made a raft for us after all the boats were lost; but the waves broke it up, and I was carried away from father and mother. I clung to a log of wood, every instant expecting to be thrown off and drowned. How I prayed to God for help! Then I saw a boat coming towards me, and I screamed as loud as I could. The boat came up; but it ran against the log, and shook me off. The cold, heavy waters swept over me, and I gave myself up for lost. My senses seemed to leave me; but I was conscious of struggling with all my might against the waves. Then some one caught hold of me, and I was taken into the boat. I did not know how I had been saved till Dr. Winstock told me; but one of these brave fellows jumped overboard, and held me up, or I should certainly have gone down."

"Who was he?" asked Paul, warmly interested in this narrative.

"Mr. Shuffles. He leaped into the water at the peril of his own life, and saved me. O, Captain Kendall, you cannot tell how grateful I am to him!" exclaimed Grace, with the utmost enthusiasm.

"Shuffles!"

"Yes; and do you know, when I was told some one had jumped into the sea after me, I thought it must have been you?"

Paul wished it had been he, but was very grateful to Shuffles for the noble service he had rendered.

"You must excuse me now, Miss Arbuckle. I must go on board and attend to my duties," interposed Paul, thinking his gig must have returned from the consort by this time.

"May I not go with him?" asked Grace, appealing to the doctor, who had been an interested listener to the conversation. "I want to see my father and mother."

"Do you feel able to go?"

"I never felt better in my life. I am quite well now."

"Then you may go."

All the clothing she had worn when rescued from the water had been dried, and though she was hardly in presentable condition to go into a drawing-room, her garments, with the addition of the surgeon's great coat, were sufficient to keep her comfortable. The gangway stairs had by this time been rigged so that the female passengers could get into the boats without difficulty, and Grace was handed into the gig by her devoted friend. The oarsmen pulled to the Josephine, and when the ship's company discovered that Miss Arbuckle was a passenger, they cheered her lustily. She was assisted on board, and immediately conducted to the cabin by the captain.

Under the exciting news of the safety of her daughter, Mrs. Arbuckle had for the first time left her berth. As Grace entered the cabin, she clasped her to her heart, and mother and daughter wept in each other's embrace. Each had a story to tell of the experience of the dreadful occasion, and all devoutly thanked Him who ruleth over the stormy sea for the lives which had been saved.

At the custom-house on shore, Mr. Lowington reported the calamity, and handed in a list of the survivors' names. A steamer was immediately despatched to the aid of the fisherman, and preparations made for the reception of those on board the squadron. The whole town was soon informed of the disaster, and the benevolent inhabitants threw open their doors for the sufferers. As soon as the principal returned, all the boats of the ship and her consort were lowered, and conveyed the passengers to the shore, with the exception of the Arbuckles, who had decided to remain in the Josephine for the present. They were landed in a sort of triumphal procession by the boats; and never were sailors prouder of their achievements on the main than were the young tars of the Academy squadron. They were regarded with wonder and astonishment by the crowds of people who had gathered on the wharf to witness the debarkation of the unfortunates. The order and discipline of the boats' crews, the tidy and trim appearance of the officers, were warmly praised. They were complimented with many a cheer, and kindly invited to the houses of the people; but the order had been given that no one should leave the boats.

Every possible kindness and care was bestowed by the people upon the unfortunate passengers, and Mr.

Lowington was satisfied that he had committed them to worthy hands. But the students were not satisfied with what they had done. Many of the poor people had lost all they had in the world by the catastrophe, and had not even clothes enough to keep them comfortable. The good Samaritans of Harwich were already collecting money and clothing to supply their needs, and the boys, when they heard of this movement, were anxious to take part in it. By the law of God, the more we do for our fellow-beings, the more we love them and desire to serve them. It was promptly voted that the five hundred and fifty-four guilders, or about fifty pounds sterling, — the balance of the fund raised for the benefit of Captain Schimmelpennink, after the wreck of the Wel tevreeden, — should be devoted to the wants of the sufferers. The principal was very happy to encourage this benevolent spirit in his pupils, and, adding ten pounds to the amount, sent a committee, consisting of Flag-officer Gordon, the two captains, and the treasurer of the fund, on shore in the commodore's barge, to tender the money to the chief officer of the customs, who was foremost in the good work.

By this time the gale, which was from the southward, had subsided, the clouds had rolled away, and the sun came out as if to smile upon the generous deeds of that day. The barge, with the American flag at the stern and the flag-officer's pennant at the bow, pulled from the ship to the consort, and then to the shore. The officers composing the committee were dressed in their best uniforms, and when they landed they produced a decided sensation. They walked up to the custom-house, and discharged their duty with becoming correctness and dignity, making an impression which was in the highest degree flattering to the young gentlemen.

Just at sunset, the fishing sloop, towed by the steamer sent out after her, entered the harbor. The barge and the first cutter of the ship were sent to land her passengers. Again friends found friends among the last company of the survivors; and, alas! others found them not, for many were "in the deep bosom of the ocean buried." The whole truth was known now. Ninety-two had been saved, and about thirty had been lost.

The mission which had brought the squadron into the port of Harwich was accomplished, and before it was fairly dark, the ship and her consort were standing out of the harbor under all sail. The usual routine on board the vessels was restored. The sickening details of death and disaster had become in a measure familiar to the students, and it almost seemed as if nothing had happened, though all were conscious of possessing an increased experience of the perils and calamities of human life.

In the cabin of the Josephine all was not as it had been before, for the Arbuckles occupied the state-room of the professors. They had, to a great degree, recovered from the effects of the disaster, and were quite cheerful. At Harwich, Mr. Arbuckle had telegraphed to his friend near London, directing him to forward all their clothing to Havre, where its arrival would free them from the imprisonment to which they were doomed for the present.

While at anchor in Harwich harbor, boats had been constantly passing between the ship and her consort, and, at the request of Mrs. Arbuckle, Shuffles had visited her in the cabin of the Josephine. She expressed her gratitude to him with enthusiasm, in which her husband and daughter heartily joined.

"I wonder that you dared to leap into the water in the dark, and in the heavy sea," said Grace, admiringly.

"I feel almost as much at home in the water as I do on the land," replied Shuffles, delighted with the generous warmth of the fair Grace. "The fire made light enough to enable me to see you."

"Did you know it was I who fell from the log, or spar, whatever it was?"

"How should I?"

"My father and mother were picked up near the steamer."

"But I did not see them. They were taken up by one of the Josephine's boats; and, you know, on board of the ship we were not even aware that they had been saved."

"I'm sure I shall always remember you," added Grace.

"I dare say, if I had known it was you who had fallen from the spar, I should have been all the more willing to go in after you," said Shuffles, gallantly.

"Thanks; you are very kind," laughed Grace.

Paul, who was present, thought so too, and again wished that he had himself been favored with the blessed opportunity vouchsafed to the coxswain of the commodore's barge.

"I only tried to do my duty," continued Shuffles. "In your case, it was the second time that our boat had run into a spar, and knocked a person from his support. I was mortified, vexed, and desperate, and I was determined not to let another be sacrificed to the clumsy handling of the boat."

"Whose fault was it?" asked Paul.

"I don't know that it was any one's fault. We could not see the spars to which the persons were clinging. We all did the best we knew how; but mistakes will happen."

"Who was the officer of the barge?" asked the captain.

"Mr. Ellis, the second lieutenant."

Paul asked no more questions, for this answer seemed to explain the whole matter. Shuffles turned to leave, and again Grace and her parents expressed their obligations to him. Paul could not find any fault with the fair girl, when she extended her hand at parting to the gallant coxswain, and said several very pretty things to him; but he had a faint suspicion that she was slightly overdoing the matter. It was certainly quite unnecessary that she should give him her hand more than once — a favor which she did not extend to him except upon extraordinary occasions; and it was equally needless for Shuffles to say that he should have been all the more willing to jump into the sea, if he had known Grace was the person in peril. But these were only flashes of thought which the noble-minded captain repelled as soon as he was conscious of their existence.

That night, after the ship was in the offing, and

had laid her course for the Straits of Dover, Shuffles was not a little surprised at being summoned to the main cabin, into the presence of the principal. Of course the students, while not actively employed, had talked of little except the burning of the steamer since the tragic event occurred. Every incident and every detail of the rescue of the passengers had been thoroughly discussed; and nothing had been so much talked about as the conduct of Ellis, in charge of the barge, especially in comparison with that of its coxswain. The lieutenant's action had been freely and disparagingly criticised.

Some of these unfriendly remarks had been wafted, in the excitement, to the ears of the subject of them. Ellis, though in the main a very good fellow, was not above the weakness of human infirmity. Though it did not appear that Shuffles had made any direct charge against him, he suspected that the criticisms had come from him. He was vexed and angry. Shuffles was just then the lion of the squadron. While all had done well, no one, except the coxswain of the barge, had particularly distinguished himself. His name and praise were on the lips of every generous shipmate. Perhaps Ellis was disturbed by a feeling of envy or jealousy; but, be this as it may, he centred the whole weight of his indignation upon Shuffles, for the disagreeable remarks in regard to himself which were circulating through the ship.

"I hear that you are talking about me," said he to the supposed offender, whom he called into the waist for the purpose of expressing his mind as freely as the occasion seemed to require.

"I haven't said a word against you," replied the coxswain, quietly.

"Yes, you have; the fellows are full of it. Didn't you say that I was no more fit to command a boat than I was an army?"

"Most decidedly I did not."

"What did you say, then?" demanded the indignant lieutenant.

"The most that I remember to have said was, that our boat was very unfortunate in running into the spar on which that man was floating."

"Well, whose fault was it?"

"I don't know that it was any one's fault."

"I do. It was your fault. When I ordered you to back water, you tossed the starboard oars."

"The oars were right over the man's head. If we had backed they would have sent him to the bottom."

"You always know better than your officers. If you had obeyed your superior in the boat, that man would not have been lost."

"I don't think it was my fault."

"You mean by that it was my fault."

"I didn't say so," replied Shuffles, who was by this time satisfied that it was useless to argue the point.

"That is what you mean, and what you have been saying to all the fellows. Then you left your place, and went into the bow of the barge, giving me the tiller lines — a piece of impudence which I should have resented at any other time."

"I should not have done it at any other time, Mr. Ellis."

"You actually took command of the boat, and winked me out of sight."

"I did not intend any disrespect."

"Perhaps you didn't, and I should not have thought anything of it, if it hadn't been for the stories which have been told since," replied Ellis. "You may be a bigger man than I am, but it don't become you to say so."

The lieutenant turned on his heel, and left Shuffles very much annoyed by the sharp words of his superior during the interview. He had done nothing to justify the abusive speech of the officer.

"He's a lubber," said Little, stepping up to him, after hearing a portion of the conversation.

"He is very unfair," answered Shuffles, more in grief than in anger.

"He came within one of using me up, and I don't feel much obliged to him. We shouldn't have saved any one if it hadn't been for you, when you took the command out of his hands, and managed the boat yourself."

"Did you think I took the command away from him?"

"I did; and all the fellows thought so, and were glad you did."

Shuffles was more annoyed than before, as Little desired he should be. He had not intended to supersede his superior; though perhaps he had spoken authoritatively in the excitement of the moment. For this offence he was summoned into the presence of the principal. Ellis had complained of him to the captain. It was hard, after he had done so well, to be accused, or even suspected, of disrespect to his officer, and the "old Adam" of his nature prompted him to resent this treatment.

CHAPTER V.

THE BAG OF GOLD.

SHUFFLES was the lion of the day, but it made very little difference what the seamen thought of him, if he had failed to secure the approbation of the principal and the officers. The fact that he had been called to the bar, after what had passed between himself and Ellis, to answer to charges, indicated that he had incurred the displeasure of Mr. Lowington. The complaint against him had at least been heard, and notice enough taken of it to call him up. He was a reformed young man, and he had been struggling for months to overcome the evil in his nature. He had been tempted on every hand, but thus far he had conquered. The very efforts he made to live a good and true life rendered him sensitive to every imputation.

Besides striving to keep his conduct above reproach morally, he was also struggling to attain a high position in the ship. He had studied very hard, and been exceedingly careful in the discharge of all his routine duties, so that, during the two months of the present term which had elapsed, not a single mark for bad conduct, and hardly a failure in the lessons, had been noted against his name. This was his record, and anything better was scarcely possible. Now he was to be charged with disobedience of orders. He was willing to acknowledge that he was technically and constructively guilty. He had, in the enthusiasm of his humane labors, asked Ellis to take the helm, and had gone into the fore sheets without orders, the better to do the work for which the barge had been sent out.

If Shuffles was troubled and embarrassed, the principal was more so. The second lieutenant had made a formal complaint to the executive officer, which had been reported to the captain, and by him referred to the highest authority on board. It was patent to Mr. Lowington, and to the officers, that Ellis was not equal to the position to which he had been assigned. In the ordinary routine of the ship he was faithful and capable, but, when left to his own resources, he lacked energy and judgment. He was a particular friend of Captain Haven, who had ordered him to the barge, satisfied that the skill of the coxswain would counterbalance the deficiency of the officer.

It was evident that somebody had been making trouble in the ship; but the boys were so ready to talk, and to criticise, that the special agency of Little had not been noticed, for it was true that he had been very industrious in stirring up strife. The rogue had cunningly directed the thoughts of his shipmates until poor Ellis was under a heavy cloud. At the same time, Shuffles was extravagantly lauded, and it was generally understood through the vessel, that if the coxswain had not taken the command out of the hands of the second lieutenant, Miss Grace would certainly have been drowned by Ellis's bungling.

The complaint, which the second lieutenant felt

obliged to make in self-defence, had come to the principal, and he was compelled to notice it. Little had actually forced the case into the cabin, where he had from the first intended it should go. It would be very hard to censure Shuffles; but if an inferior were permitted to take the command away from his officer, all discipline would soon be at an end. But the principal received the alleged offender with a pleasant smile, and the case did not look at all desperate.

"Shuffles, I find there is some misunderstanding between you and the second lieutenant," the principal began, stating the question as mildly as possible.

"I am very sorry for it," answered Shuffles.

"So am I, for your conduct had been so noble that I was pained to hear any complaint against you."

"I don't think there is any just ground for a complaint against me, sir."

"You are reported, in the first place, to have spoken very disparagingly of the conduct of your officer in the barge," added the principal.

"It is not true, sir. I have not uttered a word against him," replied Shuffles, indignantly. "I do think the boat was handled in a very bungling manner, but I have been careful not to say so."

"Entertaining this opinion, may you not have said something which indicated your views?"

"I have not said anything about Mr. Ellis, or the handling of the boat, on board the ship. I did say in the cabin of the Josephine that I was mortified, vexed, and desperate, because we had twice run into a spar, and knocked a person into the water; but I added that it was not any one's fault. If any one has heard me say a word about Ellis, either way, I should like to see him."

"I am satisfied on that point," said the principal. "Ellis says you took the command of the barge out of his hands."

"I did ask him to take the tiller ropes, and he did so. I also went forward to haul in the person with the boat-hook. If he had ordered me not to do so, I should have obeyed. I was only working to save the life of the girl."

"I know very well that you had no intention to do anything wrong," added the principal, kindly.

"If Mr. Ellis had gone into the bow of the boat, as the other officers did, he would have seen where to go, and what to do. As he did not do this, I did it myself. I meant no disrespect or disobedience, and I have told him so."

"I am satisfied you did not."

"I was excited, and, perhaps, I spoke sharper than I should. I am willing to apologize — I have already explained," continued Shuffles, struggling to retain his self-possession, though he was very indignant at the charges.

"I will send for Mr. Ellis," said the principal.

The second lieutenant was called. He came in "riding a high horse." The coxswain of the barge had taken the command, had gone to the bow of the boat, and given his directions to his officer. He had actually ordered him to take the tiller ropes. If officers were to be treated in this manner, he did not wish to have a command.

"Mr. Ellis," said the principal, rather disgusted by

the strong expressions of that officer, " did it occur to you that the command had been taken from you at the time you allege it was done?"

"No, sir. It was not a time to think of anything but the poor people who were drowning around us. I did not wish to say much to Shuffles after what he had done in the water; but I did tell him that he had not obeyed my orders; and I think that was the reason why the man was lost, and why Miss Grace was thrown from the spar."

It is not necessary to follow this discussion through all its details. Both the lieutenant and the coxswain had endeavored to do their duty; but it happened then, as it often does in the world, that the superior in ability occupied the inferior position in rank. The zeal of Shuffles to save the lives of the sufferers in the water had surprised him into doing what he would not have done in a less trying position. The principal endeavored to patch up a peace, which the lieutenant was unwilling to accept, unless it involved a censure of his inferior.

"Shuffles, you have certainly overstepped the routine of your duty," said Mr. Lowington, very gently. "You have exceeded the letter of your duty, while you have been faithful to the spirit of it, and I acquit you on all the charges. You may go."

The coxswain touched his cap, and retired. He was not satisfied even with this mild decision.

"Mr. Ellis; I do not like the spirit you exhibit in this unpleasant affair," added the principal, turning to the lieutenant when Shuffles had gone.

"Almost every fellow in the ship says that I am to

blame for the loss of that man. My orders were not obeyed, and I am sure it was not my fault," replied Ellis, somewhat mollified by the decision given to the coxswain.

"I do not know whether it was your fault or not. Probably it will never be known in this world. But I do think the boat was mismanaged."

"So do I, sir; and because the coxswain did not obey my orders."

"On the contrary, I think, after all I have heard, that if he had obeyed your orders, not only the man, but also Miss Arbuckle, would have been lost. Instead of going into the fore sheets, as you ought to have done, and as Shuffles did when you neglected to do so, you drove your boat blindly forward."

"Then you think I am to blame, sir?" replied the astonished Ellis.

"I do; but you did the best you knew how, and I do not hold you responsible."

"Then I suppose I don't know anything," added the lieutenant, bitterly, "and that Shuffles knows everything."

"We are all liable to err, and we ought to be satisfied if we get the credit of our good intentions. You should not have made this complaint."

"But all the students were talking about me."

"It does not appear that Shuffles has criticised your conduct in any manner. Whatever strictures have been made upon your action appear to come from the crew of the barge. I noticed that all the officers of the boats went into the bows, where they could see, not only the persons in the water, but the objects to which they were clinging; and it does not appear that any mistakes were made by them. I cannot, and do not wish to, control the opinions of the students. If they think you made a blunder, you must stand or fall by your own conduct; you must be judged by your own action. I am not informed that any have insulted you, or spoken disrespectfully to you; if they have, that is a matter for discipline, but not their opinion of your conduct. You may go."

Ellis left the cabin, more dissatisfied than when he had entered it. If others had a right to their opinions, so had he; and he still believed that Shuffles's disobedience of his orders had produced all the mischief. He was not without a reasonable share of self-esteem, which would not permit him to condemn his own conduct in a matter which was at least open to doubt.

Both Shuffles and Ellis were dissatisfied, though neither of them had been actually blamed for his conduct. It was one of those instances where a Christian spirit and a Christian humility would have healed the wound. It was the severest trial which the reformed young man had experienced since he turned over the new leaf. He had been adjudged guilty of technical disobedience of orders, and his new-born sensitiveness revolted at the decision. If he had heard what the principal said to Ellis after he left the cabin, he would have considered himself fully justified; but strict discipline would not permit the seaman to listen to the censure of the officer.

Ellis would inform all the other officers of the decision of the principal. Its tendency would be to prejudice them against him, and to induce them to display their authority more offensively than they would otherwise do. They would be likely to bully him in self-defence. He had been highly honored before this complaint was made, by being sent, without an officer, to the relief of the fishing vessel, in a heavy sea and a gale of wind, but he felt that he could not thus be distinguished again. He could not help feeling that he had fallen into disfavor.

For two months he had been struggling for a position in the cabin. The prize was almost within his grasp. Another month of persevering effort would bring the success he coveted. Though he realized that his present unhappy frame of mind would lead him into trouble, he found it hard to rise above it. For an hour he planked the deck in the waist, thinking of his great sorrow, as he regarded it. The ship's company would soon be talking about what he had been, instead of what he was. Thousands of people, in like manner, out of the abundance of their own imagination, make themselves miserable.

"I should like to see him disobey my orders, and take the command out of my hands!" said a well-known voice, as a couple of officers passed him; and Shuffles could not help believing that the remark was intended for his own ears.

The speaker was the fourth lieutenant, and the words were addressed to Ellis, who had doubtless been telling his grievances to him.

"I did not want to make a row there, when men and women were dying around us," replied the magnanimous Ellis, as the couple paused at the foot of the mainmast.

"Mr. Ellis," said Shuffles, stepping up to the two officers, and respectfully touching his cap, "I did not intend to take the command of the barge, or to disobey your orders. If I did anything wrong, I beg your pardon."

"If you did!" sneered Ellis, who was smarting from a deeper wound than the coxswain; "when you acknowledge that you did do wrong, it will be time enough to accept your apology."

"I say I did not intend to be disrespectful. I asked you to take the tiller ropes, and you did not object. When I went forward, you did not object."

"It was no time then to have a row with a coxswain," added the second lieutenant, contemptuously. "When you have acknowledged that you did wrong, and that your disobedience of orders made the mischief in the barge, I shall be happy to accept your apology. Until then you will not address me except in the line of your duty."

Shuffles's self-respect, as well as his opinion of the facts, would not permit him to make this humiliating acknowledgment. He touched his cap again, and retired in silence. The officers moved on, and a derisive laugh from both of them did not escape the ear of the sensitive sufferer. He felt that he had made all the atonement in his power for his constructive offence. He had been haughtily repulsed. He could do no more.

"I say, Shuffles, the nobs are rough on you," said Little, who had been watching his victim, as he intended he should be, and as he already regarded him, during the entire evening.

"They are, indeed," replied Shuffles, sadly.

"Let them say what they please; every fellow in the ship, except the nobs in the cabin, believes in you, Shuffles," continued the little villain.

"I am much obliged to them for their good opinion;" but Shuffles did not feel much comforted by it.

"Instead of apologizing to the second lieutenant, I should give him a walloping when I caught him in the right place."

"I shall not do anything of that kind. Mr. Lowington said I had been guilty of disobedience of orders; and I am willing to apologize for it; but I am not exactly ready to be kicked for it."

"You won't make anything by trying to keep on the right side of such fellows. I'll tell you what it is, Shuffles: your old friends were your best friends."

"What old friends?"

"Wilton, Monroe, Adler, and the rest of them. They are willing to stand by you now, and do so to the end."

"What are you driving at, Little?" demanded Shuffles, suddenly and sharply, of his companion; for the "lamb" was shrewd enough to see that the little rascal meant something by his persistent flattery, and by his allusion to former associates, whom he had in a measure discarded.

"I don't mean anything in particular; only I hate to see a good fellow like you imposed upon by such numheads as Ellis," replied Little, not thrown off his guard by the sudden charge of the other. "It made me mad to hear you apologize to that flunky."

"I did it to show that I had no ill will against him."

"O, get out! Tell that to the marines! Do you mean to say you love him for reporting you to the first lieutenant?"

"Perhaps he thought it was his duty to do so," replied Shuffles, very doubtfully.

"Perhaps he did; and then, again, perhaps he didn't," sneered Little. "Ellis will fall overboard one of these days."

"If he does, I shall be willing to go in after him."

"Do you mean so?"

"I do," replied Shuffles, struggling to keep the Christian spirit alive in his heart.

Little was disgusted. Shuffles would not be likely to join the Knights of the Golden Fleece while he cherished such sentiments as these. But the gallant conduct of the coxswain, as manifested in saving the passengers of the steamer, and his handling of the barge in the gale, had increased his popularity among the crew, and rendered him all the more desirable as the leader of the runaway cruise. The conspirator was satisfied that the time had not yet come for making a convert of him to the philosophy of the knights; yet he expected it to come in due time.

Shuffles went below with a faint suspicion that Little was up to some mischief, and was endeavoring to whip him in to take part in it. He was glad that he had not encouraged any such approaches; for he was still firm in his purpose to be true and faithful, though the path just then did not seem so easy and pleasant as before. It was hard to be suspected, when he had only tried to do his duty.

Ellis was still pacing the deck; indeed, he had been

impatiently waiting for some time to have Shuffles leave the deck. He wished to speak with Little in private. Still smarting under the censure of the principal, he was anxious to gather some testimony to prove that the coxswain, and not himself, had been to blame for the loss of the man from the spar.

"Little," said he, in gracious and condescending tones; for he knew how to obtain the right kind of testimony.

The little villain turned and touched his cap.

"I suppose you have not forgotten how you went overboard this morning."

"I think not."

"Don't you remember also that, just before you went over, I gave an order to the coxswain to back water?"

"Yes, sir. I remember it distinctly, for it occurred to me at the time that you ought to have said, 'Stern, all,' instead of, 'Back water.'"

"Never mind the words I used. What followed? What did the coxswain do then?"

"He ordered the starboard bank to toss oars," answered Little, promptly.

"Exactly so. Did he do so immediately?"

"Well, I think it was pretty soon."

"Pretty soon! The boat would go twenty feet in half a second."

"I know he stood up, and looked ahead, before he gave the order."

"Just so; and if he had repeated the order the instant I gave it, we should have backed clear of the man."

"Perhaps we should," replied Little, coolly.

"You know we should."

"I suppose we should, then," answered the pliable rogue.

"Then the boat swung round, and you and Shuffles got hold of the man."

"I know that part of the story very well. When the boat lurched, I held on to him, and Shuffles let go."

"Precisely so; and if Shuffles had not let go, you would have hauled the man in."

"I don't blame him for not holding on. It was not his fault," added Little, dropping his voice down to a whisper. "I suppose he told you why he let go."

"No."

"Didn't he, though?"

"No."

"Then I guess I won't say anything about it. It will only make trouble, and get me into a scrape," said the immaculate Little, in the same low tone.

"What do you mean?"

"Never mind it now."

"Yes, but I shall mind it now."

"I don't like to say anything. Shuffles is a good friend of mine, and I wouldn't do him any harm for all the world," answered the prudent villain, who, it need hardly be said, was preparing for Shuffles's admission to the order of the Knights of the Golden Fleece.

"What do you mean?" demanded Ellis, his curiosity raised to the highest pitch.

"I thought you knew all about it, or I wouldn't have said a word."

"All about what."

"Didn't Shuffles tell you, though?"

"Not a word."

"I had much rather you would not ask me any questions. Shuffles is a friend of mine."

"I don't care if he is. He is no friend of mine, and if there is anything wrong about this business, I want to know it."

"I did not say there was anything wrong about it," protested Little, mildly, as though he intended, after proper persuasion, to let the whole truth come out.

"You implied it."

"I did not intend to imply it, for if Shuffles has not said anything about it yet, he will do so when he gets ready."

"Perhaps he will; but if you don't tell me what you mean, I will report the matter to the principal before I turn in."

"Don't do that," pleaded Little, as naturally as though he had been in earnest.

"Are you going to speak, or not?"

"You won't say anything about it — will you?"

"I make no promises."

"O, come, don't be hard on a fellow. You will get me into a scrape."

"I am an officer, and I tell you to speak."

"If Shuffles don't say anything by the time we get to Havre, I will tell you all about it."

"That won't do. Now or never, to me."

"Very likely Shuffles has told the principal all about it."

"I will go and ask him whether he has or not," said Ellis, taking a step towards the companion way.

"Don't do that!" begged Little. "I think he must have mentioned the matter to you, only you don't know what I mean."

"Tell me what you mean. I shall understand you then."

"Didn't he say anything to you about a bag of gold?" whispered the rogue.

"A bag of gold!" exclaimed Ellis, opening his eyes.

"That's what's the matter!"

"He didn't say a word to me about it, and I'm sure he did not to the principal. What about it?"

"The man that was lost off the plank had a bag of gold in his hand."

"Do you mean so?" demanded the astonished officer.

"I know it. He told me so while we were on the spar together in the water. When Shuffles got hold of him, the man gave him the bag of gold, and that was what made him let go — to put the money behind the back-board, I suppose, for I didn't see anything of it. The man was a Dutchman, I think from his talk, though he spoke bad English. He was groaning about his money while we hung to the spar."

"Did he tell you he gave it to Shuffles?" asked Ellis, eagerly.

"Well, he did not know Shuffles's name, and I

suppose he had never been introduced to him. He told me he gave it ' zu dem mann in dem schiff.' "

" Is this so, Little?"

" Do you think I would lie about it?" demanded Little, with proper indignation.

Ellis knew that he would lie in some cases; but it was too monstrous to suppose he would utter a deliberate falsehood in a matter of so much importance. Besides, he was very willing to believe the story.

" It's a strange yarn," mused Ellis.

" Perhaps it is; but you have it for just what it is worth."

" How much was in the bag?"

" I don't know; the Dutchman did not tell me. Now, what are you going to do about it, Mr. Ellis?"

" I shall do what I think proper," replied Ellis, haughtily. " I will think the matter over, and decide upon my action to-night."

" I was a fool to say anything about it. I have got myself into a sweet scrape. Shuffles will kill me for blowing on him, on the one hand, and I shall be blamed for not telling of it before, on the other."

" It does not much matter what Shuffles says or does, after this; if you are blamed for not speaking about the gold before, you can say you supposed Shuffles had told the officers all about it."

" I suppose I can," sighed Little, who appeared to be very much dissatisfied with himself.

" It is a plain case enough. Shuffles intended to keep this money. Now it can be sent to the heirs of the man who was lost."

Little thought it was not likely to be sent to them, and he went below with the feeling that there would soon be " the jolliest row that ever was," as he would have expressed it, and that the lion of that day would be in the brig the next day.

CHAPTER VI.

THE LITTLE VILLAIN.

IN less than half an hour Ellis had told the story of the bag of gold to his friend the captain. The lieutenant was excited. Not only had a large majority of the students condemned his management of the barge, but the principal had squarely told him he had blundered. Shuffles, the coxswain, was a lion, and he, the lieutenant in command of the barge, was a "donkey." Shuffles had done everything; he had done nothing: Shuffles was a hero; he was a blockhead. Public sentiment on board of the ship was giving him a bad name.

All this was a mistake, in his opinion. He was willing to acknowledge that the boat had been badly managed; but Shuffles — who was a very capable fellow he would not deny, and was popular with the students — had disobeyed his officer's commands, which fully and satisfactorily explained the whole matter. It was stupid on the part of the ship's company not to see it. His friend the captain, who had never been especially fond of Shuffles, could see it. The fourth lieutenant, who was a fellow of excellent judgment and discrimination, could see it. At least neither of these officers had made any unfriendly comments upon his conduct.

The revelation of Little would turn the tables; it would convince all the fair-minded fellows that Shuffles, instead of being zealous to save the lives of the passengers of the steamer, had actually been feathering his nest with a bag of gold, torn from the hands of a perishing German. Instead of hauling in the man, he had hauled in the money, and let the man go. If he had held on to the man, instead of the gold, Little would not have been dragged overboard, and the German would have been saved. It was a plain case, in his excited state of mind, and his jealousy of Shuffles would not permit him to entertain a doubt in regard to the guilt of the coxswain.

Captain Haven listened attentively to the story, as it was minutely related by Ellis. If it had not been dark on deck when the conversation took place, the lieutenant might have seen the incredulous smile upon the face of his superior. While the captain lacked entire confidence in Shuffles, being unable wholly to forget his former record, he was not prejudiced against him. He gave him credit for trying to do well, and believed that he had actually reformed, but was too fresh a convert to be entirely reliable.

"What do you think of all this, captain?" asked Ellis, who was surprised that the commander did not join with him in condemning the conduct of Shuffles.

"I think it is a silly story. There is not one word of truth in it," replied Captain Haven. "If you have any regard for yourself or your reputation, you will not mention it to any one."

Ellis was confounded by this honest and decided

opinion. It seemed just as though his friend the captain had gone over to the enemy.

"Little told me the story, and says it is all true," stammered Ellis, taken all aback by the decision.

"Little would rather lie than tell the truth," added the captain.

"There is nothing improbable in the story."

"It is all improbable, and would have been from the lips of any fellow, but is especially so from those of Little."

"Was it strange that the man tried to save his gold?" persisted Ellis.

"No."

"Is it improbable that a man under such circumstances should have a bag of gold?"

"No."

"What is there improbable about the story then?"

"It is improbable that Shuffles should have taken it, and said nothing about it," replied the captain, impatiently.

"I think that is the most probable part of the story. He wanted the money: any fellow would want it if he could get it. I don't think he meant to drown the man for the sake of the gold, or anything of that sort. The German handed him the bag, and he could not do less than take it."

"But where were you all this time? Didn't you see anything of the operation?"

"I was looking out for the boat, and it is not strange, in the flurry of the moment, that I saw nothing of it."

"Don't say anything more about it, Ellis," laughed the captain.

"But I believe the story, strange as you think it is."

"Where is the money now?" asked Captain Haven.

"I don't know; I suppose Shuffles has concealed it somewhere."

"Ellis, if you tell this story, it will hurt you more than it will Shuffles. It may, of course, be true, but I do not believe it. You have complained of the coxswain of the commodore's barge; and this story, started by you, will look like persecution — like an intention to injure Shuffles. If you demand it, I must report the matter to the principal."

"I am willing to do what you think is best."

"Then keep still."

"And let Shuffles keep the money, and enjoy the reputation of being a hero?"

"Just now Shuffles is on the top of the wave. He has behaved nobly, so far as Miss Arbuckle is concerned; you cannot deny it."

"I don't wish to deny it."

"And you are under a cloud."

"Perhaps I am, but you know it was not my fault; Shuffles disobeyed orders, and —"

"We will not open that question: the principal has settled it. I will keep an eye on Shuffles, and you can do the same. By and by, when we go to Paris, he will be flush with his gold, if there is any truth in this story."

"But the bag of gold is somewhere in the ship. If we can find that, it will be proof enough."

"Keep an eye on him, and if we can find it we will

do so. Don't say anything more about it, Ellis. Do your duty faithfully; treat Shuffles as handsomely as you know how; and if there is anything wrong, it will come out in due time."

Ellis was not pleased with this slow method of dealing with the exciting question; but he had so much confidence in Captain Haven's judgment that he could not well disregard his advice. He was so eager to overwhelm Shuffles that he could not help believing the strange story. As it was his watch below, he went to his state-room and turned in. The matter still vexed him, and he could not sleep. He had hardly closed his eyes when he was called to take his place as officer of the deck.

Little was in his quarter watch. The young rascal was in the foretop with Greenway. He was telling, in his mysterious manner, what progress he had made in "ringing in" Shuffles as a member of the order, — declaring that he was sure to have him, when the word was passed for the story-teller to report to the officer of the deck.

"Little, did you invent the yarn you told me this evening?" said Ellis, sternly.

"No, sir; I only told you the truth," protested Little.

"Have you said anything to your shipmates?"

"Not a word; and I don't intend to do so."

"Don't do it. I believe there is not a word of truth in the story. Where is the bag of gold now?"

"That's more than I know. I suppose Shuffles has stowed it away where he can find it when we go on shore."

"Can't you find it?"

"I don't know."

"You can overhaul his berth when he is on deck," suggested Ellis.

"I haven't anything against Shuffles; and I don't want to expose him," added the innocent Little.

"You have made a charge, and now you must prove it. Keep your eye on Shuffles, and you may be able to do so. If you have trumped up this yarn, I will report you to the principal. I have already told the captain, and he don't believe the story."

"Have you, though?"

"I have. He wants the proof; and you must find it, or he will have you in the brig before you are a week older. Return to your duty."

Little did not like the idea of being committed to the brig himself. He hoped to see Shuffles there, disgusted with the life of a lamb, and desperate enough to join the knights.

"What did he want of you?" asked Greenway, when the little villain returned to the foretop, where he was on the lookout.

"He wanted to ask me if he might join the order," replied Little, in a matter-of-fact tone.

"Get out! What's the use of lying?"

"I have been with you fellows so much I can't help it," chuckled Little.

"No, but what did he want?"

The cunning rogue knew his companion too well to trust him, and "stuffed him up" with a tale invented for the occasion.

At seven bells in the morning the squadron was off

Boulogne, and from the tops the English and the French coasts could be seen. The wind was fresh and steady from the westward, but the vessels were close-hauled, and the prospect of reaching Havre that night was not very good. The regular recitations were carried on as usual through the day. Little did not for a moment forget the wicked purpose he had in view. It was not strange that he failed in his lessons, for his thoughts were all given to the anticipated cruise of the Josephine. It had been fully decided by the leaders of the enterprise that the consort must be captured during the stay of the squadron at Havre, or the lateness of the season would compel them to abandon it. The seamanship of Perth and his knowledge of navigation were discussed with renewed interest, and the feeling was stronger than ever among the dissatisfied ones that a more able commander was required. Shuffles fully met the demand of the occasion, and Little was urged by Greenway to " hurry up his cakes," if he intended to bring him into the conspiracy.

Little was very willing to expedite the business, for old as he was in mischief and iniquity, his present scheme was so utterly mean and vile that it kept him in a fever heat of anxiety, and he wished to have it brought to a head as soon as possible, for his own sake as well as for the success of the mad project. Shuffles and he were occupants of the same messroom, the former having the lower berth on one side, while the latter had the upper one on the other side. The bag of gold, which had so strangely come into his possession, was just then concealed under Shuffles's berth. The mattress rested on slats, beneath which there was a space of two or three inches, to allow them to spring.

The bag had been placed in this recess, in the absence of any other convenient place in the mess-room; but the rogue had not intended that it should remain there for any length of time. Perhaps the place he had chosen to conceal the treasure had suggested the dastardly plan by which the reformed student was to be dragged into the conspiracy. Little was alone in the mess-room, his half of the watch being off duty — "soldiering," as the young tars usually termed it. As he had done twenty times before, he raised the mattress to satisfy himself that the gold had not been disturbed. He improved the opportunity to place it in a more conspicuous place, so that it could be seen the instant the mattress was raised. Having satisfied himself that the money was both safe and in the right place, he went on deck and found the second lieutenant, who was also "soldiering."

"I have found it," said he, in a whisper.

"What! the bag of gold!" exclaimed Ellis, a smile of satisfaction lighting up his face.

"Yes; come with me, and I will show it to you. But I wish you would take the captain with you; he thinks I lied, and I want him to see for himself."

Ellis approved of this prudent policy, and by the time Little had returned to his mess-room, Captain Haven had been duly informed of the astounding discovery. Both of them hastened to the steerage, and entered the room where the little villain was waiting to receive them.

"There it is," said Little, raising the mattress, and revealing to the astonished captain the bag of gold under the slats.

"Are you satisfied, Captain Haven?" asked Ellis, triumphantly.

"That is certainly a bag; but whether it is a bag of gold, or not, I don't know," replied the commander, stooping down to take up the treasure.

"Excuse me, Captain Haven," interposed Little, in a very low tone, as all of them were obliged to speak, so as not to disturb the classes in the steerage. "I hope no one will touch the bag till Mr. Lowington has seen it. It will be better for him to see with his own eyes than with yours."

"I am not going to be deceived. I shall know what is in the bag before I say anything to anybody about it," replied the captain, glancing at Little, and perhaps suspecting that he had filled up the bag with old iron, to accomplish some purpose of his own; but Little offered no objection to his examination of the treasure.

Captain Haven took the bag from the recess, untied the string, and poured out a portion of the contents. They were coin, and, without a doubt, real "shiners."

"How long has this bag been here?" asked the captain, astounded at this apparent evidence of the guilt of Shuffles.

"I don't know," replied Little, satisfied with the impression he had produced. "I found it there just before I reported the fact to Mr. Ellis."

"Whose berth is this?"

"Shuffles's."

"Is it certain that he placed it there?" asked the captain.

"I don't know who placed it there; but if you please, Captain Haven, I wish you would put it back, and call Mr. Lowington. I want him to see for himself."

"That will be the better way," added Ellis.

"Perhaps it will," replied the captain, as he turned down the mattress, and led the way out of the room.

The commander, followed by Ellis, passed through the group of students engaged in study and recitation. Shuffles was at the mess-table, near the door of his room, puzzling over a problem in algebra.

"What is the number of your berth, Shuffles?" asked Captain Haven, as he passed him.

"No. 48, Gangway D," replied the student, looking up at the officer, and wondering why the question was put to him.

The captain made no explanation, but left the steerage by the door which led into the main cabin. Little did not follow him; but the moment the door closed behind Ellis, who brought up the captain's rear, he hastened back to the mess-room. He was a cool calculator, disposed to make the most of his opportunities. If any one has thought that he was a fool to squander such a quantity of hard coin in making a doubtful convert to the order of the Golden Fleece, he has done the little villain great injustice. Besides being a rascal of large pretensions, he was an economical one. He intended to catch the fish, and save his bait at the same time.

Raising the mattress once more, he took the bag

from its hiding-place. Wrapping it up loosely in his handkerchief, he went up the fore ladder to the deck. It was necessary instantly to dispose of the bag, and he had made his preparations beforehand to do so. Abaft the foremast was the fire engine. He had unscrewed the plate which covered one of the cylinders, and, raising it up, he dropped the bag upon the plunger. Screwing down the plate again, he returned to the steerage. Those of the crew who were on deck at the time were on the top-gallant forecastle, or in the rigging, examining the French coast, and the officers were too far aft to observe his actions. Little worked with his usual cunning and adroitness, and when he had accomplished his purpose he was satisfied that no one had seen him.

Mr. Lowington had not yet made his appearance in the steerage. Either the captain had not found him in the main cabin, or he was telling him the story which implicated Shuffles; but the crash could not long be delayed. The victim still sat at the mess-table, working up his algebra. The question which the captain had asked him suggested a greater puzzle than the problems. Why had he been asked the number of his berth? Was there anything wrong about the bed? The students were required to keep the mess-rooms and their furniture in good order, and it was possible that his berth was not in a tidy condition. He was anxious to know what the matter was, and he asked permission of Dr. Winstock, who was the temporary instructor in mathematics, to go to his mess-room. The request was granted, and he repaired to his quarters. The bed was somewhat tumbled in his berth. The quilt was not smoothed down as nicely as he had left it in the morning; but it seemed to him that this was a very small matter to make a fuss about.

The captain had come from his mess-room, and gone to the main cabin, just as though he intended to report the disorder of his berth to the principal. Ellis was with him too; and Shuffles did not lose sight of the fact that the second lieutenant claimed the captain as his friend in an especial manner. This was the beginning of the persecution to which he was to be subjected by the malice of the officers. They were seeking occasions to find fault with him, and to get him into trouble. He was to be doomed to a black mark for neglecting to take proper care of his berth. It was vexatious in the highest degree, and if he had not been too manly to cry, he would have wept over his misfortunes.

But Shuffles had not been reading his Bible, and attending to the instructions of the chaplain, to be broken down by so insignificant a trifle as a black mark. It might lower his grade a degree when the offices were assigned. He had been striving after the Christian spirit, and this was the time when he needed it most. He knelt down on the floor of the mess-room, to adjust the bedclothes in the berth. It was the attitude of prayer; and, almost involuntarily, he whispered his petition for strength to support him in the trials to which he was to be subjected, though he little knew the weight of the charge which was to be preferred against him.

While he was in this lowly posture, his door was

darkened by the appearance of Mr. Lowington and the captain, still closely followed by Ellis. As he saw them, he rose, bowed, and as the unexpected visitors stepped aside to allow him to pass out, he retired. He had arranged the bed properly; but it was almost incredible that the principal had been brought to the room to witness so trifling a departure from the regulations of the ship.

Captain Haven stooped down and raised the mattress; but the bag of gold was not there. He pulled the bed out of the berth, and removed the slats on which it had rested. The gold had taken to itself wings, as it has the reputation of doing in a more figurative sense than on the present occasion.

"It is not here," said Captain Haven, as much confounded now at not finding it as he had before been at finding it.

"I see it is not," replied the principal, mildly, and perhaps with a hope that, after all, Shuffles would justify his expectations.

"But it was here twenty minutes ago," protested the captain.

"Isn't there some mistake about it?"

"There can be no mistake, sir. I took up the bag myself, and poured out some of the sovereigns into my hand," replied the captain, warmly.

"Why did you not take the bag away when you discovered it?" asked Mr. Lowington.

"Because I wished to have you see it just where we found it."

"Shuffles has been in here, sir," interposed Ellis. "He was here when we came in, and down on his knees before his berth. I don't wonder the gold is not here now."

It was a plain case to the second lieutenant. Shuffles had seen the captain and himself enter the mess-room, and, taking the alarm, he had removed the bag to some other hiding-place.

"It is possible that Shuffles has removed the bag," said the principal.

"I know he has!" persisted Ellis. "I saw it with my own eyes, only a little while ago, in this very place."

"So did I," added the captain.

"As he was in the room when we entered, he cannot have carried it far. It is either on his person now, or concealed in some other place within the apartment," suggested Mr. Lowington.

This proposition was self-evident, and was readily accepted by the two officers.

"I have no doubt it is hidden in this room," added Ellis.

"It must be," responded the captain.

"Mr. Ellis, you will stand in the gangway, and keep your eyes on Shuffles while we search the room," continued the principal.

The gold was not in the mess-room, as the reader knows, and no amount of tumbling over the mattresses and overhauling the lockers could bring it to light. The search was as thorough as though the salvation of the ship depended upon its strictness.

"Are you entirely satisfied that the money is not here now, Captain Haven?" asked the principal, after they had ransacked every hole and corner in the mess-room, and also in the one on the other side of the gangway.

"I am, sir."

"Then there is only one other alternative — that it is concealed upon his person."

"I don't exactly see how that can be, since the bag must have weighed eight or ten pounds, and he could hardly carry it in one of the pockets of his jacket or trousers."

"I should prefer to find the bag before any charge is made," added the principal, thoughtfully. "If you have seen and handled the bag, of course there can be no mistake."

"Certainly not, sir."

"Ellis, direct Shuffles to report to me in the main cabin," said Mr. Lowington, as he left the mess-room, attended by Captain Haven. "See that he comes without delay, and that he has no opportunity to dispose of the bag."

Ellis was willing enough to deliver this order; but, though he was actuated by a bad spirit, it is only justice to him to add that he believed with all his might Shuffles was guilty.

"You will report immediately to Mr. Lowington in the main cabin," said he to the unhappy victim of the conspiracy.

"What is it now?" asked Shuffles, who was confident the worst charge that could be trumped up against him was the neglect to keep his berth in proper order, and he was prepared to submit meekly to the black mark, which had been the chief bugbear of his existence for two months.

"I am not permitted to say," replied Ellis, haughtily.

"I will report to the principal immediately," added Shuffles, with dignity, as he closed his book.

"Without an instant's delay, if you please."

Shuffles bowed, and walked towards the cabin door, closely attended by the second lieutenant, who could not be blamed for discharging his duty to the letter of his instructions. The little villain who had been the author of all this mischief kept himself at a respectful distance, but he was a close observer of all that transpired. In half an hour, more or less, Shuffles would be in the brig. The coveted member of the order of the Golden Fleece would be in condition to be approached. The shame and degradation of the ship's prison would overwhelm him; he would fall a victim to the clever trick, and be a warning to all the crew not to set up for saints.

How could so small a boy be so great a villain! Such things are mysteries.

Shuffles had been thinking, reading his Bible, praying, since the night before. He was still determined to be gentle and submissive, to forgive his enemies, even Ellis, and conquer them by the mighty power of love. In this frame of mind, he entered the main cabin, to be censured for the disorder in his berth.

CHAPTER VII.

CABIN AND CROSSTREES.

MR LOWINGTON had often pointed with pride and pleasure to Shuffles as an exemplification of the results of his system of instruction and discipline. He was obliged to write hundreds of letters in reply to inquiries from anxious fathers and mothers, and for the last two months Shuffles had been his model student. Many distinguished men, Americans as well as foreigners, visited the squadron, and were full of questions in regard to the system. Proudly he pointed to Shuffles, Pelham, McLeish, and others, as individual examples, while the perfect discipline of the ship's company exhibited the general effect. A majority of these students had been sent to the Academy squadron because they were unmanageable in ordinary institutions.

Shuffles had apparently fallen, and the principal was almost as sad as he would have been if the culprit had been his own son. He had felt a fatherly interest in him, and had observed with the deepest solicitude the struggles of the reformed student to be true and faithful. He had not failed to encourage him, while the chaplain had made him his pet, and watched his upward progress with a zeal bordering upon enthusiasm. The principal was sad, and tried to find some way to escape the conclusion which had been forced upon him. The story which Captain Haven had related to him was monstrous. It appeared that Shuffles, instead of reporting the fact that a large sum of money had fallen into his hands, had appropriated it to his own use, had concealed it, and really intended to rob the heirs of the drowned man of their inheritance. The gold had come into his possession without the knowledge of his shipmates. It had tempted him, and had triumphed over his principle, over his sense of honesty and justice. It was the old story, and the student had been wrecked, as tens of thousands of others are in the great world.

"Shuffles, I think you must know why I have sent for you," said the principal.

"Yes, sir, I do," replied the culprit.

"I hope you will be able to explain your conduct."

"I can only say that I left my berth in good order the last time I was in the mess-room. I may have been careless; but I will try to do better in future."

Mr. Lowington looked at him with a keen glance of inquiry. There was nothing in the face of the culprit which enlightened him.

"For what do you suppose I sent for you?" he asked.

"Because the bedding in my berth was not in good order," replied Shuffles, glancing involuntarily at Ellis.

"That was not the reason I sent for you. I wish it were nothing more serious than that."

Shuffles drew a long sigh, as his heart seemed to

rise up into his throat. He tried to think of something else which could be charged upon him; but the confusion of the moment did not enable him to recall the events of the past, and he waited to hear the complaint.

"Can you think of no other charge which might be preferred against you?" continued the principal.

"I cannot, sir. I have not intended to do anything wrong."

"Have you any secret which you have tried to conceal from your shipmates?"

"Any secret?" replied the culprit, puzzled by the question.

"While you were engaged in rescuing the passengers of the steamer, did any event occur which you have tried to keep to yourself?"

"No, sir," answered Shuffles, very promptly. "I apologized to Mr. Ellis for my disobedience of orders, and assured him I intended no disrespect."

"Did you, indeed? I was not aware of it," added Mr. Lowington, glancing at Ellis.

The coxswain might also have said that his apology was not accepted; but he preferred to suffer himself rather than place his officer in a disagreeable position. This was his interpretation of the divine command, "Love your enemies," which he had more than learned by heart.

Mr. Lowington derived some hope from the replies and from the manner of Shuffles. There was nothing in his words or his looks to indicate guilt. The principal then questioned him very particularly in regard to his conduct when the attempt was made to save the man on the spar, and the coxswain minutely detailed his own actions.

"I took hold of the man's arm and tried to pull him into the boat. I got hold of him near the shoulder," said Shuffles; "but the man did not seem to help me any. I tried to bring his hand up so that he could grasp the gunwale of the barge; but he either could not or would not lift it. Then the boat lurched in the sea, and I lost my hold. I was obliged to let go, or be thrown overboard as Little was."

"Didn't the man give you something before you let go?" asked Mr. Lowington, coming nearer to the point than he had before.

"Give me something?" repeated the culprit. "He gave me a hard pull, and had nearly wrenched my arms off. That's all he gave me. I don't know what you are driving at, sir."

"Didn't the man hand you something, which he was anxious to save."

"No, sir; he did not. I don't know what you mean," continued Shuffles, glancing first at the captain and Ellis, then at Mr. Lowington. "I see that I am charged with something; I have not the least idea what it is. The man in the water gave me nothing, and I don't know that he gave anything to anybody. I did not see him do so."

"Have you any money about you?"

"No, sir," replied Shuffles, promptly, as he involuntarily turned out his trousers pockets, and then those in his jacket.

"Have you, at any time since the burning of the steamer, had in your possession a bag of gold?"

"No, sir."

"Have you seen one?"

"No, sir."

Then the case was tried in due form. The charge was repeated by the principal, and, for the first time, Little appeared as the chief actor in the tragedy. He was sent for, and told the same story he had related to Ellis. The man on the spar informed him that he had given his bag of gold to some one in the boat, and that was the reason, it appeared, why Shuffles had failed to haul him in. Little declared that he knew nothing at all about the matter except what the man had told him. He had been directed to search for the bag; he had done so, and found it under the berth. Unlike many forward witnesses, he did not presume to know too much. What he knew he was sure of; and he had no theories or suppositions to introduce. Captain Haven and Ellis had both seen the bag of gold, and examined its contents, so that his testimony was fully confirmed.

It is not necessary to say that Shuffles was at first appalled and confused by the graveness of the charge, in which, so far as he was concerned, there was not one word of truth; but, conscious of his innocence, he soon recovered his self-possession. He did not attempt to stand upon the defensive. He was all submission, which made it the more difficult for the principal to resort to vigorous measures. The culprit looked and acted like a truthful boy, and, in spite of the evidence, Mr. Lowington was incredulous. There is something in innocence which resists all proof, and seems to assert itself in spite of all testimony against it.

Little was questioned over and over again. What he knew, he knew; and what he did not know, he would not say anything about. The meagre, naked fact that the man told him he had handed the bag of gold to the person in the boat who attempted to pull him in, and the equally bare fact that he had found the bag in the space under Berth 48, Gangway D, were all he knew. Beyond these he would not go. He had not seen Shuffles do anything strange on board. He had not heard him say anything. Shuffles and Little were required to leave the cabin, but to be within call.

"Are you satisfied, Captain Haven?" asked the principal.

"No, sir, I am not," replied the commander, frankly.

"Are you, Mr. Ellis?"

"I don't see what has become of the bag; but all except that seems to be plain enough," answered the lieutenant.

"Sifting the matter down to its narrowest basis, the charge rests only upon the evidence of Little," added Mr. Lowington. "His testimony is confirmed by yours, so far as the bag of gold is concerned. That the money was found under Shuffles's berth does not prove that he placed it there. I am confident the bag of gold is on board of the ship. All else is in the dark. One word more: I believe Shuffles is as innocent of the charge as I am. Captain Haven, you will pipe to muster. Mr. Ellis, send Shuffles to me."

In a moment the boatswain's whistle sounded through the ship, and all hands repaired to their stations. Shuffles reported in the cabin, but was required to remain there. All the instructors, adult forward officers, the stewards, the chaplain, and the surgeon, without being informed of the charge against the coxswain, were required to search the steerage for a bag of gold. Every locker was turned out, all the bedding was taken from the berths, and every aperture, crack, and corner, every article of clothing, and even every pot and pan in the kitchen, was examined. Of course the bag was not found.

Then every officer and seaman was searched; and, after the crew had been ordered into the rigging, the deck and all its appliances were overhauled. Even the fire engine was examined, but the professors who performed this part of the search were not even aware that the plates covering the top of the cylinders through which the plungers' rods passed, could be removed. Little had an awful fit of trembling, when, from the foretop, he looked down upon this operation on the engine; but the agony was soon over, and no discovery was made.

The search created a tremendous sensation among the students, and vainly they asked each other for information in regard to it. Little, for his own sake, said nothing, and the two officers had been instructed to keep their own counsel. When the examination was concluded, the ship's company were dismissed, and returned to their duties on deck and in the steerage. Of all who were observing these movements, none were more perplexed than the officers who were in the secret. It was singular that the bag had not been found. Mr. Lowington returned to the cabin, where the culprit was impatiently waiting to hear the result of the charge.

"Shuffles, you know all the testimony in this case. Can you say anything to relieve yourself or explain the matter?" said the principal.

"I cannot, sir. I know no more about it than any one else."

"Have you had any difficulty with Little?"

"Not a particle, sir. He professes to be one of my best friends. Now, I do remember that he said something to me about my old friends, and I suspected, for a moment, that he was trying to draw me into some mischief."

The principal inquired very particularly into the circumstances of this interview, but nothing definite could be deduced from it. He was not willing to believe that Shuffles was guilty, and he dismissed him until further inquiry should elicit more evidence. The intended victim of the conspiracy, strange as it may, perhaps, seem, was much less disturbed by the charge preferred against him than he had been on the night before. That complaint had a foundation; this one had none. He was rather amused than concerned by it, though he was exceedingly anxious to get at the root of the whole matter. The captain had seen the bag of gold, so that there was a root to it somewhere. He had no suspicion of the infamous trickery of Little, and was more willing to believe that the young villain was playing some practical joke than that he was seeking to injure him.

At eight bells in the evening, the lights on Cape la Hève, at the mouth of the Seine, were in sight, and a French pilot boarded the ship soon after. Though the vessel was actually in charge of a quarter watch, all hands were on deck. Those who were to go on duty at ten o'clock seldom turned in on these short passages, for they had six hours below, in good weather, after twelve. The ship's company had hoped to approach their destination by daylight; but as the head wind, during the day, deprived them of this pleasure, they made the most of the night. The coming on board of a pilot is always an interesting event. The usual surprise of men of his calling at finding a ship worked by a company of boys was duly and properly manifested, and the boys enjoyed his astonishment. He talked a mongrel English, for Havre has an immense trade with the United States, and a large portion of his business was with American ships.

While so many of the students were amusing themselves with the pilot, Shuffles and Little were perched upon the fore crosstrees, whither they had gone to finish a conversation begun upon deck. The coxswain had taken the earliest opportunity to approach the little villain for information on the subject which interested him so deeply.

"What made you say the man gave me that bag of money?" asked Shuffles, as he met Little in the waist.

"What made me?" replied Little, lightly. "Do you know why the Dutchman called his son Hans?"

"No, I do not."

"Well, de reason why I calls my son Hans is because dat is his name. And the reason why I said the man gave you the bag, was because he did."

"That's all nonsense, Little."

"Perhaps it is; but didn't the captain see the bag? Didn't he open it and look at the gold? I don't know anything about it except what the man told me. If he lied to me, it is not my fault. Do you think it would be my fault if he lied to me?"

"Certainly not."

"I should say not," added Little, triumphantly, as though that settled the question forever.

"But the man did not give me the gold," protested Shuffles.

"I don't know anything about that, I tell you. Don't I keep saying so? If the man lied to me, that was not my fault, as you have yourself acknowledged. If he didn't give it to you, he must have given it to Ellis; and between you and me, Shuffles, after his treatment of you, I think he is mean enough to do such a thing."

"Ellis was standing up in the barge, at the time, and the man could not have given the bag to him; and I am sure he did not give it to me."

"O, dry up, Shuffles! You are a good fellow, and I know it, if the rest of the fellows don't. You were smart when you hid that bag, after the flunkies went for the principal."

"I didn't hide it," replied Shuffles.

"What's the use of taking the trouble to deny it to me? It's honor bright between us, and I would be keelhauled before I would say anything about it. Didn't I see you go into our mess-room two minutes after Ellis and the captain went out? I might have watched you, if I had been mean enough to do so, and seen where you put the spondoolicks."

"I'm sorry you didn't."

"I wouldn't do such a thing. I'm not one of the lambs. Only the spoonies would get a fellow into a scrape. I say, Shuffles, I will go halves with you, and help you out."

"You don't believe what you are saying."

"Don't I? You will believe it yourself by the time you are put in the brig, if you don't now."

Little proceeded to rehearse the testimony again; and not being as impartial as the principal, it is almost a wonder he did not convince Shuffles that he had concealed the bag.

"I see just what you are up to, Shuffles," added the conspirator. "You are going to quit when we get to Havre, and have a good time with that money. I should like to go with you, if I had the stamps."

"Have it as you please," replied Shuffles, who found it useless to deny anything.

"Won't you take me with you?"

"I will when I go."

"That's right; I thought you would get tired of those spoonies."

"Suppose I am tired of them — what then?" added Shuffles, wishing to draw out his companion.

"Go on shore, travel on your own account, and have a good time. You know how to do it better than any fellow in the squadron."

"Is there any little party getting up for such an excursion which I could join?"

"Perhaps there is; I didn't say there was," replied Little, who was burning to gather in his suspected shipmate.

"How are they going?" asked Shuffles, taking the fact for granted.

"You must ask them; I don't know anything about it," laughed Little. "I had an idea you were getting up a party yourself, by your laying in the funds to pay the expenses."

"No; but if there is anything of the kind going on, I should like to know it."

For the first time since he had any principles to lean upon, Shuffles was embarrassed by them. Three months ago, he would not have scrupled to worm himself into the confidence of any shipmate for the purpose of discovering his plans and intentions. He wished to do so in the present instance, but his conscience revolted at the thought of a lie, either spoken or acted. What Little had said to him the day before, as well as what he hinted now, assured Shuffles that some mischief, in the shape of a runaway expedition, was brewing. It did not appear in what manner the bag of gold was connected with it, but there was evidently some connection between them.

"What do you want to know for?" asked Little.

"If the plan suits me, I might want to join, after what has happened," replied Shuffles, sorely tempted to deceive the rogue at his side. "The officers are all down upon me, as you have seen, and now I am charged with appropriating this money."

"I wouldn't stand it. Would you really like to join a party?" asked the little villain, eagerly.

"I don't know yet, till I hear what the party is, and where they are going," answered Shuffles; and this answer almost choked him, for he realized that it was not in accordance with the high standard he had set up for his guidance.

"One of those twelve-oar barges would be just the thing for such an excursion," suggested Little. "We can go up the Seine, and land where we please. What do you think of it?"

"Is that the idea?"

"That's the idea. The crew of the commodore's barge are all first-rate fellows, and you are the best one in the crowd."

"How is it to be managed?" asked Shuffles.

"Just as soon as we get to Havre, the boat will be sent off for something. If we all understand each other, all we have to do is to pull up the river, and — let them wait till we get back," chuckled Little.

"Will the barge's crew all go?" asked Shuffles.

"I will see that it is all right with them. You are the coxswain of the commodore's barge, and without you we couldn't do a single thing," added Little, apparently with a generous burst of confidence.

"We can talk it over after we get into the boat," suggested Shuffles. "But suppose there should be an officer with us?"

"If there is, we shall put him on shore at some convenient place, where he won't get back to the ship too soon."

The only part of the programme that seemed to be improbable, was the fact that some of the steadiest and most reliable boys in the ship belonged to the barge's crew; and Shuffles suggested this difficulty to his companion.

"There are only two fellows we can't approach —

Willis and Hewins. We shall put them ashore with the officer, if there is one. We shall be eleven against three, and we can have it all our own way," replied Little.

All obstacles were removed, and Shuffles was satisfied that he had discovered a mischievous scheme. He even suspected that an attempt had been made to "break him down," so as to induce him to join the party. The fact that he was coxswain of the barge, in which the enterprise was to be carried out, helped him out in the solution of the problem. It all looked plausible enough, and he was satisfied so far; but he wished to know more of the details of the affair. Little was perfectly willing to give them, inventing them as he went along, for the reader needs not to be told that the scheme was "bogus;" that he had no more intention of running away in the barge than he had of capturing the ship. If Shuffles would join in the supposed expedition, he would not hesitate to take part in going off in the Josephine.

But Shuffles had not yet squarely and unequivocally joined the party, though Little was very much encouraged by his seeming willingness. He felt that the coxswain must be disgusted by his recent experience; and, as he had fully relied upon his acquiescence, he was the more ready to interpret favorably his words and his actions; but he was too cautious to say anything about the real issues, or even to hint at the Knights of the Golden Fleece.

"But where are you going to get the money to pay your expenses?" asked Shuffles, after all other difficulties had been removed by the ingenuity of his shipmate.

"That's one of the reasons why we want you to join us," replied the little villain, eagerly.

"Have you been relying upon that alone?" asked the coxswain.

"This is a new thing, you see. We haven't talked it over till to-day."

"But suppose I don't go — what will you do for money then?"

"I don't know," answered Little, blankly. "I suppose we shall have to give it up."

"Haven't you any money?"

"No, not a red."

"It is very strange that you should get up such an enterprise without thinking of any way to pay the expenses."

"We are not so green as that. We have depended on you to furnish both the brains and the money for the expedition. That bag of gold will keep us going for a month, at least."

"I dare say it would."

"I think you had better divide it among the fellows before we start."

"Perhaps that would be the better plan. I will consider it."

"You have not said fairly that you would join us, Shuffles."

"I will go with you in the barge," replied Shuffles, who, as coxswain of the boat, would be obliged to do so.

The reformed student was not satisfied with himself, for he felt that he had deceived the rogue; but he regarded it as a duty he owed to himself, if not to the ship, to ferret out the mystery of the bag of gold. He had obtained some leading ideas on the subject during this interview, and when all hands were called to take in sail and moor the ship, he was glad to escape the little villain, and return to the deck.

He did not believe the rogue had matured the details of a runaway trip without providing the means to pay the expenses. They were going up the Seine in the barge, but of course their objective point was Paris, or some other large city in France. Shuffles was satisfied that the bag of gold was to constitute the exchequer of the party. Who had it, or where it was, he had no idea; but he was confident that when the expedition started, the gold would be in the boat, or in the pockets of the runaways. If the money was not found by that time, it would be discovered then.

Whatever Little may have thought, Shuffles was not disgusted with the life he led. Even with trouble hanging over him, and with enemies in his path, he believed that a good life was happier than a bad one. He was pleased with the information he had obtained, but not with the means by which he had obtained it. He felt that he ought to have trusted to the truth alone to redeem him from disgrace and suspicion.

The pilot took the ship into the Little Roadstead, before the inner harbor of Havre, which is left high and dry at low tide. The sails were furled, and she came to anchor. The Josephine came in just abreast of her, and followed her example. As soon as the work was done, and everything put in ship-shape order, Shuffles touched his cap to Mr. Lowington, and asked an interview with him. In the state-room of the principal, he told freely all that had transpired between himself and Little.

However much Mr. Lowington disapproved of the means by which Shuffles had obtained his information, he was too great a lover of discipline, and too anxious to discover the bag of gold, to neglect the opportunity now presented to him of exposing guilt and defeating a mischievous scheme. He promised Shuffles that on the following evening the barge should be sent to the shore without an officer, so that the whole party of conspirators could be captured. The details would be arranged in due time.

Shuffles turned in, satisfied that the bag of gold would be unearthed before another day elapsed.

CHAPTER VIII.

SOMETHING ABOUT THE GEOGRAPHY AND INSTITUTIONS OF FRANCE.

THE morning light revealed to the students on board of the squadron all that could be seen of Havre. The wind came from the north-west, and the vessels were sheltered by the headland, from which projects Cape la Hève, so that the roadstead was tolerably smooth, and the motion not uncomfortable. The lighthouses on the cape are erected upon a high, rocky cliff, three hundred feet above the level of the sea, and its scenery was very attractive to the tourists who had so long been looking out upon the low lands of Holland and Belgium. The rocks on the cape were the favorite resort of Bernardin de St. Pierre, author of "Paul and Virginia," who was born at Havre.

The Seine at its mouth is about four miles wide. The tide rises and falls twenty feet on an average, and the current is very rapid. The entrance to the river is obstructed by sand-bars, piled up by the swift flow of the waters; but most of them are above Havre. The tide phenomenon, which prevails in the Amazon and some other rivers, called the *bore*, may be observed in the estuary of the Seine. The wave, sometimes four feet high in the spring tides, rushes furiously up the river, and vessels not properly prepared to meet it are liable to be swamped by its violence.

The harbor in front of the city is a small inlet, the mouth of which is protected by jetties, or breakwaters, extending from the opposite shores towards each other, so as to leave only a narrow passage for vessels. At low tide, the water nearly all runs out of this basin, where, at high tide, ships float in eighteen or twenty feet of water in the deepest parts. From this harbor, called the *Avant-Port*, open the immense docks which receive all the shipping, as at Liverpool, Bristol, and other places. The French, in their efforts to compete with the English, have devoted a great deal of attention to the subject of navigation, and to the improvement and safety of their harbors. At all the principal ports of the empire, a system of tidal signals has been established, by which vessels coming in are apprised of the depth of water in the channels.

Between the jetties of Havre there is hardly water enough at low tide to float a jolly-boat, and the depth is precisely indicated to the approaching vessels by this marine telegraphy. The apparatus consists of a mast, with a yard across it, upon which black balls are hoisted. One ball at the intersection of the mast and yard denotes a depth of ten feet between the jetties. Each ball under this one, and on the mast, indicates an additional depth of three and a quarter feet. Each ball hoisted above the first adds six and a half feet to the depth indicated by the single one. Each ball on the left yard-arm denotes an extra depth of ten inches; on the right, twenty inches. Sometimes certain signal flags are used to convey the same idea. When the state of the sea is such as to render it dangerous for vessels to enter the port, a red flag is hoisted, instead of the balls.

The system of buoys and beacons on the French coast is similar to that adopted by England and the United States, but it is more comprehensive. In entering a harbor, all red buoys are to be left on the starboard hand, and the black ones on the port. Beacons below the level of high water are painted white, and each one has its number, and the name of the rock or shoal which it marks, painted upon it.

The docks of Havre were the especial care of the first Napoleon, and have been greatly improved and enlarged by his successors. The largest of them contains an area of fourteen or fifteen acres. The regulations for vessels within them are very strict. No fires or lights are allowed on board, and it is even forbidden to smoke on a ship's deck. Mr. Lowington was not willing to dock the two vessels of the squadron, for this step involved the necessity of boarding all hands on shore, and it would be impossible to keep up the discipline under such circumstances. It was his intention to lie in the roadstead as long as the weather permitted, or until the students started for Paris, and then go into the docks, leaving the adult forward officers to attend to the business. It was Saturday now, and he expected to leave Monday afternoon.

Early in the morning Mr. Arbuckle was landed from the Josephine. The baggage of his family, which had been hurried forward by his friends in

London, had already arrived. It was passed through the custom-house, and taken on board. The ladies of the party were thus able, for the first time, to appear on deck.

Immediately after breakfast, the signal, "All hands, attend lecture!" appeared on board of the ship. Mr. Arbuckle's family wished to be present at this exercise, for they were deeply interested in the routine of the Academy squadron. Places were assigned to them in the captain's gig, and they were warmly welcomed on board of the ship by the principal. Grace had entirely recovered from the effects of the disaster, and looked like a new being. She inquired for Shuffles as soon as she went on board, and again poured forth her thanks for the important service he had rendered to her.

"Mr. Lowington, I desire your coöperation in carrying out a little plan of mine, to express my gratitude to the brave fellows who have done so much for me and mine," said Mr. Arbuckle, as the students were piping into the steerage to hear the lecture on France.

"I think it is hardly necessary to express your gratitude any further than you have done so, but I shall be happy to aid you."

"I intend to give a dinner to all hands on board of the Josephine this afternoon, if practicable, and another to the crew of the barge which saved Grace, on Monday," added Mr. Arbuckle.

"I will consent, but I must name two conditions — that you give them no wine or money," laughed the principal.

"I will agree to give them no wine, or anything stronger than coffee. In regard to the money, I will do that through you, or with your knowledge and consent."

"Money is really the root of all evil with our students. When their pockets are full, we cannot so easily control them. They run away, or otherwise break through our wholesome discipline; and wine was not made for boys."

"You may be assured I will not transgress any of your rules, Mr. Lowington. I shall take the liberty to invite all the officers and crew of the Josephine as soon as they return to their vessel. Will you do me the favor to invite the officers and the crew of the barge for Monday?"

"I will, with pleasure," replied Mr. Lowington, as he conducted his guests to the steerage.

Mr. Arbuckle, anticipating the consent of the principal, had ordered the entertainment for the Josephine at the Hotel de l'Europe, while he was on shore. He was a very wealthy man, as he was a very liberal one. He was deeply impressed with his obligations to the squadron, and the dinners to which he had invited those who had been directly instrumental in saving the lives of his family were only the beginning of what he intended to do, and of what, so far as the circumstances would permit, he did do.

On the foremast, in the steerage, hung a large map of France, and before it stood Mr. Mapps, the instructor in geography and history. He was involuntarily rubbing his hands, for this gentleman was now in his element. Like many other teachers, he took greater pleasure in talking to the whole school than in the dry details of single classes.

"Young gentlemen," he began, taking up his pointer, "France is a great country; and so eventful has been its history, that the brief period allotted to this lecture will only permit me to skim over the subject in the most unsatisfactory manner. In shape, France is an irregular pentagon, whose five sides are approximately bounded as follows: On the north-east by Belgium and the German provinces of Rhenish Prussia and Bavaria; on the east by the German province of Baden, by Switzerland, and the kingdom of Italy; on the south by the Mediterranean Sea and Spain; on the west by the Bay of Biscay; and on the northwest by the Atlantic Ocean and the English Channel.

"The distance from its most northern to its most southern point is six hundred miles. From its most eastern to its most western point it is five hundred and eighty-two miles, though between the Bay of Biscay and the Italian frontier the distance is only three hundred and sixty miles. It has a coast line of one thousand five hundred and thirty miles. It has an area of two hundred thousand square miles. It is larger than the ten eastern and middle states of our own country united. Add Indiana, and the area of the eleven states would about equal that of France. The four states of Georgia, Alabama, Mississippi, and Louisiana have also about the same territory as France. Its population exceeds that of the United States by about seven millions.

"France has every variety of surface, from the low and marshy land of the west to the mountainous regions of the east and south. Most of it presents about the same physical features as New England, the country being diversified by frequent elevations. Its highest mountains are on the eastern and southern borders. The Pyrenees, between France and Spain, are a continuation of the Asturian Mountains. This range extends through Europe, being connected with the Alps by the Cevennes, Côte d'Or, Vosges, and Jura chains. On the east are the Alps, subdivided into a great many minor ranges, as the Pennine, the Graian, and the Cottian Alps. The highest peak of the Pyrenees in France is about eleven thousand feet. Until the recent annexation of the Italian provinces of Savoy and Nice, Mount Olan was the highest mountain in France; but now Mont Blanc, in Savoy, the highest in Europe, lies within its limits. Its height is fifteen thousand seven hundred and fifty feet. I hope you will see it.

"Let me call your attention for a moment to the interior mountain ranges of France," added the professor, pointing to them on the map. "The Cevennes and Côte d'Or ranges divide the country into two unequal parts, and form the water-shed between the Atlantic and the Mediterranean Sea. From the Cevennes branch out the Auvergne Mountains, which extends north-west in the centre of France.

"Among these mountains rise the principal rivers, the Seine, the Loire, the Garonne, and the Rhone. The Rhine separates France from Germany on the east. The Meuse, Scheldt, and Moselle rise in this country, and flow into Belgium and Germany. The Rhone, five hundred and thirty-four miles long, rises in Switzerland, and flows into the Mediterranean. In passing through the Jura Mountains, it descends into a deep chasm, and at low water disappears from view; but when the river is high the water flows over the rocks. The place is called the *Perte du Rhone.* It is navigable three hundred and sixty miles, and is connected with the Rhine, Seine, Loire, and Garonne by canals, so that boats on one of these rivers can make their way to either of the others, and merchandise may be transported from Paris to Marseilles, or from Strasburg to Bordeaux.

"The Seine, about five hundred miles long, rises in the Vosges Mountains, and is navigable for small craft for three hundred and fifty miles. The Loire, six hundred and forty miles in length, rises on the Spanish side of the Pyrenees, and is navigable for boats about four hundred miles. The Garonne, three hundred and eighty-four miles long, also rises in Spain, and is navigable to Toulouse, about a hundred and fifty miles from the sea. All these rivers are noted for the beauty of their scenery and the lovely landscapes which border them. The navigation of them is very much interrupted by shoals; the Loire, near its head waters, is sometimes left high, and dry, and at others so overflowed, that, on account of its furious current, it is impassable. Great efforts have been made to improve these rivers by dikes, dredging, and dams; but in the American sense of the word, they can hardly be considered navigable.

"With this meagre view of the face of the country, let us glance at its political divisions and its government. France formerly contained thirty-three provinces, with the names of many of which you are familiar, as Normandy, Brittany, Lorraine, Champagne, Picardy, Poitou, Anjou, Burgundy, Gascony, and Dauphiné. You still hear these terms used; but they have now no political significance, and no such divisions are legally recognized. They have been cut up into smaller territories, called departments. France now contains eighty-nine of these divisions, which are practically equivalent to counties in the United States and England, each having its specific name. The ancient provinces include from one to five of these departments.

"Each department has a government of its own, at the head of which is a *prefect*, who is assisted by a council. The eighty-nine departments are subdivided into three hundred and seventy-three *arrondissements*, two thousand nine hundred and forty-one *cantons*, and thirty-seven thousand five hundred and forty-eight *communes* or villages. Each *arrondissement* has a sub-prefect, who is responsible to the prefect of the department, and the communes are governed by a mayor and a town council. Each *arrondissement* has its high court, and each canton its police court.

"The government of France is nominally a constitutional or limited monarchy; but practically it is an absolute monarchy. Doubtless all the forms of the constitution are complied with; but it hardly admits of any independent action on the part of the people. The crown is hereditary in the Bonaparte family, though females are excluded from the throne. The constitution recognizes five powers in the government, of each of which I will say a word.

"*First.* The emperor is vested with the entire executive power. He is not responsible for the acts of the government, according to the pleasing fiction of monarchies. He cannot be arrested or held to answer for any of his acts; but his ministers must bear the blame when anything goes wrong. He appoints and discharges his ministers, pardons criminals, and all honors and dignities in the state are derived from him. He is commander-in-chief of the army and the navy, and may make war or peace at his imperial pleasure. He negotiates treaties with other powers, and nominates the persons who are to fill the offices in the empire. All the courts are conducted in his name, and he has the sole right to introduce legislative business, and no law is voted upon unless approved by him. No person can be employed in the public service without taking the oath of allegiance, not to France, but to the emperor. You perceive that he may have it all his own way.

"*Second.* In the discharge of his executive functions, the emperor employs eleven ministers, who hold office at his majesty's pleasure. Their duties are strictly defined by imperial decrees, and correspond with those of similar officers in our own country, except that there is a Minister of the Imperial House — of which we have no need — and a Minister of Public Instruction, and of Agriculture, Commerce, and Public Works, which we include in other departments. The Minister of State is the Premier, and communications between the emperor and the other ministers, as well as the Senate and legislative body, must be through him.

"The emperor and the ministers constitute the executive branches of the government. The legislative branch, which is under the control of the executive, is composed of three bodies.

"*Third.* The Council of State is composed of between forty and fifty members, appointed by the emperor, and holding office at his pleasure. They present to the legislative body the business upon which it is to act, draught laws, and introduce bills, under the direction of the emperor and his ministers. Certain of their number are appointed to advocate the bills offered, and to defend the governmental action. They receive a salary of twenty-five thousand francs, or five thousand dollars.

"*Fourth.* The Legislative Chambers, or, as formerly called, the Chamber of Deputies, is the nearest approach to a popular body to be found in France. The members are elected by the people at the rate of one for thirty-five thousand voters. This body is composed of three hundred and seventy-six members. They are chosen for six years, and receive five hundred dollars for every month of actual service. It is the duty of this body to discuss and accept or reject such bills as are laid before it by the Council of State, and to vote the money for the use of the government. This body cannot receive petitions from the people, and is called together, adjourned, and dissolved by the emperor.

"*Fifth.* The Second Assembly, usually called the Senate, is composed of men of eminent gravity, who are supposed to act as a check upon the legislative body, and in some respects corresponds to the

Senate of the United States, or the House of Lords in England. The Senate cannot have more than one hundred and fifty members. The cardinals of the Catholic church in France, the marshals, and the admirals, are members in virtue of their positions, and the others are nominated by the emperor. The dignity is for life, and cannot be revoked, though members may resign. They receive a salary of thirty thousand francs, or six thousand dollars, a year. The Senate acts upon all measures passed by the inferior legislative body, and no bill can become a law without its sanction or approval. — Well, Captain Kendall, what do you wish?" asked the professor, when he saw that the commander of the Josephine was trying to propose a question.

"I was reading last evening that the Constitution of France was modified by the *senatus-consulte* of November 2, 1852. What does *senatus-consulte* mean?"

"The Senate, with the advice and consent of the ministers, may propose any change in the Constitution; and when such change is approved by the emperor, it is called a *Senatus consultum*. The Senate is declared to be the guardian of the Constitution, of religion, public morals, freedom of conscience, individual liberty, and equality of all citizens before the laws. This body alone has the right to receive petitions from the people; and being appointed for life, with a handsome salary, the members are not likely to disturb his majesty by any pertinacious attempts to redress grievances. Under a good man on the throne, such a government might be just and equal; under a bad one, it might be the worst it is possible to conceive of.

"As in Belgium, all religions are tolerated, and the Roman Catholics, Protestants, and Jews are assisted with money stipends, by the government, for the support of the clergy. Before the revolution the Catholic church in France held one third of the landed property. The government took possession of its real estate, and the money now paid for the maintenance of religion seems to be a commutation for the former revenues of the church. Of the population of France, thirty-five and a half millions are Roman Catholics, one and a half millions are Protestants, and one hundred and fifty-six thousand are Jews. The Catholics receive from the government ten million dollars a year, the Protestants three hundred thousand dollars, and the Jews in their proportion. Besides these sums, each sect has its own private resources, and the total revenue of the Catholic church is estimated at twenty million dollars.

"The Catholic church in France has seventeen archbishops and sixty-seven bishops. The archbishop of Paris has a salary of ten thousand dollars, the other archbishops four thousand, and the bishops three thousand dollars. Six of these prelates are also cardinals, and in virtue of this office receive an additional stipend of two thousand dollars, besides being *ex officiis* senators, with a further salary of six thousand dollars. Other Catholic clergy, including vicars-general, canons, *curés*, and *desservants*, or curates, receive from five hundred dollars down to one hundred and eighty dollars a year.

"Great improvement has been made in the French system of education within the last generation. It is under the charge of the Minister of Public Instruction, who makes an annual report of its condition and progress. In Massachusetts there are about one hundred and ninety pupils in the public schools for every thousand of the population. In France, in 1832, there were fifty-nine to a thousand; in 1863, one hundred and sixteen to a thousand. In 1866, thirty per cent. of the conscripts, or drafted soldiers, could not read. But the intelligence of the people in different departments of France varies as much as in different parts of the United States. In fourteen of the eighty-nine departments only seven per cent. of the conscripts could not read; in thirteen others, fifty-eight per cent. could not read; and other departments vary between these — the highest and the lowest.

"France is divided into sixteen districts, each having its academy or university, in which the higher branches of learning are pursued, including theology, law, and medicine. In 1863, there were eighty-two thousand establishments for primary instruction, — equivalent to the high, grammar, and primary schools of the large towns of the United States, — which instructed two million six hundred thousand children. These are supported by the communes, but are not entirely free, only one third being admitted without charge, and two thirds paying small tuition fees. Normal schools for the preparation of teachers are provided in nearly all the departments. The average annual salary of female teachers in France is one hundred and thirty dollars. They do not board at the Grand Hotel!

"France is noted for its institutions of learning, among the most celebrated of which is the Polytechnic School at Paris, where naval, military, and civil engineers are educated. There are many establishments for the special instruction of students in the practical sciences, particularly those relating to the various departments of engineering, the mines, manufactures, forests, agriculture, and similar topics."

"What is the French Academy?" asked Terrill. "I see it mentioned on the title-page of all the French dictionaries."

"It was established in 1635, by Cardinal Richelieu, for the care of the French language. It was composed of forty members, who met three times a week in the palace of the Louvre, to regulate the use of words. After fifty years of debate, it completed, in 1694, the Dictionary of the French Language, which has been the basis of all subsequently issued. It has been abolished and revived several times, and now exists under the title of *Institut de France*. It includes five academies, each of which has in its charge one or more branches of art, science, and letters. It has two hundred and seventeen members, — each of whom receives a salary of three hundred dollars, — and seven secretaries. It has also certain honorary members, who are not paid, and over two hundred correspondents, who assist in collecting valuable information.

"*L'Académie Française*, composed of forty members, has the care of the French language, and all that relates to grammar, rhetoric, poetry, and the classics. It gives a prize of two thousand dollars every year to the author of the best work on public morals, and another of the same sum to the person of the laboring classes who is adjudged to have performed the most virtuous action. Every other year it makes a present of three hundred dollars to some needy genius who deserves such encouragement.

"*L'Académie des Inscriptions et Belles Lettres*, with forty members, devotes itself to the study of laws, history, chronology, medals, inscriptions, monuments, and ancient documents. It gives prizes for the best essays on the topics within its control.

"*L'Académie des Sciences* has sixty-five members, and has the natural sciences in its care. It gives prizes for papers on physiology, statistics, mechanics, and kindred sciences, and one to the best scholar in the Polytechnic School.

"*L'Académie des Beaux Arts* has the fine arts in its keeping, and gives prizes for the best painting, sculpture, engraving, architectural design, and musical composition.

"*L'Académie des Sciences Morals et Politiques*, attends to moral and general philosophy, political economy, statistics, law, and history, and gives one prize every year for the best production relating to its branches.

" Once in five years the *Institut* bestows the government prize of two thousand dollars for the most useful invention which has appeared within that period. It will thus be seen that this grand institution fosters and encourages noble deeds and useful inventions, as well as art, science, and literature.

" The army of France on the peace footing is composed of four hundred and four thousand men; on the war footing, seven hundred and fifty thousand men. The soldiers are drawn by conscription, and are liable to be drafted at the age of twenty-one. One hundred and sixty thousand men are drafted every year, of whom one half serve for five years in the regular army and four years in the army of reserve. The other half serve five years in the army of reserve and four in the *National Garde Mobile*, the latter of which can be called into actual service only by special law or the decree of the emperor. A drafted man may escape service by paying five hundred dollars to the government for a substitute.

"The French navy contains three hundred and sixty-eight vessels, afloat or in process of building, including transports and despatch boats; but not more than one third of this number are effective sea-going war vessels. The approaches of the French coast are guarded by twenty-seven forts and three hundred and forty-four batteries. The navy is composed of about fifty thousand officers and seamen, and every seafaring man, between twenty and forty years of age, with a few exceptions, is liable to be drafted into its service.

"Young gentlemen, as I am not half done, you may take a recess of fifteen minutes," added Mr. Mapps, as he folded up his papers, and retired from his rostrum.

The students went on deck, but in a quarter of an hour were piped back again.

CHAPTER IX.

AN EPITOME OF THE HISTORY OF FRANCE.

"IN order to give you an idea of the productive industry of France, young gentlemen, I will mention a few of the articles in the order of their importance," continued the professor, as he resumed his place. "First, silk goods; second, wines; third, woollen goods; fourth, fancy goods, including toys, gloves, wood work, umbrellas, &c.; fifth, linen goods; sixth, dressed skins; seventh, cotton goods; and, eighth, brandies and other spirits. Its principal imports are corn and flour, raw cotton, raw wool, and lumber.—Who is the present emperor?" asked Mr. Mapps, with sudden energy, as if he were as glad to escape dry details as his pupils.

"Napoleon III.!" shouted the crowd of students.

"Who is he?"

"The nephew of his uncle."

"Who was his uncle?" laughed the professor.

"Napoleon Bonaparte."

"Napoleon I. Who was Napoleon II., since the present emperor is Napoleon III.?"

"Napoleon Bonaparte's son, the King of Rome, or Duke de Reichstadt, as he was called in Austria," replied Paul Kendall. "He died when he was twenty-one. His father abdicated in his favor in 1814, but as the allies never admitted his title of Napoleon II., he did not assume it."

"When the present emperor was recognized by the governments of Europe, no objection was made to his title. Napoleon I. had four brothers — Joseph, King of Naples and of Spain, Louis, King of Holland, Jerome, King of Westphalia, and Lucien, who declined the throne of Italy. The first emperor, you know, married Josephine, the widow of Viscount Beauharnais, who had two children, Hortense and Eugene Beauharnais. Louis, King of Holland, married Hortense, and the present emperor is their son. He was born in Paris, in 1808, and led an eventful life. He was educated principally in Switzerland, and has been concerned in several insurrections.

"He had been a great favorite with his imperial uncle as a child; and the emperor, setting aside the natural descent, had named his brother Louis as his successor. The death of his elder brother in 1831, and of the Duke de Reichstadt in 1832, made him heir to the throne of Napoleon I. This fact stimulated his ambition, and fired his soul with a desire to win the imperial honors. He used every effort to conciliate the French people, and wrote books to demonstrate the necessity of the empire; but not satisfied with this slow process of spreading his 'Napoleonic ideas,' he sought to vitalize them by a revolution.

For attempting to get up a rebellion in 1836, at Strasbourg, he was sent an exile to America; but he returned to Europe in less than a year. In 1840 he made another effort to create an insurrection at Boulogne, for which he was condemned to perpetual imprisonment. After a confinement of six years, he escaped from the fortress of Ham, and resided in England, until the revolution of 1848, when he hastened to Paris, again to seek his destiny. He was chosen a deputy to the National Assembly, and then elected president of the republic.

"His government was, nominally, republican, but he was steadily at work to carry out his personal schemes. He began to exercise his power rather arbitrarily, and some differences between the president and the deputies, which soon grew into a rupture, ensued. Suddenly, on the night of December 2, 1851, Paris was declared to be in a state of siege by the president; the Assembly was dissolved, and nearly two hundred of the members arrested, the leading ones being taken from their beds, and hurried to prison. People who were disposed to defend them were shot down by the soldiers. This was the *coup d'état*. At the same time a decree, granting universal suffrage, was promulgated, and Louis nominated himself to the presidency for ten years. He had the good fortune to be elected, which was not very strange, under the circumstances. But the dignity of Prince President did not satisfy him, and he still bent himself steadily to the purpose of reëstablishing the empire. He won over a sufficient number of partisans to accomplish his purpose; and then the Senate called upon him to assume the title of Emperor; which, however, he was not willing to do, until the people had again gone through the formality of an election. By a vote of nearly eight millions for him, to about two hundred thousand against him, he was chosen hereditary emperor. On the 1st of December, 1852, he accepted the imperial dignity, and assumed the title of 'Napoleon III., Emperor of the French.'

"He married Eugenie Marie de Montigo. They have only one child, Napoleon Eugene Louis, who is styled the Prince Imperial, born in 1856. The emperor has two cousins at court — the Princess Mathilde, daughter of Jerome, and Prince Napoleon Joseph, son of Jerome — who married Clotilde, daughter of Victor Emmanuel II., King of Italy. He has been nicknamed 'Plon-plon,' and visited the United States a few years ago.

"Napoleon III. has a larger 'civil list,' or income, than any other monarch in Europe. He has an annual revenue from the government of five million dollars, besides which he receives the income of the crown domains, amounting to three millions more. He also has the free use of several palaces, parks, mansions, and forests, which are kept in good condition at the expense of the nation. But though his total revenues are about eight million dollars, his expenses exceed his income, and he is in debt to the extent of twenty millions of dollars.

"If the emperor should die, his son would succeed him, with the empress as regent, if the event should occur before the prince imperial is old enough to ascend the throne. If his majesty should die without a male child living, the throne passes into the family of his uncle Jerome, in which contingency Prince Napoleon becomes the sovereign, if living; if not, his oldest son, Napoleon Jerome, and then his second son, Louis Jerome. There are, therefore, four persons living who are in the direct line of succession, three of whom are now small children. Napoleon's brother Jerome first married Miss Patterson, a Baltimore lady, but the emperor compelled him to cast her off. He afterwards married Catharine of Würtemburg, who is the mother of the Prince Napoleon. The first wife has a son, Jerome Napoleon Bonaparte, now living, I believe, in Baltimore. For the very interesting story of this family, I refer you to the 'New American Encyclopædia,' in the libraries of both vessels of the squadron.

"I have time and you have patience for only a very brief sketch of the history of France. To the ancients the country was known as Gaul, or Gallia, which it is still called in poetry. The Franks, whose Latin name was the Franci or 'Freemen,' were a confederation of German barbarians, who, after the decline of the Roman empire, gathered in vast numbers in Gaul, and the present name of France is derived from them. Their leader was Pharamond, who was succeeded by Merovœus, from whom the first line of French kings were styled Merovingian kings; but the period of reliable history commences in 481, with Clovis, his grandson, who conquered the country, drove out the Romans, and, marrying Clotilda, a Christian princess, established Christianity in his dominions. He made Paris his capital, and introduced the Salic law, excluding females from the throne, which prevails to this day. His successors were weak men, and, in 690, Pepin d'Héristel, mayor of the palace, obtained the control of the government, though not of the crown, His son Carl, known as Charles Martel, who won immense renown and popularity by his victories over the Saracens, that invaded France from Spain, succeeded him, and ruled both the nation and the nominal king. Martel's son Pepin shut up the last of the Merovingian monarchs in a convent, and took the title of king. Being only four and a half feet in height, he was called ' Pepin le Bref.' Pope Zachary confirmed his title, and he was the first of the Carlovingian kings.

"Pepin had two sons, Carl and Carloman, the former of whom succeeded to the throne, and became the illustrious Charlemagne, the ablest sovereign of his age. He carried on a merciless war with the barbarous Saxons for thirty-two years, and finally compelled them to embrace Christianity; conquered the greater part of Italy, and the north-eastern portion of Spain. His dominions not only included France and these conquests, but the whole of Germany, what is now Belgium and Helvetia, or Switzerland. He styled his realm the "New Empire of the West," and elevated France above the highest power and civilization of his time.

"This great king was succeeded by his son Louis, who, after a weak and useless reign, divided the realm among his sons. They immediately began to quarrel about their inheritance, involving France in a bloody war, which was finally settled on the plains of Fontenay, where one hundred thousand men are said to have perished, including most of the ancient nobility. The empire was then divided among the rival brothers. Charles the Bald received the western part of France, Lothaire Italy and some of the southern sections of France, while Germany was apportioned to Louis.

"While the kings were quarrelling for the sceptre, the power of the nobles was greatly increased; the dukes and counts proclaimed their rights and dignities to be hereditary, and Charles the Bald admitted their claim. Then was established what is known in history as the Feudal System. In 912 the Normans from Scandinavia, who had before made incursions into the country and burned Paris, established themselves on the west coast, in that part which, from them, has since been called Normandy. They were pirates and robbers, and, being very troublesome, were bribed to depart. They soon returned, and Charles the Simple, to conciliate the invaders, ceded the country they occupied to them.

"At this time Hugh Capet, the most powerful nobleman in France, secured the control of the government, and, on the death of Louis V., seized upon the crown, in 987, being the first of the Capetian race of kings. He was a skilful ruler, and considerably enlarged his territories by conquest and diplomacy. His successors held the throne for nearly four hundred and fifty years. During this period Normandy had become a powerful dukedom, and William the Conqueror invaded England from his domain, and conquered it. The first, second, and third crusades to the Holy Land took place, in which many French as well as English knights engaged, and hundreds of thousands of the nobles and their followers perished by disease and in battle. Louis IX., commonly called St. Louis, was one of the most eminent monarchs who sat upon the throne. He engaged in two crusades, and proved himself to be both a saint and a hero. He died on one of these ill-fated expeditions.

"Charles the Fair was the last king of the Capetian direct line. He was the last of the three sons of Philip the Fair, all of whom died without male children, and the crown devolved upon Philip VI. of Valois, his cousin-german. Philip the Fair, besides the three sons who reigned in succession, had a daughter Isabella, who was married to Edward II. of England, and her son came to the British throne as Edward III., whom you will remember as the father of Edward the Black Prince. On the death of Isabella's third brother, Charles IV. (the Fair) of France, Philip of Valois was recognized and supported as king. But Isabella's son, Edward III., was a nearer relative, and claimed the throne in right of his mother, making war upon France in order to obtain it. This was the beginning of those frequent conflicts between the two nations. Edward invaded France, fought the great battle of Cressy in 1346, in which he signally defeated the French.

"During the reign of Philip VI. Dauphiny was annexed to France by its last count, on condition that the king's oldest son should be styled the dauphin. Normandy had also been wrested from the successor of William the Conqueror, in 1204, by Philip II., and added to the domain.

"Philip VI. was followed by his son John II., who was entirely routed at the battle of Poictiers, by the English under the Black Prince, and taken to London as a prisoner, where he died. Charles V., his successor, improved the condition of the country, and drove the English from nearly all their possessions in France. He was a good man, a wise statesman, and was the founder of the royal library at Paris, now the largest in the world, which he commenced with about nine hundred volumes; and as this was before the invention of printing, it was the largest collection of books extant. His son, Charles VI., was a weak ruler, and during his reign Henry V. of England invaded the country, and defeated the French in the memorable battle of Agincourt, in 1415. By the treaty of Troyes, Edward was to succeed to the throne of France after the death of Henry; but both of them died soon after the arrangement was completed.

"Charles VII., son of Charles VI., claimed the throne. though Henry VI., the infant king of England, was also proclaimed sovereign of France, under the regency of his uncle. The English laid siege to Orleans, the capital of the old province of that name. It is nearly in the centre of France, seventy-five miles from Paris. The situation of the country was desperate, and the nation seemed to be on the point of falling into the hands of England, when Joan of Arc, or the Maid of Orleans, appeared, and pretended to be divinely inspired to overthrow the national enemy, and conduct Charles to Rheims to his coronation. She was a simple country girl, twenty-seven years old, but her zeal and energy roused the people; she represented the national spirit, and inflamed the soldiers with a fury which enabled them to beat the invaders. She was dressed like a man, fully armed, and rode a horse into Orleans, actually compelling the English to raise the siege and depart. She afterwards fell into the hands of the enemy, and was burned alive at Rouen for witchcraft. Her example had fired the national spirit, and the people dislodged the English from all their possessions in France except Calais. Charles, obeying the command of the Maid of Orleans, proceeded to Rheims, then in possession of the enemy, captured it, and was crowned there.

"Louis XI., his successor, was a crafty king, and a bad man, though the pope gave him the title of 'Most Christian,' which has since been annexed to the appellations of the French kings. Charles VIII. was a mild and polite king; he conquered Naples, but lost it. He had no son, and was followed by Louis XII., Duke of Orleans, who derived his right to the throne from Charles V. (the Wise). He was a good man, popular with his subjects, but unfortunate in his projects. He retained the ministers of his predecessor in power, though they had treated him badly, declaring that it was unworthy of the king of France to punish them for injuries done to the Duke of Orleans. The Chevalier Bayard — '*sans peur et sans reproche*' — and Gaston de Foix, eminent generals of that day, figured in this reign.

"His nephew, Francis I., Duke of Angoulême, followed him. He was fond of war, panting for glory, and was a rival with Charles V. of Spain, for the vacant throne of the emperor of Germany. He was not successful, and the two candidates became bitter enemies. Francis first attacked the kingdom of Navarre, and won and lost it in a short time. Francis quarrelled with the Duke of Bourbon, High Constable of France, who in revenge went over to his enemy, Charles V.; and when the French king marched into Italy, he was defeated by Bourbon, taken prisoner, and sent to Madrid, where he was detained until he had submitted to disgraceful terms of peace. Neither of them kept his promises, and a long period of war ensued. Francis struggled to retain his possessions in Italy, but the emperor's power was too great for him. During this reign occurred the Reformation, which excited the fears of all the Catholic rulers, who soon made tremendous efforts to exterminate the heresy. Francis left his kingdom in a flourishing condition, though he was always engaged in war. The thirteen years of the reign of his son Henry II. were also filled up with wars with Charles V. and Philip II. of Spain: he recovered Calais from the English, and redoubled the persecutions of the Protestants, or Huguenots, which induced the civil wars that shook the nation for the next thirty years.

"His son, Francis II., who was the first husband of Mary Queen of Scots, next ascended the throne, but lived only one year after his accession, and was succeeded by Charles IX., ten years old. His mother, Catherine de Medici, a wicked woman, reigned as regent for him. The Protestant religion had by this time become widely spread, and some of the most distinguished nobles of the realm professed it; among them the celebrated Prince of Condé and Admiral Coligny. At the head of the Catholics were the Duke of Guise and the Cardinal of Lorraine, who were brothers, and influential men in the government.

They were cruel and vindictive to the Protestants, who engaged in a conspiracy to destroy them, but were discovered, and twelve hundred men of the reformed faith were sacrificed. Civil war followed, and the Protestants under Condé and Coligny were defeated several times by the Catholics. In 1570 an amnesty, with liberty of conscience, was granted to the persecuted sect, but only to lure them to their destruction. On the occasion of the marriage of Henry of Navarre, who was of the reformed religion, to the king's sister, Coligny and other influential Protestants were induced to visit Paris. A few days later, on the morning of St. Bartholomew's day, an indiscriminate massacre of the Huguenots was commenced. The admiral was among the first to fall, and the number slaughtered has been variously estimated at from twenty-five thousand to seventy thousand. The butchery began at Paris, but extended through France.

"Henry of Navarre was thrown into prison, but afterwards escaped. The massacre, instead of exterminating the Protestants, strengthened them, and they became a powerful party, with Henry and Condé at its head. When Charles was succeeded by his brother, Henry III., the latter found it best to grant them some privileges, which incensed the Catholic party, and they formed a league again to destroy the heretics. The king finally joined it, and took the field against the Huguenots; but the Duke of Guise usurping his authority, Henry caused him and his brother, the Cardinal of Lorraine, to be assassinated. This deed fomented a rebellion against him, and he was himself murdered by a Dominican friar.

"Henry III. had no children, and the throne passed, in 1589, to a new line of kings, the first of which was Henry IV., the Huguenot king of Navarre, who, however, abjured his faith, after having fought its battles bravely, in order to obtain the throne. He was a descendant of the Constable of Bourbon, from whom the name of this line of monarchs is derived, and which exists at the present time. He was the first of the royal Bourbons of France. But the Catholic League, under the Duke of Mayenne, one of the Guises, declared the Cardinal of Bourbon to be king, under the title of Charles X. Henry defeated the army of the League in the famous battle of Ivry, in 1590. His subjects refusing to acknowledge a Protestant king, he was absolved by the pope, and embraced the Catholic religion; but to the Huguenots, by whose arms he had won the throne, by the Edict of Nantes, he granted all their rights and privileges as subjects, and made them eligible to all offices of honor and profit. He did a good work for France in developing its resources; but having formed an aggressive scheme against the other powers of Europe, with the aid of the Duke of Sully, his famous minister, he was assassinated, in 1610, just as he was about to take the field to carry out his ambitious project.

"Mary de Medici, his widow, ruled as regent for her son Louis XIII., who was only nine years of age. The kingdom was soon in disorder, from which it was relieved by Cardinal Richelieu, who became prime minister when the king was of age. His chief purpose was to subdue the nobility, exterminate the

Huguenots, and restrain the power of Austria. He persecuted the Protestants, drove them into rebellion, and they attempted to establish an independent state, with Rochelle for its capital. The cardinal laid siege to that city, which, after a stubborn resistance of a year, during which fifteen thousand perished, was obliged to yield, and the power and influence of the sect in France was lost. Richelieu, in spite of his deceit and severity, raised the nation to the highest degree of power and glory. He was the real ruler of the country, and Louis' XIII. hardly appears to be recognized.

"Louis XIV. succeeded his father at the age of five years, under the regency of his mother, Anne of Austria, who made Cardinal Mazarin, an artful Italian, the chief minister of state. At the death of the cardinal, Louis himself, at the age of twenty-two, took the reins of government into his own hands. He became a powerful sovereign, and greatly extended the limits of France. He was aggressive in his policy, and united the other states of Europe against him; his treasury was drained, and the league to dethrone him soon involved him in reverses, by which he lost nearly all he had won. In this war occurred the great battle of Blenheim (in Bavaria), in which the English Duke of Marlborough was engaged. The peace of Utrecht closed the conflict. Louis revoked the Edict of Nantes in 1685, and hunted the Protestants out of France. He reigned seventy-two years.

"The next king was Louis XV., great-grandson of his predecessor, who succeeded at the age of six, with the Duke of Orleans as regent. During his reign occurred the war of the Austrian Succession, and the French and Indian war in America. Louis died in 1774, after a reign of profligacy and tyranny, which lasted fifty-nine years, and was followed by his grandson, Louis XVI., a monarch of good character, but lacking decision. His situation was a very trying one. The treasury had been depleted by the wars of his predecessor, and the finances of the nation were almost hopelessly embarrassed. The people had been trodden down, until they had become turbulent and desperate, and the king stood between them and the nobility, the former demanding reform, and the latter crying out against it. The war of the American Revolution took place at this period, and France assisted the young republic, struggling for its life. On the return of the French officers who had been in America, they brought with them something of the spirit of the people whose cause they had espoused, which added to the flame of discontent. The example of the United States was before them. The government was despotic; the taxes were burdensome; the nobility were aiming at greater power; the clergy and other privileged classes were exempted from taxes, and the wide-spread infidelity of influential men, which encouraged great latitude of thought and expression, — all these things combined to produce the French Revolution.

"The king and some of his ministers were disposed to grant reforms, but he was too slow and uncertain. He called together the Notables (a body selected by himself), after all attempts to regulate the finances had failed; but they afforded him no relief.

The States General were called together, but the nobility and clergy were in the majority. The deputies of the people, with such of the privileged orders as would join them, took affairs into their own hands, and declared themselves to be the legislative power of the land, under the title of the National Assembly. Of this body the brilliant and eloquent Mirabeau was the popular leader. It assumed the sovereign power, and not only the nobility and clergy, but the king himself, were deprived of their authority. The dismissal of Necker, a minister, from office by Louis, lighted the fire of active rebellion. The Bastile, or state prison, was torn down by the people; rabbles of furious men and women committed outrages upon property, and violence was the order of the day. The nobles fled, the army fraternized with the people, and the royal family was driven from Versailles to Paris by the mob, but were protected by Lafayette, who commanded the National Guard.

"The National Assembly, which now held its sittings in Paris, nearly stripped the crown of its power, abolished all the privileges of the clergy and nobles, established religious liberty and the freedom of the press, confiscated the property of the church, suppressed convents, and divided France into departments. In the midst of these commotions, Louis and his family attempted to escape, but were captured and brought back to Paris from the frontier. The National Assembly finally completed a constitution, which the king accepted, and dissolved in 1791.

"A year later, another body, called the National Convention, assembled, and its first act was to abolish the monarchy and declare France a republic. The king was arraigned at their bar, and sentenced to death. He was executed on the guillotine in January, 1793, for no crime of his own, and his death will ever be a reproach to the nation. Then came the bloodiest days of the French revolution. The Convention was divided into two parties; the first, and more violent one, styled the Mountain party, on account of their high seats in the hall, was under the lead of Robespierre; and the other, more moderate, called the Girondists, because their leaders came from the department of the Gironde, was led by Brissot and Condorcet. The former obtained the ascendency, and resorted to the most revolting massacres. They condemned and executed Marie Antoinette, Louis's widow, in the most barbarous manner. The Girondists were brought to the guillotine, and the dominant party indulged in the most bloody and abominable excesses. The Christian religion was suppressed; Liberty, Equality, and Reason were decreed to be the only French deities; the churches were plundered; Sunday was abolished, and a calendar making every tenth day a day of rest was established. New parties arose, with Danton in one, and Robespierre in the other, and as each came into power it butchered the other. Robespierre died on the guillotine, to which he had brought so many others. The Jacobins — revolutionary clubs of the most violent tendencies — were suppressed.

"In 1799 four different constitutions had been framed. By the last the executive power was vested in three consuls, the first of whom was Napoleon Bonaparte. This remarkable man had already, in a great measure, achieved his military reputation. He had rapidly worked his way up to the rank of brigadier general in the army of France. In the erratic course of the National Convention, it had, in 1795, by its assumptions of power, incurred the displeasure of the populace, who turned their fury upon it. The Convention had five thousand regular troops, and, after one general had failed, Napoleon was designated as their leader. The people advanced, thirty thousand in number, towards the Tuileries, pouring in a murderous fire of musketry, to which the young general replied with artillery, of which he had an abundant supply. In less than an hour, by his decision, energy, and skilful combinations, he achieved a complete victory for the Convention. In 1796 he was appointed to the command of the army of Italy, and conquered the country. The Austrians attempted to check his victorious career; but he repeatedly defeated them in some of the most brilliant victories on record, and finally compelled Austria to submit to hard terms, as the price of peace, in the treaty of Campo Formio. His return to Paris was a triumphal procession, and he was received with the most unbounded enthusiasm.

"The French revolution was regarded with alarm by the powers of Europe, and they combined to repress the disorder it occasioned. The sovereigns trembled for the stability of their own thrones, and hastened to defend them by attacking France. Austria had been subdued and silenced; Italy was a French province; and during the absence of Napoleon, the Directory, then the executive authority under the Convention, had created the army of England, intending to invade and conquer England. The command of this force was given to the young Corsican; but he had a project of his own, which he persuaded his superiors to substitute for the uncertain scheme they had devised. This was the conquest of Egypt and the East. With his fleet and army he crossed the Mediterranean, capturing Malta on the way, ascended the Nile, took Cairo, defeated the Mamelukes in the battle of the Pyramids, and attempted to carry his successes into Syria, where he was checked at Acre by the English. In the mean time, Nelson had almost annihilated the French fleet in the tremendous naval engagement at Aboukir. The plan was a failure, though Napoleon 'whitewashed' it, so that it did not look so bad to the French.

"Privately returning to France, he was elected First Consul. From this point his history becomes that of the French nation. He was the 'idol of the army,' and in its strength he was strong enough to do as he pleased He expelled the Legislative Council, and formed a new constitution. Another coalition of the European powers was formed against France; but Napoleon defeated the Austrians at Marengo in 1800, compelling them to make peace with him; and in the course of two years he made terms with most of the other powers. In 1802 he was made consul for life, and devoted his attention to civil affairs, reforming the laws, restoring the Catholic religion, and developing the industrial and commercial resources of the country. He displayed splendid abilities as a ruler, and raised France to the highest degree of power and influence. In 1804 he was proclaimed hereditary emperor, and was crowned December 2 — a day for which his nephew has manifested a partiality. In the following year he went to Milan, and was anointed King of Italy.

"The peace was of brief duration. The powers of Europe, incited by England, formed a third coalition against Napoleon; and he defeated and captured the Austrian army at Ulm, and achieved his memorable victory over the combined Russians and Austrians at Austerlitz, where three emperors were present. But just before this last event, Lord Nelson won the great naval victory of Trafalgar, in which the English admiral was killed. By the peace of Presburg Austria again submitted to humiliating conditions. The King of Naples having incurred the displeasure of the emperor, Napoleon deposed him, and made his brother Joseph King of Naples, and placed his brother Louis on the throne of Holland. He also formed of several of the German states the 'Confederation of the Rhine,' of which he was chosen Protector, and made Kings of the Electors of Bavaria, Wurtemberg, and Saxony. This increased power and influence caused a fourth coalition, in which England, Russia, Prussia, Austria, and Sweden joined against him, and was followed by the battles of Jena, Auerstädt, Pultusk, Eylau, and Friedland; and Napoleon, having taken Dantsic and Konigsberg, concluded the peace of Tilsit. Prussia was deprived of a portion of her territory by this treaty, which was erected into the kingdom of Westphalia, and the emperor's brother Jerome was placed on the throne.

"Napoleon was greatly elated by his marvellous

successes, and was disposed to be the dictator of all Europe. By his movements he drove the royal family of Portugal to Brazil, and took possession of the country. Having a difficulty with the pope, he annexed a portion of his territory to Italy, and occupied Rome. In 1808 he sent his brother-in-law, General Murat, to Madrid, and then proclaimed his brother Joseph King of Spain, giving Murat the vacant throne of Naples. The Spanish people, objecting to this arrangement, rose in arms against the invaders, and were assisted by England with men and money. The Peninsular War, as it is called, in which the Duke of Wellington distinguished himself, raged for five years. In 1809 another war with Austria ensued, in which Napoleon, after several victories, entered Vienna, and afterwards utterly routed the Austrians at Wagram. By the treaty of Vienna, Francis I. of Austria lost considerable territory, and promised his daughter Maria Louisa in marriage to Napoleon, who was divorced from Josephine, and married her. A new difficulty with Alexander of Russia led the emperor to invade the dominions of the former with an immense army of over four hundred thousand men. Napoleon defeated the Russians at Smolensk, and obtained the advantage over them at Borodino; but his enemy burned Moscow, and he was compelled to retire, amid the snows of a Russian winter, in which the greater part of his army was lost. Napoleon returned in disguise to Paris, deeply humiliated by his failure. The next year he raised another army, to break up the fifth and most powerful coalition; but his star had begun to wane. He was defeated at Lutzen, was more successful at Bautzen and Dresden, but was completely routed in the awful battle of Leipsic, where four hundred thousand men were engaged. Napoleon escaped, and went back to Paris, whither his allies followed him. His case was hopeless; the people, and even many of his own generals, turned against him, and he abdicated in favor of his son. The emperor was sent to the Isle of Elba, with a salary of one million two hundred thousand dollars, there to live in state as a prisoner.

"When Louis XVI. was guillotined, he left a son, the dauphin, Louis Joseph, eight years old. He was sent to prison, and kept there till he died, two years after his father. His remains were privately buried, and all traces of his grave obliterated. Though his death was certified by four physicians, four members of the Committee of Safety, and twenty officials of the prison, several persons have claimed to be the dauphin, and among them, the Rev. Eleazar Williams, in the United States. As the last king, therefore, had no male heir, Napoleon was succeeded by Louis XVIII., brother of Louis XVI., the deceased dauphin supplying the wanting numeral. Ten months later, Napoleon, encouraged by the republicans of France, escaped from Elba, and returning to his capital, Louis fled amid the storm of applause that greeted the emperor, But the allies gathered an immense army, and moved towards Paris again. Napoleon, with two hundred and fifty thousand men, hastened to confront his old enemies on the field. He entered Belgium, defeated Blucher at Ligny, and despatched Ney to confront the English, under Wellington, at Quatre Bras, who, however, was repulsed, and fell back upon Waterloo where the decisive battle was fought. It was a momentous conflict, involving the destiny of France and the peace of Europe. The French were partially successful at first, but the day ended in their utter rout and total dispersion. Napoleon hastened back to Paris, which was soon in the hands of the allies, and the fallen chief abdicated again, after a reign of just one hundred days. He attempted to escape to the United States, but, finding it impossible, he gave himself up to the captain of an English war ship. He trusted to the magnanimity of England, and was sent to St. Helena, a prisoner, where he died.

"Louis XVIII. returned to his throne. France was reduced in territorial limits, heavily mulcted for the expenses of the war, and compelled to maintain a large force of allied troops upon her frontier for three years. The king was liberal in his views, but between the two violent parties his situation was a difficult one. He was succeeded by his brother, in 1824, who reigned as Charles X. He was not so liberal as his predecessor, and when he attempted to dissolve the Chamber of Deputies, suppress the newspapers, and alter the election law, the people rose up against him, and after a revolution of three days, the king's troops were overpowered. The liberal deputies assembled, declared the throne vacant, and invited Louis Philippe, Duke of Orleans, to accept it. Charles X. fled, and the new monarch was crowned. He was a man of decided ability, though he did not carry out the principles of the men who elected him. His measures were arbitrary, and he was not a popular sovereign. During his reign, Algeria was completely subjugated, and Abd-el Kadir brought to Paris a prisoner, in 1847. The people were discontented under the heavy taxes imposed upon them, and the oppression of the government. *Reform banquets* were held all over the country for counsel and agitation. One was appointed to be held in Paris, on Sunday, February 20, 1848. The police were directed to prohibit the meeting. The friends of reform postponed the banquet for two days, when vast crowds assembled, which soon came into collision with the troops, of whom eighty thousand had been hurried into the city. The insurrection soon became general, and the National Guard refused to act, or joined the people, who had erected numerous barricades in the streets. Louis Philippe attempted to quell the tumult by conciliation, but it was too late; and, abdicating in favor of his grandson, he fled with his family to England. A provisional government was formed, and Louis Napoleon was afterwards elected president. The subsequent history of France I have already related to you in speaking of the present emperor."

Some of the students yawned heavily, but to most of them the narrative, long and statistical as it was, had been full of interest, for in a few days they were to behold the locality of some of these stirring events.

CHAPTER X.

THE KNIGHTS OF THE GOLDEN FLEECE AT WORK.

"THAT was a tremendous long yarn," said Lieutenant Terrill to Captain Kendall, as the professor finished his extended remarks.

"Rather long, but I think we need not complain, if Mr. Mapps does not," replied Paul. He has taken a great deal of pains to gather up his facts, statistics, and descriptions, and to arrange them in a connected narrative. For my part, France already has a greater interest to me for what he has said, though I don't care much about hearing the names of the kings before the time of Louis XVI."

"How did you like the lecture, Miss Arbuckle?" asked Terrill, as the two officers approached her seat.

"Very much indeed. I think you students are remarkably fortunate in having such a preparation for seeing the countries you are to visit," replied Grace. "Now, when you go to Paris, you will know what everything means."

"Exactly so," added Mr. Arbuckle. "When I first visited St. Chapelle, in Paris, and was told when and by whom it was built, I felt no interest at all, for I had forgotten all about St. Louis. Now you have been told all about the geography, history, and government of the country. When you enter the *Place de la Bastille*, you will know where you are. This review is a capital thing for you."

"I think it is, sir," replied Paul, as the party went on deck.

The Josephine's boats returned with her crew to the consort. An early dinner, or rather lunch, was served, and all hands in both vessels went on shore to see the city, which, however, has no particular attractions to the tourist who has seen the docks of Liverpool. It has a population of seventy-five thousand, and is mostly of modern construction. The students examined the docks, walked upon the North Jetée, which is the principal public promenade, visited the splendid Hôtel de Ville, or City Hall, and its beautiful garden, and took an outside view of the house in which Bernardin de St. Pierre was born.

"Tom Perth, our time has come," said Little, as he met the chief of the Knights of the Golden Fleece on the Jetée. "We must go it this very night, or never. Everything is fixed for us."

"So I was thinking," replied Perth.

"Have you heard the programme for to-night?"

"I was told that the coast would be clear on board of the Josephine."

"Mr. Arbuckle gives a big dinner at the Hôtel de l'Europe to-night to all on board the Josephine, and there will be no one left in her except the under-stewards and the cook."

"Briskett, the head steward, and the boatswain and carpenter will be there — won't they?" asked Perth, with interest.

"You keep your ears closed, I think. Mr. Arbuckle insisted that every man and boy on board should attend his party. They say he is going to have a band of music, and it will be the biggest time ever heard of. He is going to do the same thing for the crew of the commodore's barge on Monday; but I reckon I shall not wait for that. Here comes Greenway. We must whisper the thing round, and be ready to start to-night. We shall never have such another chance."

"What's up?" asked Greenway, as he joined the interesting couple.

He was told what was " up," and he also was ready to strike when the iron was hot.

"How about that bag?" inquired Greenway, who alone had been made the confidant of the little villain in regard to the gold.

"Dry up!" muttered Little, sharply. "You were not to mention that to any fellow."

"What bag?" demanded Perth.

"Never mind that now. When we get off I will tell you all about it. We have no time to talk about it now. Have you heard anything concerning the arrangements for to-night for the Josephines?" said Little, turning away the attention of his companions from the prohibited topic.

"I have only heard that the boats of the ship are to bring off the Josephines after they get through with their spree."

"That's so. We are to take the consort's boats back, and hoist them up. Then, at nine o'clock, we are to come ashore, and take the fellows off in four of our boats," added Little, who had carefully investigated all the arrangements.

"Then all we have to do is to drop on board of the Josephine, up anchor in the dark, and go to sea," said Perth.

"The thing won't do itself, I can tell you," Greenway objected. "How shall we get all the knights into the same boat? How shall we get rid of the officers? What's to prevent the other boats from the ship coming between us and our game?"

"Sure enough!" exclaimed Perth, who was not brilliant at scheming.

"What's to prevent it?" replied Little, quietly. "The new knight."

"The new knight!"

"That's the term I used."

"Who is he?"

"Bob Shuffles."

"Do you mean to say that you have been talking to that 'lamb' about our affairs?" demanded Perth, angrily.

"I didn't say it, and don't mean to say it," answered Little, who, in coolness, self-possession, and dignity, as well as in the cunning art of diplomacy, was vastly more than the equal of the acknowledged leader of the order. "I think I know what I am about a good deal better than some of the rest of you. You are all ready to go, Tom Perth, but if you don't have some one to lay out the work for you, you couldn't do a thing; that's so. I don't ask any place or power for myself; but I don't want to see the thing bungled as it was at Cowes, when you were going off so finely."

"Do you mean to say that was my fault?" demanded Perth.

"I don't care whose fault it was; the affair was a failure. You were going into your boat while Fluxion was in his berth below."

"Don't fight about it," interposed Greenway.

"I don't want to fight, and don't intend to do so," continued Little; "but I want this business better managed than it was before. You snapped at me because I said something to Shuffles. You don't know what."

"You had no right to speak to him without letting some of us know it," persisted Perth.

"All right; I'm under censure, and I submit," said Little. "You are the chief, Perth. Go ahead, and put the thing through."

"You needn't get mad about it."

"I don't intend to get mad. Tell me what to do, and I'll do it. The coast will be clear to-night. If you let this chance slip by, you will never go: take my word for that."

"I don't see how we are to get the knights on board of the Josephine," added Perth, after he had considered the matter a little. "Do you know what boats are to be sent for the Josephine's fellows?"

"I don't," replied Greenway, as Little did not afford the information.

"Do you, Monkey?"

"I do; I have a friend at court who tells me what I want to know."

"That's Ellis," said Greenway.

"No matter who it is. I got the order just as it was given by the captain to the first lieutenant."

"What boats are they?"

"The commodore's barge, the first cutter, the professors' barge, and the second cutter."

"I don't see that this arrangement will help our plan any. The knights are scattered in all these boats."

"You are a Louis XIII., and you need a Richelieu," laughed Little. "You have the problem; all you have to do is to solve it. Given thirty Knights of the Golden Fleece in four boats, to get them all into the same boat, when only eight of them are to be found in any single boat."

"I did not intend to do the thing in this way," replied Perth, vexed at the raillery of his companion.

"Did you intend to do the thing in any way, Mr. Commander of the Order?"

"Of course I did."

"All right; then we will obey orders as faithful knights, Sir Tom Perth. What is your plan? if you don't object to stating it."

"I don't object to stating it, though I have not fully made it up yet," added Perth. "Of course such an affair as this can't be carried out without a great deal of contrivance. You can't tell beforehand how things are going to be, and what you do is liable to go wrong."

"We know all that," interposed Little, impatiently. "But in this case we do know how things are going to be. The Josephine will be left to-night with no one on board of her but the cook and two waiters."

"I was going to tell you my plan, but if you don't want to hear it, I don't care about telling it," replied Perth, rather curtly.

"Let us know what it is," said Greenway.

"We are going to Paris Monday, I believe."

"Monday night," added Little, who seemed to know everybody's plans.

"Just so, and the darker the better. One of these railway carriages here has about four compartments, which seat six or eight each. We must contrive it so as to have all the knights get into the last carriage. By hurrying up a little we can easily manage that. But if we happen to get two or three other fellows in, it won't much matter; we can give them the slip. What do you think of that plan?" asked Perth, who seemed to think he had invented a big idea.

"I don't see through it yet," answered Little, too coldly to please the commander of the expedition.

"Don't you? Well, you are not so sharp as I thought you were," sneered Perth.

"I see what you mean plainly enough, but I want to hear the whole plan before I give an opinion."

"What do I mean?" inquired the leader in embryo, incredulously.

"You intend to unshackle the car, and be left behind, of course."

"What, in the station?"

"No; after you get a mile or two out of the city."

"I should do it when we are in some lonely place on the road. Then we can just make our way back to Havre, go on board the Josephine, and put to sea without any delay."

"That's what you mean. But there are some trifling obstacles," suggested Little. "In the first place, we shall all be locked into the compartments."

"Bah! Locked in! What do we care for that? Isn't there a window big enough for a man to get out, to say nothing of a boy?" added Perth, contemptuously. "When we were going from Bruges to Brussels, I got out of the window on one side, went over the top of the carriage, and came in again at the window on the other side, just for the fun of it."

"There may be no difficulty about that; but if the last carriage should be a mail car, or something of that sort?"

"No matter if it is. We can break up the train, and when it stops, all we have to do is to get out and make tracks for Havre."

"All right; grant that you get clear of the train, and find your way back to this city; what then?"

"You know what then as well as I can tell you. We will take the Josephine and be off. We should be out of sight of land before morning, and then they couldn't find us any more than they could a needle in a hay-mow."

"Do you know what they are going to do with the two vessels while we are in Paris and Switzerland?" asked Little.

"They are going to put them into the dock. There I may be lame," replied Perth, candidly. "But I don't think they will dock the vessels till the next day."

"Perhaps they won't; but if you have any gumption, you will see they are very likely to do so; and then what becomes of your little plan?"

"I shall be dished, of course, unless we can get the schooner out of the dock. The forward officers will live on shore."

"They will take their meals on shore, but sleep on board, and be in our way at the very time we want to go. The tide will be high at about five on Monday; and, in my opinion, the vessels will be docked then, before we start for Paris."

"If they are, of course our chances are small. You don't like my way; now tell us what yours is," growled Perth.

"You snapped me before I had time to say anything about it. You are the commander; and all we have to do is to obey your orders when you give them."

"You are a good fellow, Monkey," added Perth, stepping down from the high horse.

"All the fellows know that without being told; and you find it out when you get into a tight place," answered Little, modestly.

"But let us know what your plan is."

"It can't be carried out without Shuffles; so it is no use to talk."

"Do you mean to tell us Shuffles will agree to anything that isn't pious?"

"Yes, I do."

"O, get out!"

"Out of the knights?"

"No; but has Shuffles fallen from grace?"

"He is ready to go in with any fellows for a good time. He finds he don't get any credit for being a lamb. I have had a talk with him since we came ashore."

"I saw you were pretty thick with him."

"If I was, he don't know any more about the

knights than I did before I joined," answered Little, significantly.

"I don't understand you, Monkey."

"Then don't snuff at me till you do understand. Shuffles is coxswain of our boat; and if he is a lamb, he isn't a baby. He knows what he is about; and I'll bet my eyes you couldn't go off in any boat with him in it, unless he consented."

"Will he consent?"

"He has consented."

"You don't mean so!"

"If I didn't, I shouldn't say so," protested Little. "You see I bamboozled him. We are up to one thing, but he thinks we are up to another."

"Tell us what you mean in plain English. If you haven't blown upon us, it is all right."

"Perhaps I don't know enough not to blow on you. If you think so, you had better strip off my spurs."

"We know you are all right, Monkey," interposed Greenway. "Let us know what you have done."

"Now you are decent I will tell you all about it," replied the little villain, complacently. "We want Shuffles;" but he was careful not to say to the commander of the knights what he wanted of him. "By slow degrees I led the lamb to believe that the crew of the commodore's barge were going off without asking leave. The officers have made complaints against him, and he has been charged with something which has not come out yet. That's what's the matter. Shuffles is disgusted and dissatisfied, and he is willing to go on a runaway cruise in the barge."

"Are you sure he isn't bamboozling you?" sug

gested Perth. "He is an old rogue, and I don't believe he has lost his tact since he became pious."

"I know what I'm about," was all the reply the immaculate Little would condescend to make to this implied imputation upon his own cunning. "He has consented to go; and I rather think he will like the Josephine better than the barge. He will be as willing to be hung for an old sheep as for a lamb. No matter for that. After he gets us off in the boat, I don't care whether he joins or not. He can do as he pleases. He has promised to fill up the barge with the fellows I send into her.

"But he won't let thirty of us get into her."

"That we must tinker up so as to make it come out right. If you will leave the affair to me, I will promise to have all the knights on board of the Josephine," replied Little, confidently. "I don't ask to be captain, or anything of that sort."

"That's fair. What do you say, Greenway?"

"It is for you and Wilton to decide. You are the leaders."

"I'll let you know in half an hour or so," added Perth, who wished to communicate the situation to his associate in authority.

The commander of the Knights of the Golden Fleece — for this was the position to which Perth had been assigned — had a long consultation with Wilton, who without talent for anything in particular except making blunders, was regarded as the second in rank. Wilton always growled, and of course he did so when informed that Shuffles was to have a part in the programme, for, in his estimation, the reformed student was a traitor, who had deserted "our fellows" and gone over to the enemy. But when it was shown that the only practicable scheme which had yet been devised could be carried out only with his assistance, he assented to the proposition, as he would have done to anything after he had gone through the formality of growling at it. Little, therefore, was immediately apprised of the acquiescence of the high and mighty second in command, and directed to carry out his arrangements to suit himself.

"But remember that, when the knights are safely on board of the schooner, you are to be the same as the rest of the fellows," added Perth, careful to guard against any usurpation on the part of the wily little villain.

"I don't want any office; you needn't be afraid of me," answered Little, meekly, "I am willing to do the work, and let you bear off all the honors."

"O, we don't mean to ignore you, Monkey, or anything of that sort," protested Perth. "If you do a good thing for the order, you shall not lose anything by it. We shall want a second lieutenant as soon as we get off."

"I don't ask for anything; I go for the good of the whole, and not for myself, like some of the rest of the fellows."

"Do you mean me, Monkey?" demanded the commander.

"I don't mean anybody."

"Shut up, now!" interposed Greenway. "If you are going to be snubbing each other in that way, we shall be in a row all the time, and I would rather not go."

"We will be good friends, Monkey," added Perth.

"Till we get on board the Josephine, we will," said Little. "We shall have time enough to fight it out there."

"We won't fight anywhere. Now, what are we to do?" demanded Perth.

"Tell every knight to be in the waist close together when the boats are piped away. That's all I want you to do," answered the self-possessed little villain, complacently.

They separated, and before the students had returned on board the squadron, each of the knights had been instructed to be at the appointed place, and to be prepared to go on board of the consort. They had been too well drilled in keeping the mysteries of the order to talk upon the exciting anticipations. To be in possession of the Josephine, and free from the restraints of discipline, formed a brilliant prospect. It would be ten times more agreeable than going to Paris, tied to the skirts of the professors' coats; but they expected to visit the great city in their own time. Freedom from restraint was their ideal of perfect bliss; but the fancy was never to be realized, and their hopes were to be rudely jarred.

At five o'clock, the ship's boats left the jetty. The Josephine's boats were manned by the crew not at the oars, and pulled off to the consort in charge of the second lieutenant. They were hoisted up to the davits, and everything left in good order. The barge and first cutter from the ship conveyed these hands to the Young America.

Three hours must elapse before it would be time for

the boats to go on shore and bring off the Josephine's people. The knights were highly excited, but they were extremely cautious. All of them who had any valuables, or other articles which they wished to take with them, concealed them in their clothing, or placed them where they would be available when needed. Little was a great wire-puller, and he worked hard. The problem he had volunteered to solve was a difficult one, and if the circumstances had not singularly favored him, the promise he had made to get the knights on board of the Josephine must have failed.

Towards night the weather, which had been pleasant, came up thick and misty, with a fresh breeze from the channel, which drifted in dense clouds of fog. At dark it was hardly possible to see a ship's length ahead. It was chilly and uncomfortable, and most of the students retreated from the cold blasts on deck to the steerage and the cabin. They had been walking all the afternoon on shore, and with their sea legs on, which makes it all the more fatiguing. Those who were not excited by the prospects of the stolen expedition were tired out. Not a few of this class grumbled at the idea of being obliged to pull a boat to the jetty in the heavy sea, the dark night, and the cold wind.

Little heard these complaints, and hastened to profit by them. When the boats were merely engaged in ship's service, and not in the regular routine of discipline, any member of a crew, with the consent of the officer in charge, had the privilege of procuring a substitute. This had been the rule ever since the ship went into commission, and was intended not only to relieve an oarsman who wished to be excused, but to afford opportunities to cultivate good feeling among the students by allowing and encouraging one to do a kindness to another. On all occasions of drill or ceremony, every one of the crew was required to be on his thwart, unless excused for good reasons by the captain.

In the commodore's barge, eight of the twelve oarsmen were knights, and when the chilly "lambs" shrugged their shoulders, and did not care to pull a mile on such a night, four members of the order, very quietly, at the suggestion of Little, offered to take their places. The barge was then properly manned, and nearly one half of the conspirators were provided with a passage to the Josephine. An examination of the station bills posted up in the steerage showed that four of the eight oars in the second cutter were pulled by members of the order. This boat was therefore selected to take part in the secret service. No one wanted to pull to the jetty and back that night, and Little, while he lay on two campstools, apparently asleep, filled the "lambs'" places with conspirators. Whatever the knights thought they kept to themselves; but the rest of the crew believed that the era of good feeling had been inaugurated, for never before had fellows been so kind and obliging to their shipmates as on that cold, dark, foggy evening.

Twenty-one of the knights had thus been provided for; but as another boat could not be taken without exposing the whole scheme to defeat, it required sharp wits to dispose of the other nine members of the secret organization. As it was always stipulated that no knight should be deserted by the others while he was true to the common interests, it was necessary that not a single one should be left behind. In view of this difficulty, Little concluded to wake up and go on deck. Those who were provided with places in the boats very naturally kept themselves comfortable in the steerage, while those who had not been so cared for were as naturally nervous, and fearful of being left in the ship while the glorious enterprise was in progress. They followed the little villain on deck, to inquire of him what they were to do.

The anchor watch on the forecastle struck seven bells. In half an hour more the boats would be sent away. It was necessary to act promptly; and Little, in the course of the remaining period of probation, directed the last nine slyly to go down the ladder and stow themselves away in the bottoms of the barge and second cutter. In the deep darkness that prevailed they were not likely to be seen, and as only knights were to go in these boats, they would not be exposed. The little villain was satisfied then that he should be able to keep his promise. He whispered the arrangement to several of the crew in each of the two boats, and the programme was soon understood by all.

The only unfavorable circumstance was the fact that the second cutter was to be officered by the second lieutenant; but Adler was to go as substitute for the coxswain, and he was to dispose of the officer as well as he could. At eight bells the several boats' crews were piped away. The first cutter, in charge of the first lieutenant, went away first; she was followed by the professors' barge and the second cutter. Mr. Lowington, expecting the barge's crew would attempt to run away, had instructed each of the officers of the other boats to pull up to the jetties, and bring back the barge if she attempted to go up the river, according to the programme indicated by Little to Shuffles. The barge went last, and the principal was confident that the bag of gold would soon be found.

CHAPTER XI.

THE CAPTURE OF THE JOSEPHINE.

MR. LOWINGTON himself had unconsciously contributed more than any one else to the success of the little villain's plan. In his anxiety to discover the truth in regard to the mysterious bag of gold, he had permitted, rather than directed, Shuffles to fall in with the plan of the conspirators. His understanding of the matter was, that the crew of the commodore's barge were endeavoring to run away. Little was one of the leading spirits of the enterprise, and the gold was intended to pay the expenses of the expedition. Instead of passing between the jetties into the harbor, the barge would continue on her way up the Seine.

This was the programme as communicated to Shuffles by Little; but none knew better than Mr. Lowington the character of the coxswain's informant. Captain Haven proposed to detain the barge as soon as the crew were seated on the thwarts, and have them searched; but the principal decided that it would be safer to permit the conspirators to carry their plan a little farther. It was possible that the scheme had been postponed, or some other method adopted to execute it, for the rogues could not well help distrusting Shuffles. If the boat, therefore, went into the harbor, nothing was to be said or done, for then the presumption would be, that the gold was not on board. On the contrary, if the barge passed the jetties, and continued up the river, it would indicate that the bargemen really intended to run away, and that the gold was on board.

The first lieutenant had been placed in command of the first cutter, with instructions for the occasion. Ellis in the second cutter, and Leavitt in the professors' barge, were to coöperate with him, though the crew of these boats knew nothing of the officers' directions. Agreeably to the programme, which had been carefully arranged by the principal and the chief officers, the commodore's barge had been sent off last, and detained long enough to permit the other boats to reach the jetties in advance of her. Each barge and cutter was provided with a lantern and a boat compass, in charge of the coxswain, to whom the course had been given.

The fog was very dense, and the position of the boats could only be known by the sound of the oars. The first cutter, without waiting for the others, pulled up to the jetties, on each of which was a light for the guidance of vessels. The professors' barge followed her, and reaching the rendezvous soon after, communicated with the first lieutenant, who stationed her just beyond the jetties, in the thick fog, while he placed his own boat farther out. Though neither boat could see the other, they were within hail, each pulling an occasional stroke to prevent being carried out by the rapid tide. The second cutter, with Ellis, was expected next, and she was to be stationed outside of the first lieutenant's boat, so that he could give his orders conveniently to both of his companions.

Adler, who was an old salt, having been in the ship a year and a half, was coxswain *pro tem.* of the second cutter. His station was behind the back-board, with the compass and lantern on the grating at his feet. The boat cast off, and in a moment the ship disappeared in the thick fog. Gradually, so as not to excite the suspicion of Ellis, Adler changed the course of the boat, till he had headed her towards the Josephine, instead of the jetties which were in the opposite direction. If the second lieutenant had been a smart officer, he could have seen by the roll of the waves that the cutter was not going in the right direction; but Adler kept him busy talking until they were far enough from the ship to insure the success of the enterprise, and then he ceased to amuse the officer.

"How are you steering, Adler?" asked Ellis, when for the first time he discovered that the boat was head to the sea, instead of going before it.

"With the tiller ropes," replied Adler.

"Let me see the compass," added the officer, rising and attempting to look over the back-board.

"You needn't trouble yourself," said Adler, suddenly laying aside the respectful attitude of an inferior.

"What do you mean?" demanded Ellis, who needed nothing more than what had passed to assure him that a mutiny was in progress.

"Keep still, Ellis, and you are all right," answered Adler. "Fellows in the bottom of the boat," he added, "come out of that now, and take your places in the stern sheets."

Ellis was appalled, and could not immediately make up his mind what to do. He had been directed, with the first and third lieutenants, to counteract the movements of the barge, in which the runaways were supposed to be; but it now appeared that he was himself in the midst of another band of conspirators. The four knights in the bottom of the boat rose from their hiding-places, and came aft. One of them had a boat-hook in his hand. They seated themselves on each side of the astonished officer.

"Phillips!" said Adler, sharply.

"Ay, ay, sir!"

"Have you the boat-hook?"

"I have," replied this worthy, who had been previously instructed in the part he was to perform.

"Stand by with it, then."

"Ay, ay, sir!"

"Ellis, if you should take it into your head to yell, or anything of that sort, Phillips will crack you on the sconce with the boat-hook," continued the coxswain.

The second lieutenant therefore, being a prudent young man, did not take it into his head to yell. He was generally halting and undecided, and he had not yet made up his mind what to do; indeed, the circumstances were not favorable for him to reach a conclusion.

"Keep your weather eye open tight, you soldiers in the stern sheets, and see if you can make out the Josephine in the fog," said Adler, after the crew had pulled long enough, as he thought, to bring the boat to the consort.

"What are you going to do?" Ellis ventured to ask.

"If you keep your eyes wide open, you will find out in the course of half an hour," replied Adler, roughly.

Ellis concluded that the best thing he could do was to keep still.

"I see her!" shouted one of the hands in the stern sheets. "She is right on our beam!"

"Shut up! You needn't yell. It isn't polite," said the coxswain. "Way enough! Lay on your oars!"

Adler decided to wait till the barge came up, and board the Josephine with her crew. Ellis behaved very well, but the coxswain was not so sure that the cook and stewards on board the consort would be equally tractable.

The 'crew' of the commodore's barge took their places in the boat, alongside the ship, and neither Shuffles nor the principal had any suspicion that five extra hands were stowed away in the bottom. It was very dark and very chilly, and none but those whose duty called them to the deck were there.

"Be very careful, Shuffles," said Mr. Lowington, as the coxswain was about to go over the side. "The three boats are ranged outside of the jetties. If you happen to miss them in the fog, you must use your own judgment. If your crew attempt to use violence towards you, perhaps you had better let them have their own way. It will be easy enough to find them if they get away, for you can inform me by letter which way they have gone."

"I am not afraid of the whole of them," replied Shuffles, confidently.

"Perhaps not; but don't be rash, and don't injure any of them."

Shuffles was a stout fellow, and, in his wild days, had been the bully of the crew. Mr. Lowington had no idea of the nature or extent of the conspiracy, and did not really expect anything like resistance on the part of the twelve seamen in the barge. With him it was simply a matter of obtaining evidence, and he was satisfied, if the boys attempted to run away, the other boats would turn their flank, Shuffles would declare that the scheme was impracticable, and the barge, with the other boats, pretending they had missed the way, or something of that sort, would pull into the harbor. But the gold would be on board, and when the twelve bargemen returned to the ship, they would be searched, the guilty one discovered, and the whole affair end in strengthening the discipline of the ship. Of Shuffles' fidelity he had no doubts, and he did not misjudge him; but the coxswain was as innocent of all knowledge of the real purpose of the conspirators as the principal himself.

The crew of the barge gave way, and pulled out into the gloom and fog of the night. Of course the coxswain headed the boat for the jetties; and this course did not suit Little. But the rogue had prepared for this emergency. He had debated with himself, and with Greenway, whether to set the five knights in the bottom of the boat upon Shuffles, overpower and muzzle him, or to play another trick upon him. Shuffles was not Ellis. The former was energetic and decided. There was fight in him, if he was a lamb, and even if conquered, he would make such a row as to endanger the success of the enterprise. Besides, Little and Greenway wanted him, at the right time, to take command of the Josephine. They thought he could be brought over when the plan was explained to him. He was regarded as a tough customer, who could not be handled too cautiously.

"Did you bring the money with you?" asked Little, in a low tone, as soon as the boat was out of hail of the ship; for he had decided to be polite instead of violent.

"What money?" asked the coxswain, rather to encourage the little villain to talk than to obtain information.

"That bag of gold," replied Little, abandoning his oar, and taking a seat on the cushions near the coxswain.

"I haven't it."

"We can't go without that, Shuffles," added Little, earnestly. "We must have money."

"Certainly we must," responded the coxswain, willing to give the rogue all the rope he needed.

"Between you and me, Shuffles, I know where it is," added Little, confidentially.

Of course he did! And Shuffles actually trembled with delight when he saw the scheme working so well, as he believed. Little had said enough already to condemn him, and the coxswain was satisfied that the gold was in the barge.

"Where is it?" asked Shuffles, with an eagerness which he had no occasion to assume.

"I'll tell you, but I can't stop to explain the whole thing now. 'Pon my honor, I thought you had the bag, or I shouldn't have said so. Howe, come up here, and take my oar," added Little, calling to one of his associates under the middle board.

The knight thus addressed crawled out from under the thwart, and took his place at the stroke oar.

"What does that mean?" asked Shuffles, astonished at this addition to his crew.

"Five more of our fellows wanted to go with us, and stowed themselves in the bottom of the boat," answered Little. "You may come out, fellows. It is all right now."

The coxswain found he had gone into the business deeper than he intended; but he was not appalled, only surprised, at the increase of his crew.

"Now, where is the money?" he inquired, nervously, when the interlopers had disposed of themselves in various parts of the barge.

"Do you know Osborne?"

"Osborne? In the Josephine?"

"Yes;" well, he has it in his charge," replied Little, as though he was giving his interested companion the most important and valuable information in the world, which, in the estimation of the coxswain, it actually was.

"But Osborne is on shore with the rest of his crew."

"He is, but the gold is not."

"Where is it, then?"

"On board of the Josephine; and, before we go up the river, we must pay her a visit. We shall have a gully time. Do you know where she lays?"

"Certainly I do," replied Shuffles, who was not

exactly satisfied with the intelligence he received.
"Isn't the gold in the barge?"

"No, sir!" said Little, decidedly.

"I supposed it was."

"You were mistaken. I know exactly where it is concealed on board of the Josephine."

"Where?" asked Shuffles.

"No, you don't!" exclaimed the little villain, who, ever ready to play a trick, was always on the lookout for one. "I shall not give you any chance to back out. You agreed to go with us."

"I am with you."

"Then steer for the Josephine, and we will get the money."

The coxswain was in doubt; and while he was thinking of the matter, Little whistled as composedly as though he had no interest in his decision.

"You must say quick," said he, after a pause. "If you don't want to go with us, I am willing to give it up; but I am afraid we shall never see the gold again, if we don't get it to-night."

"How came Osborne by it?" asked Shuffles.

"I'll explain that after we get the money."

It would not make a delay of more than ten or fifteen minutes to visit the Josephine, and Shuffles decided to let the rogue have his own way. He was on the right track to obtain the bag, which possibly was on board of the Josephine, and the other boats would wait at the jetties for him. The coxswain put the barge about, and Little felt that he had won the victory.

"We are all in the same boat; can't you tell me now how Osborne happens to have this bag of gold?"

asked Shuffles. "You see it is a matter of more consequence to me than to any other fellow, for I have been accused of concealing it."

"What difference does it make to you now, if you are going in with us?" demanded Little.

"I am curious to know how I got mixed up in the scrape, when I didn't know anything at all about the matter," explained Shuffles. "But you asked me, as soon as we got off from the ship, if I had the gold."

"That was only to open the subject. I knew you hadn't it then."

"But how came it aboard the ship yesterday?"

"Osborne handed it to Greenway, who hid it under your berth."

"Greenway, do you know anything about the bag?" demanded Shuffles, suddenly.

"I do," replied the oarsman addressed.

"Do you?" added Shuffles to the stroke oarsman.

"What bag?" asked Howe.

"No; he knows nothing about it," interposed Little." No one but Greenway does."

"I think this matter is a good deal mixed," said the coxswain.

"I'll tell you about it, since you are so suspicious."

"I'm not suspicious. I'm only curious to know how the thing was charged upon me."

"I didn't know myself till we went ashore to-day," continued the ever-ready little liar. "The Dutchman on the spar told me he gave the bag to the man in 'dem schiff,'— boat, I suppose he meant. I didn't know then that any other boat than ours had been near him; but it appears that the Josephine's first cutter had tried to haul him in, and the money was handed to Osborne, her coxswain. Greenway took care of it for him; but after the row in the ship yesterday, he gave it back."

Little did not care whether his exacting companion believed this story or not, if he would only keep still ten minutes more. Unfortunately the coxswain did keep still. He was intent upon finding the bag of gold, and deemed it best, even if the money was then in the barge, to give the conspirator all the rope he wanted, satisfied he would hang himself in the end. With some difficulty the consort was found in the thick fog, and the bowman fastened to her gangway stairs with his boat-hook.

"Keep still, fellows," said Little to the crew. "Come, Shuffles, and I will show you exactly where the gold is, and you may put your own hands upon it, for I would rather have you keep it, and be purser, than any other fellow."

That was exactly what Shuffles wanted. If he could get his hands upon the treasure, he would be satisfied, and he was willing to incur any risk for that purpose. He leaped out of the boat, and ran up the steps to the deck.

"Don't move till I tell you," said Little, in a low tone, as he followed the coxswain.

"Now, where is it?" asked Shuffles, impatiently.

"The best place to hide anything is in the most exposed position," replied Little. "Do you know where Greenway hid the bag on board of the ship, after he found the officers had seen it."

"No."

"In Mr. Lowington's state-room," replied Little, chuckling. "Osborne has done about the same thing here, for he has concealed the bag in the vice-principal's room."

Shuffles did not care a straw for these revelations. He only wanted the bag of gold, and he did not pause to criticise whatever may have seemed doubtful to him in the statements. Little led him into the cabin of the Josephine, and paused before the door of the professors' apartment. It was locked, but the key was in the door.

"You know how your berth is situated. This one is just like it," said Little, opening the door. "Go in, raise up the mattress, and under the forward part you will find the bag. I will hold your lantern for you."

The little villain began to be somewhat nervous, for he heard the second cutter come alongside with some loud talking, and he was afraid Shuffles would take the alarm; but the latter was too eager to obtain the evidence of his own innocence to defer even for an instant the search for the treasure. He entered the room; Little stepped back, and hastily closed and locked the door. The coxswain was a prisoner, and, as the door opened inward, he was not likely to get out in season to defeat the enterprise, if he did at all.

Little rushed on deck, with the lantern in his hand, and called to those in the boats to come on board. The knights, intensely excited, and perhaps surprised at the success, so far, of the wild scheme, hastened on board.

"Perth, I have kept my promise. The knights are all here," said Little.

"Where's Shuffles?" demanded Perth.

"Locked up in the professors' state-room. But you had better be in a hurry."

"Clear away the mainsail and the jib!" added Perth.

He had been prudent enough to station his men beforehand, and in a few minutes the mainsail was shaking tremendously in the fresh breeze. A warping-line was made fast to the cable outboard at one end, while the other was attached to the barge.

"What am I to do?" asked Ellis, who had come on deck, and was viewing with astonishment, not to say alarm, the proceedings of the lawless students.

"Will you join us as a seaman?" asked Perth, sharply.

"What are you going to do?" asked Ellis, rather timidly.

"We are going on a cruise in the Josephine. Will you go, or not? Short stories."

"I would rather not," added the second lieutenant, who, however, did not see how he was to avoid going.

"Then you need not. Get into the barge, or the cutter."

"Are you going to turn me adrift alone in a boat?" demanded Ellis, who did not consider such a prospect very encouraging. "Where are you going?"

"To the north coast of Ireland," replied Perth, intending, by this answer, which might be reported to the principal, to deceive him in regard to his destination.

"I don't want to go, and I don't want to be turned adrift," added Ellis. "Where is Shuffles?"

"Locked up in the professors' state-room."

"Is he going with you?"

"I don't know yet. But I have no time to talk. We are going to sea at once. Choose quick. We shall buoy the anchor with the barge."

"Then I will stay in her."

"Well, behave yourself, or you will get a broken head," said Perth, sharply.

Ellis was faithful enough, but he could do nothing alone. He went over the side into the barge, to which the line from the cable had been fastened, to prevent it from drifting to sea; for the conspirators did not wish to have the second lieutenant's life sacrificed by their freak.

The mainsail was set, and the hands stood at the cable and at the jib-halyards. The cook and the two waiters had made their appearance on deck, but they did not offer to interfere with the conspirators. One of them had asked Perth what was going on, and had been informed that they were only to change the anchorage of the vessel. But Shuffles was not a waiter, and he was not disposed tamely to submit to his imprisonment. He had used his voice, and applied his heels to the door, but, as yet, he was secure. When everything was ready to let go the cable, Perth wanted to know what was to be done with him.

"If you let him out he will break about a dozen of our heads to begin with," suggested Monroe.

"He won't break mine," replied Phillips, a great, stout fellow, who had a taste for fighting; but, being one of the recruits received at Liverpool, he had never had a chance to measure muscle with Shuffles. "Let him out; if he don't behave himself, I will undertake to handle him."

"Let him out, Little; you have the key," added Perth. "We don't want him with us, if he does not join."

"He will join by and by, if you only let him stay," suggested Little, who did not wish to spare him.

"Bring him on deck, at any rate," said the acting captain.

Little, attended by Phillips, went into the cabin, and unlocked the door of the state-room.

"Did you find it?" asked the little villain, as he threw open the door.

Shuffles, who now understood how thoroughly he had been duped, stepped out into the cabin. His first impulse was to fly at Little and tear him in pieces; but he had learned to conquer such temptations, and he stood gazing at the rogue.

"Did you find the bag, Shuffles?" repeated Little; but he was prudent enough to keep under the lee of his stout companion.

"You have deceived me," said Shuffles, sharply.

"Sold you, Shuffles — that's a fact," laughed Little, as he took the bag of gold from his pea-jacket pocket, and dropped it heavily upon the table. "There is the gold, and you need not trouble yourself to look after it any more. If you believed anything I said, you were a bigger fool than I took you to be."

Little put the bag in his pocket again, and was careful to keep Phillips between himself and his victim.

"I did not think so small a boy could be so big a scoundrel," replied Shuffles, with dignity.

"Thank you! I intend to keep up my reputation. If I deceived you, you did me the same favor. You didn't intend to go in with us."

"No; I did not."

"Well, I forgive you."

"I wanted to know who had the bag of gold."

"You know now."

"Bring him up!" shouted Perth, at the head of the companion way. "Don't fool there all night."

"What are you going to do?" asked Shuffles.

"We are going on a cruise in the Josephine. Shall we have the honor of your company?"

"Where are you going?"

"To the north coast of Ireland," replied Little, as instructed by Perth.

"Are you really going to run away with the vessel?" asked Shuffles, appalled, in his turn, by the boldness of the scheme.

"Bring him up!"

"Come on deck, Shuffles, and I will introduce you to Captain Perth," added Little.

They went up the steps, and Perth put the question to him whether or not he wished to join the vessel as a common sailor. He was ashamed to go back to the ship after being so grossly duped. By remaining, he might create a diversion in favor of law and order, and, perhaps, with the aid of the cook and stewards, whom he saw on deck, save and bring back the Josephine.

"I will go with you," said he, firmly.

"Let go the cable!" shouted Perth. "Run up the jib!"

The cable ran out, and sank to the bottom, but the warping line held the barge, to which the second cutter had been made fast, and afforded the means of recovering the anchor and chain. The jib went up, and, in the gloom and fog, the Josephine stood off to the westward on her runaway cruise.

CHAPTER XII.

A FEW HOURS IN ROUEN.

THE first cutter and the professors' barge waited very patiently off the jetties at the entrance of the harbor of Havre. The second cutter, which was to form part of the "cutting out" fleet, had not appeared. Goodwin, the first lieutenant, became very anxious for the result, for the programme seemed to have miscarried somewhere. It was not possible that either boat had lost its way, for they had compasses, and the officers were experienced in managing the boats by night and in the fog.

After waiting half an hour, he sent the barge back to the ship to ascertain what had become of the other boats. On its arrival, Mr. Lowington was more astonished than Goodwin had been, when Leavitt, the officer, informed him that the two boats had not been near the jetty.

"The second cutter left the ship soon after you did, Mr. Leavitt," said the principal. "The barge followed ten minutes later."

"I don't understand it, sir," replied the third lieutenant. "My boat was within hailing distance of the jetty lights, and the barge was outside of me, within call. I am quite sure neither of them can have gone up the river."

"Possibly they have lost their way in the fog, or been drifted off by the strong tide, though I do not see how either of these things could have happened."

Mr. Lowington did not give expression to his worst fears. He suspected that the runaway party, instead of going up the river, as they had declared to Shuffles they intended to do, had altered their plans, and pulled over to Honfleur, on the opposite shore, or made a landing in the vicinity of Cape la Hève. He had not the remotest idea of the real truth. The Josephines were still on shore, probably waiting at the landing for the boats, and it was necessary to provide first for their return, for the tide would soon leave them where they could not be reached by the boats. The crews of the third and fourth cutters were piped away, and the four boats were directed to bring off the ship's company of the consort. Wherever the runaways had gone, it was obviously too late to intercept their passage up the river. The principal judged, from the absence of the second cutter, that Ellis, zealous to convict Shuffles, had detected the movements of the barge and followed her.

The three boats pulled to the jetties, and, hailing the first lieutenant, Leavitt gave him the principal's orders, as transmitted to him through the captain. Goodwin led the way into the harbor, and found the Josephines on the pier, where they had been waiting over an hour. As the night was chilly and damp, they were not very comfortable, and were in a hurry to return to their snug quarters in the consort. At the Hôtel de l'Europe they had enjoyed a splendid entertainment, at which all the delicacies of the French *cuisine* had been set before them, while a band of music played inspiring airs. Mr. Arbuckle had made a pleasant speech to them, to which Captain Kendall, the officers and the professors, had responded "in fitting terms." It was an occasion to be remembered, for it had been heartily enjoyed.

The Josephines embarked in the boats, and many of them were thankful for an opportunity to stir their blood at the oars. The little fleet passed the ship, hailing her on the way, to inform those on board that nothing had been seen of the missing cutters. Captain Kendall was directed to send out all his boats in search of them. Goodwin, in the first cutter, led the line. Terrill was in the bow, looking out for the Josephine, which it was not easy to find in the dense fog.

"Young America, ahoy!" shouted a voice from the depths of the fog and darkness, ahead of the cutter.

"Some one hails the ship, Mr. Goodwin," said Terrill.

"Where away?"

"Dead ahead, sir."

"Young America, ahoy!" repeated the voice.

"Ay, ay!" shouted Terrill, in reply.

The head boat of the line, guided by the voice, rapidly approached the barge and second cutter, moored to the schooner's anchor, where poor Ellis, chilled by the night air, was waiting for the return of the Josephines. Impatient at the delay, he was trying to hail the ship.

"Boat, ahoy!" he called, as the first cutter emerged from the fog, so that he obtained a faint view of it.

"In the boat!" replied Terrill. "Who is it?"

"Ellis," replied the second lieutenant.

"What are you doing here?" asked Terrill, as the bowman hooked on to the barge. "Where's the Josephine?"

"Where is she?" repeated Ellis, leaping into the barge. "She has gone to sea."

"You don't mean so!" exclaimed the first lieutenant of the consort.

"It's a fact. She has been gone for two hours, I should think."

It was only one, which the officer's impatience had extended into two. This was startling information, and Captain Kendall, who was also in the barge, was utterly confounded by it. Ellis told his story very briefly, and Paul ordered a crew into the second cutter to pull her back to the ship, leaving the barge to buoy the anchor. Officers and seamen were appalled at the daring of the conspirators, and opinions were freely expressed that the Josephine would be on the rocks or shoals before morning.

The boats returned to the ship with the astounding intelligence, which was soon communicated to the whole ship's company. The principal was sick at heart, and feared that he had made a fatal mistake. Mr. Fluxion and Ellis were invited to the main cabin, where the lieutenant, highly excited by the event, related his experience after leaving the ship.

"Who was the leader of this insane enterprise?" asked Mr. Lowington, with an apparent calmness which belied his feelings.

"Perth and Little seemed to be the chief ones," replied Ellis.

"Was Shuffles concerned in it?"

"I don't know, sir; but he has gone with them."

"Did you see him?"

"No, sir; but I heard his voice on deck after they sent me into the barge."

"What did he say?"

"He said he would go with them."

"Then he had not been concerned in getting up the project."

"I don't know, sir. I asked for Shuffles, and Perth told me he was locked up in the professors' state-room."

"That shows that he was not one of the original party," added Mr. Lowington, who derived much satisfaction from the fact. "Do you know where they are going?"

"To the north coast of Ireland," replied Ellis.

"Did they say so?"

"Perth said so."

The second lieutenant was dismissed, and Mr. Lowington had an anxious consultation with Mr. Fluxion.

"What do you think of it, Fluxion?" asked the principal.

"It is a mere lark, that cannot amount to much. Probably the rascals will be back in two or three days," replied the vice-principal.

"I am afraid they will wreck the vessel, and lose their lives."

"I don't think so. If they had pluck enough to run away with her, there are brains enough among them to handle her. Perth is a navigator, and Shuffles is equal to the command of either vessel."

"But Shuffles appears to be a prisoner, or, at least, not one of the party, and probably has no control over them."

"In my opinion he will soon have control over them. They will not stay at sea long; and as soon as they put into port, we shall hear of them."

But it was finally decided not to let the affair take its own course; and Mr. Fluxion, Mr. Stoute, and the adult forward officers of the Josephine were sent on shore in the professors' barge. Two steamers were to be employed to search for the runaways, which were to leave as soon as the tide would permit them to go out of the harbor. One, with Mr. Fluxion and the carpenter on board to identify the Josephine, was to go to the northward; and the other, with Mr. Stoute, as interpreter for Cleats, the boatswain, was to go to the westward.

The crew of the ship were piped to muster, and the names of the thirty absentees were discovered by calling the roll. The Josephine's hands were berthed in their vacant places, and the officers were accommodated in the after cabin. In an hour after the return of the boats, all was as quiet as usual on board; but it is doubtful whether the principal slept much that night. The next day was Sunday. Before it was fairly daylight the steamers had gone out, the fog having lifted so as to render the search more hopeful. Mr. Arbuckle and his family spent the day on board. Of course they were very much surprised and grieved to learn of the mischief which had been accomplished, and doubtless concluded that it was not always plain sailing for the principal.

The freak of the knights changed the plans which had been arranged. The majority of the barge's crew were not present to be fêted; the entertainment for them was dispensed with, and Mr. Arbuckle was permitted to propose his second move. On Monday morning the crew were piped to muster, and the liberal gentleman invited "all hands" to be his guests for three weeks in Paris and in Switzerland. He had already sent forward an agent to provide accommodations for them in Paris.

"Three cheers for Mr. Arbuckle!" called one of the enthusiastic students; and they were given with unusual zeal.

The principal attempted to remonstrate with his guest, declaring that he intended to take the students to Paris and Switzerland; but Mr. Arbuckle insisted that he should never forgive himself if he did not do all he purposed. The crew of the squadron had saved the lives of his family, and he was anxious to testify his gratitude, though he could never discharge the obligation. Possibly he was not familiar enough with the plans of the principal to understand and appreciate them, and desired to entertain the students on a grander scale, during the vacation, than he supposed the resources or the discipline of the Academy would permit.

Mr. Lowington was, of course, very anxious and troubled about the runaways; but, having done all he could to reclaim them, he was not disposed to curtail the opportunities for instruction and amusement which were presented to the faithful ones. There would be no loss of time so far as the studies were concerned.

As the morning brought no tidings of the Josephine, it was evident that she had not struck upon any of the rocks or shoals near the mouth of the Seine. The conspirators were all good seamen, whatever else they were; and as they were abundantly supplied with all the appliances for navigating the vessel in safety, there was really but little danger that they would wreck the schooner. Mr. Lowington and the vice-principal had reasoned that ship's duty would soon disgust the runaways, and they would make a port to enjoy themselves in a manner more to their taste. Keeping watch, reefing, steering, taking in and setting sail, were an old story to them, and they would seek enjoyment of a different kind on shore. Mr. Fluxion had consulted with the custom-house officers at Havre, and taken such measures as would cause the arrest of the conspirators, and the detention of the vessel when she made a French port. Mr. Lowington, therefore, expected to hear from them at Cherbourg, Brest, or Dieppe, within two or three days.

The principal, who, as a naval officer, had cruised for months after a suspected vessel, knew how uncertain were the chances of either of the two steamers finding the Josephine; but he hoped she would be found and brought back. He felt sure the runaways would not attempt to cross the ocean, for the vessel was not watered or provisioned for a long voyage. Mr. Fluxion was energetic and skilful, and the chances of the conspirators making a long cruise were very small. The vice-principal was directed, when the Josephine was recovered, to keep her present crew close prisoners on board, and compel them to "work up" their studies, in which most of them were deficient, while their shipmates visited Paris and Switzerland. Having disposed of this unpleasant business as satisfactorily as the circumstances would admit, the principal gave his whole attention to the proposed excursion, assured that, in a few days, the wild freak of the runaways would end in grief and sadness to them.

At half past ten a small steamer conveyed the students of the ship to the shore. Each of them was dressed in his best clothes, and carried his pea-jacket and little bag. They marched directly to the railroad station, where they took their seats in the carriages, which are constructed similar to those used on English railways. Some of them have seats upon the top, with a covering to protect the passengers from the sun and the rain, thus forming a kind of two-story car. The Arbuckles occupied a compartment in one of the first-class carriages, in which Paul Kendall and Dr. Winstock were invited to take seats. This arrangement was a very pleasant one to the young captain; and seated opposite his fair companion at the window of the compartment, he was not likely to devote his usual attention to the scenery on the way.

"I am so sorry Mr. Shuffles is not here," said Grace, as the train started. "I am so grateful to him, and I had promised myself a great deal of pleasure in his society during this trip."

"It is very unfortunate for him," replied Paul.

"I never was so amazed in my life as when father came to the hotel, and told us that some of the students had run away with the Josephine — the dear little ship! I love her almost as well as my own home," added she, warmly. "But I thought all your students were such good boys that they never did anything wrong. I mean with only two or three exceptions, like Mr. McLeish."

"I am sorry they are not all as good as you supposed. Almost all of them are good-hearted fellows, but a little wild," answered Paul, generously. "They are full of spirit, and fond of adventure. I sometimes wish Mr. Lowington would take the squadron to Africa or Asia, and let us hunt elephants, lions, and tigers, and go among the natives."

"Certainly he will never do that."

"Probably not; at least, not until we have spent a year or more in the waters of Europe. But I think we shall go to Smyrna, to Syria, and Egypt."

"If you do, you must tell me all about them in your letters."

"I may not be with the ship so long. I expect to graduate in the fall. But Shuffles will write you all about the cruise, and I think he would be very glad to do so," added Paul. "I dare say he can write much better letters than I can."

"I don't think they could be any better, Captain Kendall. Do you think Mr. Shuffles is concerned in that wicked runaway trip."

"I do not think so," answered Paul, very promptly.

"Why didn't they put him in the boat with Mr. Ellis, then?" inquired Grace.

"I don't know; but it is certain that they locked him into a state-room; and that proves he was not one of the party. I think he intends to induce them to come back, if he can."

"O, I hope so! It would break my heart to think he had done anything wrong. He is so brave, and noble, and self-sacrificing."

"He is a good fellow," replied Paul, with, perhaps, a little less enthusiasm than usual when he spoke of a deserving shipmate.

"You think he went with the runaways for the good of the vessel?" asked Grace.

"I think so; at any rate, I shall be very much disappointed if it appears that he is really an actor in this mischief. He means well now, and — "

"And what?" inquired Grace, when Paul suddenly suspended his remark.

"And I hope he will do as well as he means," added the captain.

Paul was about to say that Shuffles had once been a very bad boy; but when it occurred to him how mean it was to tell even the truth about the reformed student, he checked himself. If Grace "thought more" of Shuffles than he desired her to think, she must despise him, if he said anything to the prejudice of her absent friend. He honestly and sincerely believed that Shuffles was now one of the best young men in the squadron, and ought to be judged by what he was, rather than by what he had been.

"I am sure, when he comes back, he will be a greater hero than when he went," added Grace, with enthusiasm. "I am almost certain he will find some way to overcome his companions, and bring the Josephine back to Havre."

"I hope he will."

The conversation continued, as the train sped on its

way along the slope of the hill. It was a new country to Paul, and he was interested in its scenery, though his attention was equally divided between the landscape and the interior of the car, which had an attraction of its own.

"This must be Harfleur," said Paul, consulting his guide-book as the train passed through a small place.

"It is," interposed Dr. Winstock. "It used to be on the bank of the Seine, but now the current has thrown the sands up before it, so that the river is two miles distant. Henry V. of England besieged and captured the place in 1415. It resisted for forty days, but when it surrendered, the king bared his feet and legs, and marched to the church to return thanks for his victory. He then collected the people, eight thousand in number, robbed them of everything they had, except the clothing they wore, banished them, and called in English colonists to take their places."

"How very strange it is that a king who took the trouble to say his prayers should commit such a wicked act, and forget that the poor people he drove away were the children of the God to whom he prayed!" commented Grace.

"It was more than four hundred years ago, when kings had singular views in regard to their subjects."

On the route, Paul looked with interest at the homes of the poorer classes of people, which were mostly of wood, very small and very neat. The train stopped at Yvetot.

"Have you heard of the King of Yvetot, Miss Arbuckle?" asked the doctor.

"I never did. Was he the king of this village?" replied Grace.

"I suppose so, though it is difficult to tell now what he was king of. This town is celebrated in France for the title of 'Le Roi d'Yvetot,' but the students of antiquity have been puzzled to learn its origin. The story is, that Gaulthier, Lord of Yvetot, offended King Clothaire, son of Clovis. Banished from his presence, the noble endeavored to make his peace with his sovereign by throwing himself upon his knees at the feet of the king, while he was at prayers in the church on Good Friday, trusting that the holiness of the place and the sanctuary of the day of pardon for sin would move Clothaire to forgive him. When the king saw him, he drew his sword and killed the offending subject on the spot. But he repented of his crime, and as an atonement to Gaulthier, created his heirs kings of Yvetot, though it does not appear that any particular dominions were ever assigned to them."

After the train passed Yvetot, there was certainly variety enough to amuse and astonish the students. Now the carriages were hurled through long tunnels, where the cold, damp air chilled, and the darkness was deep and black, and then were carried over high bridges, commanding a wide prospect of the country. The viaduct of Barentin has twenty-seven arches, the highest of which is one hundred and eight feet, while the length of the structure is over twenty-two hundred feet. The distance from Havre to Rouen is fifty-five miles, and the excursionists arrived at one clock at the old city, where they were to remain long enough to view the ancient Gothic cathedral and the quaint structures which line some of its streets.

A lunch had been ordered at the Grand Hôtel

d'Angleterre. The house seemed to be a part of the old city, for it contained all the elements of an ancient castle — great oaken doors, floors of the same material, waxed till they were as smooth as a mirror, panelled walls, and other indications of the olden time. At the station in Rouen there was a *buffet*, or restaurant, which, like most of its kind in the larger towns of France, was very inviting; but Mr. Arbuckle took the party to the hotel rather to show its quaint apartments than because he could not provide for them elsewhere. After the lunch, the principal features of which were soup and cold chicken, the students were permitted, in charge of the professors, to visit the objects of interest. In the hotel, Mr. Mapps had occupied a short time in stating a few interesting facts in regard to the city.

France contains eight cities having a population of over one hundred thousand. In 1866, Paris had one million eight hundred thousand inhabitants, and ranks next to London. Lyons has three hundred and ninety-four thousand; Marseilles, three hundred thousand; Bordeaux, Lille, Toulouse, Nantes, and Rouen, have each between one and two hundred thousand. Fifteen other cities have from fifty to one hundred thousand people. Rouen is situated on the Seine, one hundred and three miles from Havre by water. It was the ancient capital of Normandy, and abounds in historic monuments of the middle ages. It is now the chief town of the department of the Seine Inférieure, and is largely engaged in cotton manufactures.

The students first visited the Cathedral of Nôtre

Dame, in the choir of which a small tablet in the pavement marks the spot where the heart of Richard Cœur de Lion and the remains of several of his family were buried. But the chief object of interest to the tourist is the church of St. Ouen, which exceeds the cathedral in size, and is one of the most beautiful specimens of Gothic architecture in the world. It was commenced in 1318, and finished at the end of the next century. The interior is nearly four hundred and fifty feet long; but in spite of its great size, it has a very light and graceful aspect. The stone is richly carved, and while the building is profusely ornamented, its style is pure.

"This is the tomb of Alexandre Berneval, the builder of the church," said Mr. Mapps, as he pointed to it in one of the chapels. "It is said that he murdered one of his apprentices because the young man surpassed him in the construction of one of the windows. Though he was executed for his crime, the monks of St. Ouen, in gratitude for his skilful services, buried him within the edifice."

In the Museum of Antiquities the students saw some rare curiosities. Among them were the door of the house, in Rouen, in which Corneille, the great French poet, was born, and many old documents, on which were autographs of kings, dukes, and other persons famous in history. William the Conqueror, who could not write, made his mark; but Henry I. and Richard I. affixed their signatures. The most remarkable object was the heart of Richard Cœur de Lion, which is now contained in a glass box. There can be but little doubt of the genuineness of this relic, though it seemed almost incredible that this shrivelled member could be the same that beat in the iron frame of the Lion-hearted, as he battled in the Holy Land with Saladin and the infidels.

In the Place de la Pucelle, their attention was called to a very insufficient monument to the memory of Joan of Arc. In this square she was burned as a sorceress, and her ashes were collected by the hangman, and cast into the Seine. She was treated with the greatest cruelty and injustice by the bishop, who was her judge. A pretended priest was sent to her cell, and under the guise of friendship, obtained her secrets. Though the English condemned her, her own countrymen were her betrayers.

On the return to the station, they visited the Hôtel du Bourgtheroude, where there is a number of marble bas-reliefs, representing the interview between Henry VIII. of England and Francis I. of France, near Ardres, which is called the Field of the Cloth of Gold, from a pavilion of golden cloth in which the meeting took place. Near the station, they halted at the building which commemorates St. Romain, an ancient worthy, who, like St. George of England, conquered a dragon, which was a very troublesome monster, in the vicinity of Rouen. The only person willing to attend him on his perilous expedition was a condemned criminal, who was released for the purpose. But the dragon behaved better than was anticipated, and when the saint made the sign of the cross, he gave up the conflict, and was quietly led into the town by his ghostly conqueror. Until the French revolution, the chapter of the Cathedral was entitled to claim, on Ascension Day, the pardon of one criminal, however great his crime, in grateful remembrance of the companion of St. Romain.

Taking places in the express train for Paris, the party arrived at the gay capital in two and a half hours, though the distance is eighty-six miles. The road for nearly the whole distance is on the banks of the Seine, through a beautiful country, passing over high bridges and through long tunnels. The bags and baggage of the students and other persons of the company were examined by the custom-house officers in the station, both for the *douane*, which collects the duties on imported articles, and the *octroi*, which collects certain local dues, or taxes on goods brought into the city. The officers were very civil, but very business-like in their manners. In charge of Mr. Arbuckle's agent, the tourists walked to the Hôtel du Louvre, where accommodations had been secured for them.

CHAPTER XIII.

THE KNIGHTS AT SEA.

THE darkness was deep and the fog dense when the Josephine, in charge of her reckless captors, sailed out of the roadstead. Though the crew had been billed and stationed, there was no little confusion on board, for the situation was novel and strange. Captain Perth, as we must call him, undeserving as he was of the distinction, was nervous and anxious. Doubtless he felt that he had taken a big job upon his hands; and, unaccustomed to command, he felt ill at ease. He was really the only one of the conspirators who was competent to navigate the vessel, and the entire responsibility rested upon himself.

While the crew were hoisting the mainsail, he had gone into the cabin and examined the chart. The wind was north-west, by the dog vane on the quarter, which was about the compass course he intended to run. He went over his calculations several times, in order to make no mistake; and, having done so, he felt considerable confidence in them. Returning to the deck, he superintended the buoying of the cable, and the Josephine was soon under way, with her starboard tacks aboard. If Perth was nervous before, he was still more so now, for the fog was so thick that the lookout could not see the length of the vessel ahead, and many craft were anchored in the roadstead.

"Keep her south-west, quartermaster," said he to the hand in charge of the wheel.

"Sou'-west, sir," repeated the wheelman, so naturally and respectfully as almost to assure the new commander that all was going well.

"Bring up the fog-horns," continued Perth. "Lay out on the bowsprit, and keep a sharp look out for vessels in our track."

"Ay, ay, sir," replied the crew forward; and soon the fog-horns were sounding their gloomy strains.

"Don't blow all the time, you lubbers," cried the bewildered captain. "Don't you know any better than that? Sound the horns, and then listen."

Presently a halloo was heard dead ahead, and the lookout shouted furiously to announce the fact. Perth listened, and heard the hail himself. It came from some vessel lying in the track of the Josephine, and only a short distance ahead.

"I see her!" yelled Greenway. "Starboard the helm, or we shall be into her!"

"Keep her as she is," said Shuffles, quietly, to the captain.

"But she is dead ahead!" replied Perth, with his heart in his mouth.

"If you put the helm a-starboard you will run into her," added Shuffles.

"Steady! as she is," said Perth to the quartermaster.

"Hard a-starboard!" roared Greenway again.

"Shut up your head! I see her," answered Perth; but at the same time he braced his muscles to receive the shock of a collision.

The tide, which was running out furiously, swept the Josephine clear of a large brig, which was anchored in the roadstead, though with only a few feet to spare.

"That was a close shave," said Perth, breathing easier when the peril was passed.

"It was not so close as it would have been if you had attempted to go to leeward of her," replied Shuffles, in a kind of mournful tone, which showed how little heart he had in the present working of the consort. "There is another vessel lying under her lee."

"Why don't you mind what I say?" demanded Greenway, rushing aft from the bowsprit, disgusted because his advice, or rather order, had not been heeded.

"I am the captain," replied Perth, angrily. "Go forward to your duty."

"You came within six inches of running into that brig. If you don't mind what the lookout says, what's the use of having one?" snarled Greenway.

"If I had minded what you said, we should have run into the brig. There is another vessel to leeward of her, which would have prevented us from giving her a wide berth, and the tide would have crowded us upon her," continued Perth, savagely, for he felt the necessity, at this early stage of the expedition, of defending himself. "Am I right, Shuffles?"

"You are," replied the coxswain, who, whatever his views of the runaway cruise, did not care to have the Josephine sunk in a collision, or run ashore on a sand-bar.

"Go forward to your duty, Greenway," ordered the captain, sternly. "When I want any of your advice I will ask for it."

"Humph! You needn't put on any airs here," growled the discontented tar, as he went forward.

Another vessel was reported ahead, and the Josephine, as narrowly as before, escaped running into her; but this was the last one, and the vessel was clear of the anchoring-grounds when she had passed her. The wind was fresh, and, being against the flow of the tide, it created a heavy chop sea, in which the Josephine pitched and plunged in a manner very trying to the nerves even of the experienced seamen on board of her. They were in constant dread of a collision, or of striking on one of the sand-bars which lie at the mouth of the Seine. But Perth had carefully studied his chart, and made due allowance for the swift tide, which, however, was in favor of the runaways. He caused the lead to be frequently used, and, as the depths obtained corresponded with the figures on the chart, he gradually acquired more confidence in his knowledge. The log-line was run out every half hour, to make sure of the distance sailed.

The crew had been stationed merely to enable the conspirators to get the vessel out of the harbor. The difficult problem of selecting the officers had not yet been settled, for the leaders had purposely reserved it till after the heavy work was accomplished, that the disgust and dissatisfaction of ambitious aspirants might not defeat the enterprise before its execution was commenced. But as soon as the vessel was in blue water, this exciting topic was brought up for discussion. Of the whole number on board, not less than two thirds regarded themselves as competent for high positions, and felt that they had a claim for places in the cabin. Electioneering was commenced on a large scale, but no one seemed to have any decided strength. It had been understood that Perth and Wilton were to have the two highest offices. For each of the other three next to them there were half a dozen aspirants.

Little was really the most influential personage on board, with the exception of Perth. It was generally acknowledged that by his skilful management he had achieved the success of the expedition so far. He had done all the work, but, like Richard in the play, he pretended to have no claim or desire for an office. He and Greenway had already determined to depose Perth, and put Shuffles in his place, not doubting that the latter would accept the high position. But early in the evening it was decided to postpone the election of officers till the next day, as the night, the fog, and the necessity of giving the closest attention to the working of the vessel made it inconvenient to settle the important matter.

The crew were equally divided into two watches, and Wilton and Adler appointed by Perth to serve as officers of the deck *pro tem.*, each of whom was to appoint his subordinates. Everything went well, for the Josephine was under easy sail, and the crew were generally disposed to do their duty. The watch on deck blew the fog-horns at intervals of five minutes, being on the starboard tack, according to the English admiralty orders. On the port tack, a bell is rung, instead of using the horn. Perth was too much excited to go below, even after he had resigned the deck to Wilton. The crew, while attending to their duty, were still busy discussing the claims of the various aspirants for office.

Little had been appointed second officer of the starboard watch by Wilton, who was smart enough in this instance to conciliate him in order to secure his influence. The little villain was quietly at work for Shuffles, and Greenway earnestly seconded his efforts. But it required a great deal of argument and persuasion to dislodge Perth from his position in the regards of the ship's company. Little seemed to be disinterested, and whiningly proclaimed himself to be so. His influence was strong, but the runaways were not prepared to pledge themselves to vote for him.

After the vessel had run fifteen miles by dead reckoning, she was put on the port tack, and the bell, instead of the horn, was sounded every five minutes. The foresail was set, and, the tide helping her, the Josephine made ten knots an hour. At midnight the wind died out, and all sail was set; but it soon freshened up again from the south-west, blowing away the fog, and making a fair wind. The tide had turned, and the chop sea subsided. Wilton was relieved, and Adler took his place.

"Keep her north-west," said Perth to the new officer of the deck, "and look out for lights on the weather bow."

"All right," replied Adler; "everything is going first-rate with us. That fog was a capital idea, and just fitted our case."

"We are doing tip-top," added Perth, with a yawn, for, after the hard work he had done on shore and during the evening, he was very much fatigued. "I am going to turn in now. Keep your eyes wide open, Adler, and don't let the watch go to sleep."

"Well, I think I know my duty," replied Adler, rather sharply.

"I know you do; but a caution will do no harm, for all the fellows are tired and sleepy," added the captain, as he went below.

Shuffles, who had satisfied himself that the Josephine was in no present danger of being wrecked, had gone below when the schooner went in stays and was headed away from the coast. The cook and stewards had been to him to ask what they should do. He had told them to turn in, and keep quiet. When Perth went below no one was up except Shuffles, who sat at the cabin table reading his Bible. Wilton and Little had taken possession of the professors' state-room, and the starboard watch occupied the berths in the steerage.

"Well, Shuffles, everything goes first-rate," said Perth, as he entered the cabin.

"The way of the transgressor is hard," replied the former.

"Don't preach!" added the captain, shrugging his shoulders like the Frenchmen he had seen at Havre.

"Have you considered the end of this affair?" asked Shuffles, gently, as he closed the book on the table.

"The end of it is a good time; and if we don't have that, it won't be our fault."

"Are you really going to the north coast of Ireland?"

"Not a bit of it," laughed Perth.

"Where are you going?"

"Up the Mediterranean."

"Do you mean so?"

"Certainly I do."

"But you are very sure to be captured before many days."

"Don't you believe it. We have got a fair start, and the Young America won't be likely to catch us."

"The Young America!" exclaimed Shuffles. "You are not so simple as to suppose Mr. Lowington will pursue you in the ship?"

"Why not?" asked Perth, rather anxiously; for he had not thought of any other pursuit.

"He is not so simple as you are."

"Do you mean to insult me?"

"Certainly not; I only meant to say that he would not be so foolish as to chase you in the ship. I have no doubt that, by this time, several steamers are on your track."

This was rather a startling suggestion. The idea of such a pursuit had not been considered.

"You may be sure, also, that some one in every port in France is ready to seize the Josephine as soon as her anchor touches the bottom," continued Shuffles, earnestly.

"I shall not anchor in any port of France till we are ready to abandon the vessel. I fancy I can keep out of the reach of all pursuers."

"But you are sure to get into trouble before you see the end of the affair. Let me advise you, as a friend, to go about and return to Havre. I will promise to do the best I can with Mr. Lowington to induce him to let you off easily," added Shuffles.

"Do you think I'm such a lunkhead as to back out now?" demanded Perth, with the utmost contempt in his tones and his looks. "No, sir! You have mistaken your man. I wouldn't go back if Lowington would agree not to say a word about it."

"Listen to reason, Perth. You have about thirty of the most disorderly fellows in the squadron with you. If the principal finds it hard to manage them, what do you expect to do with them?"

"They are all good fellows, every one of them; and they will do the right thing. Don't trouble your head about them. Now you have shown your colors, I should like to know what you intend to do," replied Perth.

"I don't know what I shall do."

"Do you mean to join us, or not?"

"Certainly not," replied Shuffles, decidedly; for, after his former experience in tampering with evil associates, he found it best to do his duty squarely, and let the consequences take care of themselves.

"Well, you needn't be so crank about it. What did you come with us for, if you don't mean to join? I gave you a chance to go into the barge with Ellis."

Shuffles was not prepared to answer this question, though he believed that he could give a good reason for his conduct.

"By this time you have the name, on board of the

ship, of having joined our party, and you may as well be hanged for an old sheep as a lamb," added Perth, who was not without hope that his influential shipmate might change his mind.

"I prefer to be hanged for a lamb," replied Shuffles. "I hope you will think better of it by morning, and be ready to go back."

"Make yourself easy on that point. We intend to have the cruise out whatever happens. I'm going to turn in."

"Where shall I sleep?" asked Shuffles.

"Anywhere you please. The berths are not assigned yet. Let me tell you one thing, old fellow: if you attempt to play any of your pious games on board this vessel, I'll turn you adrift in one of the boats."

"I don't understand what you mean."

"If you try to get up a mutiny, or to turn the fellows against me, it will be all day with you," answered Perth, as he entered Paul Kendall's stateroom.

What the runaway captain possibly suspected had already engaged the attention of Shuffles; indeed, he had remained on board when he might, perhaps, have saved his reputation by going into the barge, in order to use his influence and his exertions for the safety and the restoration of the Josephine. He had already hinted his intention to the cook and stewards, when he advised them to submit for the present to the new order of things. He felt morally certain that the disorderly elements of the party would soon break out in opposition to the leaders, and he was willing to wait until a divided house should insure the success of any plan he might form for the recapture of the Josephine. He selected one of the berths in the cabin for his own use, and turned in fatigued enough to sleep even under the present exciting circumstances.

The morning of Sunday dawned bright and beautiful upon the waters. The starboard watch was called at eight bells, and having had only four hours sleep, the runaway tars below were not very willing to be turned out; in fact, quite a number of them were dragged out of their berths by the port watch, who had fared still worse, having had nothing more than a " cat nap " before twelve. The change was made at last, but no such grumbling, growling, and fighting had ever been seen before in either vessel. At this time the Josephine was off Point de Barfleur, well in the offing. Perth's navigation was certainly justified by the result; and, when the fact was announced to him, he turned out to examine his chart. The vessel was very nearly on the red-ink line he had drawn on the chart to indicate the course of the schooner. Pleased with the result, he turned in again to finish his night's rest.

Breakfast was served at seven, and at eight bells, according to the sea routine of the squadron, to the two watches. The starboard watch turned in as soon as they had disposed of their meal, and Perth found it impracticable to organize the crew and elect the officers. It was decided to keep watch and watch, till everybody had slept as much as he desired. The Josephine still made her ten knots an hour, carrying all sail in the lively breeze. But everything was dull and heavy on board. The crew were sleepy and stupid, and only the most necessary work was done.

At eight bells, in the afternoon watch, the crew appeared to have slept as much as they could conveniently, and nearly all of them gathered on deck. They had begun to clamor for the settlement of the exciting question in regard to the choice of officers. Perth concluded that the time to organize had come, and he called all hands for the purpose. They assembled on the quarter deck so that the quartermaster at the wheel could take part in the proceedings, and Perth stepped upon the high threshold of the companion way to make a speech.

"Fellows, we have been in the habit of doing our work in an orderly manner, and having everything in ship-shape style. I hope we shall do so now on this cruise," he began. "We are in for a good time, and it will be our own fault if we don't have it."

"That's so!" shouted one of the crew.

"We must keep good order, and have fair play for every fellow," continued the captain. "Each one must do his share of the work, and—"

"What's this to do with the election of officers?" demanded a rude fellow.

"Perhaps nothing," replied the captain, smartly. "If you elect officers, you must obey them, or we shall all go to the bottom together."

"Let's vote," growled the rude tar, who evidently had no taste for speeches.

"This is a republican government, and we must all obey the will of the majority. I hope there won't be any growling about the result of the election. We can't all be officers, and those who are not elected must submit to those who are. That's fair play."

"Fair for the officers," responded the grumbler.

"Fair for all. How many officers shall we have? We must settle that first. I am ready to hear any motion. I don't think there ought to be many of them; at least, not cabin officers, for we have not any too many seamen to handle the vessel in heavy weather."

"I move there be a captain, and a first, second, third, and fourth officer," said Dunlap.

"Second the motion," roared the rude fellow.

The motion was put and carried without dissension. The captain was then empowered to appoint a committee to receive and count the votes. Phillips, who was the heaviest fellow and the biggest fighter in the crowd, was made chairman.

"Bring in your votes for captain," continued Perth, who, knowing that he was the only navigator among the knights, was entirely confident of his own election.

The ballots were prepared, and dropped into a travelling-bag held by Phillips. As soon as all had voted, the committee went down into the cabin to count the ballots. They were absent but a few moments.

"Attention to the report of the committee," called Captain Perth, who regarded the vote for commander as a mere formality.

"Whole number of votes, thirty," said Phillips, reading from a little slip of paper. "Necessary to a choice, sixteen. Sampson Little has two, Thomas Perth has eleven, Robert Shuffles has seventeen, and is elected."

"What!" exclaimed Perth, aghast at the result of the balloting.

"Robert Shuffles, seventeen!" shouted Greenway. "That's what's the matter!"

"I protest against this election," said Perth, fiercely.

"No, you don't," roared Brown, the grumbler. "Didn't you say just now that the fellows must stand by the vote."

"But Shuffles is not even a Knight of the Golden Fleece," replied Perth. "He isn't one of our fellows."

"No matter for that," growled Brown. "Three cheers for Captain Shuffles."

Brown and three or four others gave the cheers.

"I will not submit to this election. It is an insult to me. If the fellows don't like me, let them say so," continued Perth, who was actually beginning to realize in his mortified vanity that the way of the transgressor is hard.

"They have said so," replied the grumbler. "Can't you understand the vote?"

"The fellows like you well enough," interposed Little; "but they prefer to have Shuffles for captain. They mean to elect you first officer."

"I decline to serve as first officer."

"And I decline to have him serve as first officer," said Wilton, stepping forward, and shaking his head like a defeated bully. "The fellows promised to choose Perth captain and me first lieutenant."

"I haven't anything more to say, fellows. You can run the vessel to suit yourselves," added Perth, walking away, utterly disgusted with the proceedings.

"Captain Shuffles has been fairly elected," persisted Little, lifting his diminutive body upon the companion way, in an attitude which threatened a speech. "Stick to the vote, fellows. The majority must rule. If Perth won't be first officer, let him go into the steerage, and do his duty before the mast."

"I will not do duty any way, if I am to be insulted in this manner," said Perth, walking up to the speaker.

"Just now you talked the other side of your mouth. You believed in good order, and doing things up shipshape. I believe in it now."

"So do I," added Phillips, who had voted for Shuffles; "and if a fellow won't do his duty, I go for making him do it."

"Bully for you, Fisty," shouted Brown.

"Where is Shuffles?" asked Little.

"In the cabin."

"Shall Phillips go below, and inform him of his election? If you agree, say so," continued Little, briskly.

"Ay, ay!" replied those who had voted for Shuffles.

Phillips went down into the cabin. Shuffles was lying in his berth reading a good book, and unsuspicious of the honor which had been conferred upon him.

"Bob Shuffles!" called Phillips.

"What is wanted?" inquired the reader.

"I have the honor to inform you that you have been elected captain of the Josephine, and that the ship's company wish to see you on deck."

"What do you mean by that?" demanded the astonished Shuffles.

Phillips explained, and exhibited the paper on which the vote was recorded.

"Do you regard me as belonging to your party?" asked Shuffles, quietly.

"We have not so regarded you, but we hope you will join us now. Come on deck, and speak for yourself."

The unfortunate recipient of the "greatness thrust upon him" consented to go on deck, where he was formally introduced to the ship's company as "Captain Shuffles."

"I will accept on one condition," said the captain elect.

"What is it?" demanded half a dozen of the voters.

"That the Josephine come about, and return to Havre, where I will do my best to induce Mr. Lowington to forgive you for what you have done."

"No! No!" shouted a score at once.

"I believe Mr. Lowington would think favorably of my request, if I inform him of the circumstances," added Shuffles.

"No! no!" shouted the runaways. "We are in for a good time, and we are going to have it!"

"Will you join the Knights of the Golden Fleece or not?" demanded one of the Perth party.

"I do not know what you mean," answered Shuffles.

"I will explain it," volunteered Little, taking the commander elect aside for the purpose.

As briefly as possible the little scoundrel related the history of the order, and its object. The organization was the counterpart of the Chain League, which Shuffles had invented, and he felt that his past sins were rising up in judgment against him as he listened to the story; but his former infamy only made him the more strenuous to be faithful now.

"I will not join it," replied the reformed student.

"Don't be in a hurry to decide now. Think of it," pleaded Little. "All the fellows wanted you, and that is the reason I got you to come."

"You deceived me, Little. You told me the party was going up the Seine in the barge."

"That was a guy, of course," laughed Little. "All I wanted was to make you come."

"Where is the bag of gold?"

"I have it all safe."

"All I wanted was to know what had become of it;" and Shuffles explained his own position so unequivocally that even the little rogue could not misapprehend him. "I will have nothing to do with this scrape."

"The fellows will ship you in one of the boats, if you don't."

"Let them do so. I will not join."

"O, come, be a good fellow. You are ruined already on board of the ship, and you might as well have a good time."

"No."

Shuffles told the conspirators plainly that he would take no part with them.

"Shuffles declines; that's enough!" snapped Little. "We may as well vote again. This time I shall go in for Perth."

"I decline," said the captain *pro tem.*, sullenly, for he was still smarting under the insult.

"Bring in your votes, fellows," called Little, regardless of the words of Perth.

This time the vote was unanimous; and Perth,

after some coaxing, yielded, and was restored to his position and his temper at the same time. Wilton, after two ballots, was elected first officer. After a great deal of electioneering and many fruitless ballots, the remaining offices were filled by majorities of one or two, and Adler, Little, and Phillips were respectively elected second, third, and fourth officers. There was a great deal of grumbling at the choice, but the minority finally submitted, and there was a better prospect of peace.

CHAPTER XIV.

PALACES IN PARIS.

THE Grand Hôtel du Louvre, where the excursionists were to remain during their stay in Paris, is in the Rue de Rivoli, opposite the Louvre, which is connected with the palace of the Tuileries. There is no direct entrance from the street, as in American hotels; but the students marched through an archway into a court, surrounded by the four wings of the building, which is roofed over with glass. Opening out of this court are the various offices and other business apartments of the establishment. A broad and elegant staircase leads from one end to the portions used by guests.

The carriage of the traveller is driven into this court, and he is received by the clerk who assigns the rooms, and who occupies a small office next to that of the cashier. As the prices for rooms are different on the several floors, he is permitted to choose which he will have. A servant shows him his apartment, and his baggage is sent up on an elevator. A small blank, called *bulletin d'arrivée*, is given to the stranger, which he is required to fill out with his full name, age, quality, or profession, place of birth, habitual residence, last residence, *papiers de sûreté*, and the date and hour of his arrival. Most of this information is for the benefit of the police, who know all about every person who comes into Paris, and every one who leaves it. If his antecedents are at all suspicious, he is dogged in all his movements by government spies.

The Hôtel du Louvre has above five hundred bedrooms, besides private parlors and the public apartments. It is kept on a grand scale, and differs essentially from English, and especially from American hotels. This establishment has been surpassed by one more recently erected, which was at first called the Grand Hôtel de la Paix; but as the name trenched upon that of another public house, it is now called simply the Grand Hôtel. It contains upwards of seven hundred sleeping-rooms, and is built and furnished in the most elegant style.

The Arbuckles came up from the station in a carriage, and had gone to their rooms when the students arrived. The latter were to be disposed of two in an apartment. Commodore Gordon and Captain Kendall had decided to occupy the same room. They were conducted to No. 363, on the third floor, which corresponds with the fourth in the United States.

"This is not bad," said Paul, when the servant had left them.

"Not at all for a sky parlor," replied Gordon, as he went to the window, which opened like a couple of double doors. "We are opposite the Louvre, on the Rue de Rivoli. I like to know where I am."

"So do I. The Rue de St. Honoré is on the opposite side of the hotel, and one end of it faces the Place du Palais Royal. Now, where's the Seine?"

"I have it all here," replied the commodore, spreading out a map of Paris on the table. "There is nothing but the Louvre between us and the river, which runs parallel to the Rue de Rivoli. Now, let's see: if we follow this street to the west, we shall pass the palace and garden of the Tuileries, and come to the Place de la Concorde. Beyond this is the Champs Elysées. I know where I am now."

"Paris is a big city," laughed Paul, puzzled by the complicated map before him. "I don't think we can understand it just yet."

"We can get a leading idea. I always want to have one avenue, as a guide. Here is the Rue de Rivoli, beginning at the Place de la Bastille, and ending at the gardens of the Tuileries, or continued by the Avenue des Champs Elysées, to the Arc de Triomphe, about three miles and a half."

The commodore was satisfied with the idea he had drawn from the map, and the young officers turned their attention to the immediate surroundings. In the room hung a framed placard containing a tariff of the hotel prices, with such information in regard to the establishment as it was needful for the guest to possess. The price of this apartment, written in ink, was five francs and fifty centimes a day, and *service*, or servants, one franc and fifty centimes. There were several *bureaux*, or offices, in the house, at which the keys were to be left, each in charge of a servant who attended to the wants of the guests in his division.

The room was elegantly furnished for a hotel. The carpet was of fine quality; the bed was adorned with an elaborate canopy; wrought muslin draperies half concealed the windows, and on a marble mantel rested an immense mirror and a marble clock; and the chairs and divan were upholstered with velvet.

The students, satified with their quarters, went down stairs to the reading-room, where the party were to assemble for dinner. It was an elegant apartment, and like the spacious dining-room adjoining it, was a copy of one of the principal halls of the palace of Versailles. From the reading-room opens the restaurant, where breakfasts and suppers are served to order. When the guest seats himself at a table, a card is brought to him, on which he writes his name, the number of his room, and the articles he desires. These cards are sent to the office, and the traveller's bill is made from them, so that there can be no dispute. A fixed price per day is never charged, and the guest is required to pay only for what he orders. The bill is made out with the items for each day, the charge for room and service being repeated for each new date.

The prices are tolerably reasonable, though the everlasting "bougie" is a swindle. The first charge is two francs for two candles, which must be paid for though the guest remain but one night. Some travellers put them in their trunks, and require the waiter to remove those provided at the next place at which he stops. If you have a bath, you are charged for a piece of soap, which, however, you may take with you. Tea or coffee, with bread and butter, is one franc and a half; a beefsteak, or other extra dish, two francs.

The *table d'hôte* is served in the great *salle à manger*. Guests are admitted by ticket, which may be purchased in the reading-room for seven francs, or ordered by card, and charged on the bill. The dinner consists of a limited variety, and every dish on the "*menu*" is offered to the guest. A bottle of "*vin ordinaire*," or common claret wine, is placed at each plate, and included in the price. One does not care to go through the tedious forms for so indifferent a dinner more than once, when the restaurants afford a better meal for half the money.

A special dinner had been prepared for the students, from which were excluded the wine bottles, though the claret is often drank freely by those who are temperance men at home, for it is hardly stronger than new cider. The boys worried through the forms, and the frequent changes of plates, with very little interest, and perhaps would have preferred plain beefsteak to "*poulet aux champignons*."

"Young gentlemen," said Mr. Mapps, near the head of the table, when the dessert had been served, "I am directed by the principal to make a few explanations. Paris, in the time of Julius Cæsar, was only a few mud huts on the small island in the Seine now called the Ile de la Cité. It increased in size and importance rapidly, and was occasionally the residence of the Roman emperors. In the reign of Clovis it was fortified, and a church to St. Genevieve, the patron saint of Paris, was erected. In the reign of Hugh Capet the city was greatly enlarged, and many churches were erected. Since this period it has continued to increase in size and elegance.

"Paris is situated on both sides of the Seine, one hundred and eleven miles from its mouth. It is built on a plain, though there are several elevations within and around it. The river is crossed at various points by twenty-six bridges, two of which are iron, two are suspension, and the rest of wood or stone. The stream is here navigable only for small steamers, boats, and barges. The ground on which the city is built is generally so level that the drainage is difficult, and until recently no adequate system of sewerage was adopted. There are two hundred and seventy miles of sewers, completed or under construction. Six large galleries, called " collectors," three on each side of the river, carry off the refuse matter. The principal one is three miles long, eighteen feet wide, and sixteen and a half feet high. Into this immense sewer lead the smaller ones. Boats float up and down these galleries, with men employed to keep them from being blocked up. They are ventilated with air-traps, and lighted with oil lamps. These under-ground avenues surpass any similar works in the world, and the sewers of Paris are almost as celebrated as the streets. Everything in this city is economized, and the sewers are visited by the rat-catchers, who drive a good business in the skins of these animals.

" Paris is supplied with water from several sources, — from streams ten to twenty-five miles distant, from the Seine, from which it is pumped to a height sufficient for distribution, and from the artesian wells of Grenelle and Passy. The latter is over eighteen hundred feet deep, and supplies three and a half million gallons of water a day. Not more than one fifth of the houses in the city are supplied by pipes extending into them. The rest are furnished by carts, which go from door to door.

"The streets of the city have been vastly improved within a few years. A company, chartered by the government, was authorized to purchase the real estate in certain localities, to pull down the old houses, lay out new streets, and erect buildings upon them, making their profit on the sale of them. In this manner, as well as by the direct enterprise of the government, the aspect of certain sections of the city has been entirely changed. As you came into the hotel, you observed, beyond the Place du Palais Royal, that the buildings were in process of demolition for a considerable distance. A new street is to be made there, and several others are planned in this vicinity.

"The government of Paris is vested in the prefect of the Seine, who is assisted by a council of sixty, all of whom are appointed by the emperor. Under the prefect are twenty districts, each in charge of a mayor and two deputy mayors. These districts are subdivided into *quarters*, each of which has its *commissaire de police*. The prefect of police is the equal in rank of the prefect of the Seine, and is independent of him. He has under his orders about forty-six hundred agents, thirty-seven hundred of whom are *sergents de ville*, or patrolmen; the others are the secret police, about which so much is said — men who make your acquaintance in the hotels, *cafés*, and other public places, to ascertain whether you intend to demolish the government of Louis Napoleon. Your servant, courier, commissionaire, interpreter, or waiter may be one of this class, but you don't know it; and if you have no evil designs you need not know it. The *sergents de ville* are the men whom you saw in the street, wearing cocked hats, dress coats with broad skirts, with wiry-looking swords at their sides. To assist in keeping the peace there are four thousand gendarmes, and a regiment called the *garde de Paris*, of nearly three thousand men. Within and around the city are forty thousand troops, who may be called into service when the ordinary force fails. Paris is surrounded by a circle of fortifications thirty miles in extent, and seventeen detached forts, each of which is of great strength.

"A franc of French money is usually reckoned as twenty cents of our currency, though its actual value is eighteen and three fourths cents. Accounts are kept here in francs and centimes. One hundred centimes make a franc. And these terms alone are used in giving prices. Your newspaper costs ten centimes; your fare from the railroad is two francs fifty centimes. The silver coins are the half franc, the franc, the two-franc piece, and the five-franc piece. The gold coins are the Napoleon, or twenty-franc piece, the half Napoleon, or ten-franc, and the quarter Napoleon, or five-franc piece. Forty-franc pieces are also in use, and other gold coins are occasionally seen. The copper coins are the sou and two-sous pieces. You constantly hear of centimes, but never see them. The sou is five centimes. The Bank of France issues notes of one hundred, two hundred, five hundred, and one thousand francs, which are legal tender throughout the empire.

"The French use a decimal system of weights and measures. Of weight, the unit is the *gramme*, which is fifteen and four tenths grains Troy. The *kilo gramme,* or a thousand *grammes,* is equal to about two and a quarter pounds Avoirdupois. In measures, the *metre* is the unit, and is found by taking one millionth part of the quadrant of the earth's circumference on a meridian, or the distance from the pole to the equator. It is equal to thirty-nine and thirty-seven hundredths inches; or three and a quarter feet is near enough for rough calculations."

Mr. Mapps took his seat, and Mr. Arbuckle rose. By permission of the principal, he invited the party to visit the *Cirque de l'Impératrice.* A circus is a very delightful affair to boys, and they promptly applauded the brief speech of their liberal friend. The party formed a procession in the court-yard of the hotel. A lieutenant of police — a very trim-looking personage, wearing a chapeau, a long coat, and a thin sword, which mysteriously depended from his side, for he wore no belt — was in waiting, with four of the dashing-looking patrolmen, to escort the party; for Mr. Arbuckle had influential friends in Paris, who had secured government assistance to enable the visitors to see the city without annoyance.

The tourists, in ranks four deep, passed out of the court into the Rue de Rivoli. At the head of the procession walked the commodore, with one of the captains on each side of him, the lieutenant of police on the left of them. Of course such a display of blue cloth, shoulder straps, and arm bands made a sensation, and the Parisians paused to look at it. The four *sergents de ville* flanked the column, and kept the way clear for it.

For a long distance on the Rue de Rivoli, the sidewalk is covered by the buildings which overtop it, and form a long arcade. On the opposite side of the street were the beautiful gardens of the Tuileries, brilliantly lighted with gas, the fountains sparkling in its glare. At the end of the gardens, as it was too early for the performance, the procession crossed the street into the Place de la Concorde. It is a magnificent square, perhaps the grandest in the world; in the centre of which is the Obelisk of Luxor, presented to the government by the Viceroy of Egypt, and brought from Thebes. On each side of it is an elaborate fountain.

"Young gentlemen," said Mr. Mapps, as the students gathered around him, "in this square, formerly called the Place Louis Quinze, stood the statue of Louis XV., which was pulled down and melted into cannon by a decree of the National Convention. Here, also, near the obelisk, was placed the guillotine on which Louis XVI. was beheaded. Here, too, perished his queen, Marie Antoinette, his sister, Madame Elizabeth, Madame Roland, Robespierre, Danton, and many others. Here was raised the statue of Liberty, and the square was then the Place de la Révolution. After the restoration, it was proposed to erect a fountain on the spot where the king was executed; but Châteaubriand declared that all the water in the world could not wash away the blood which had been shed there. In 1800 it received its present name, which, however, has been changed for brief periods several times."

The march was resumed, and the procession passed into the Avenue des Champs Elysées, on each side of which the grounds are laid out in walks and grass plots. A certain portion of it is devoted to out-door shows, such as one usually sees around a circus in a country town in the United States; as "Punch and Judy," puppets, weighing apparatus, and organs. The students entered the circus, which is a large, circular building, seating three or four thousand people. The audience was composed of people of all nations, and some of the students were rather surprised to find themselves near a group of Arabs, in white garments and turbans. The performance was rather inferior in skill and daring to those seen in our country, and the "great American rider," who manœuvred three horses, won the most applause. Of the three clowns, two were Americans, who, though they could not speak a word of French, won the laurels of the evening by their grotesque and agile feats. There was a savor of home about the scene when they got off the venerable joke, "Did you never see a horse's tail before?" "No, I always saw it behind!" The Frenchmen looked blank — did not see the point; but the boys, for old acquaintance' sake, applauded heartily when they heard the witticism.

At the close of the performance the students were conducted to a *café chantant*, of which there were two or three in the vicinity of the circus. The audience sit at little tables, in the open air, at which refreshments, such as coffee, cakes, and lemonade, are sold, no fee being charged for admission. In front of them is a kind of little covered stage, gaudily painted, and flashing with light, upon which comic songs, dances, and other light performances take place. The students were treated to cake and lemonade by Mr. Arbuckle.

Still under the guidance of the police, they were led to the Jardin Mabille, which is a beautiful garden, similar to the Cremorne in London. It contains numerous walks, arbors, grottoes, with lights fantastically arranged, and the effect is suggestive of fairyland. Though an admission fee is charged, the restaurants are a prominent element in the entertainment. In one part of the garden there was a large kiosk, of fanciful architecture, gaudily adorned with paint and gilt, in which a large orchestra, consisting of not less than forty pieces, discoursed music for the multitude. Around this kiosk was enclosed a circle floored for dancing; but before the Terpsichorean revels commenced, Mr. Lowington was careful to withdraw his students. There were thousands of people in the place, apparently as respectable as any in the city, while a strong force of *gendarmes* was scattered through the premises to preserve order.

Leaving this gay scene, the students returned to the Hôtel du Louvre, weary enough to retire. At seven o'clock the next morning, all hands were mustered in the court-yard of the hotel, and marched to the Halles Centrales, or Central Market, which covers several acres of ground. They consist of a series of sheds, or *pavillons*, under one glass roof, with stands for fish, flesh, and fowl, for eggs, butter, cheese, and vegetables. Under the market are immense vaults for the storing of produce, from which extend an underground railroad to the several railway stations. The students gazed with interest at the busy scene, and many observed with critical attention the articles exposed for sale, which, however, did not materially differ from those seen in the markets at home. The beef and mutton were very nicely prepared for market, and the veal was exceedingly white and plump; but it is "blown up" to give it this inviting appearance.

One stall was a "cold victuals" stand, where baked, boiled, roast, meat pies, and other food, which had already seen service on the table, were arranged with Parisian skill and taste to tempt the appetites of the poorer classes. The vast heap of cooked provisions, gathered from the tables of the rich, had evidently been sorted over, so as to make huge dishes of similar material. Parts of patties and pies from different sources had been ingeniously united so as to form consistent whole ones; and drumsticks, wings, breast-bones, and second joints of chickens, which had never looked each other in the face, still less were parts of the same body corporate, were so tastefully arranged on plates that they seemed to have been recently cut from the same *corpus*.

Adjoining this immense establishment was the Halle au Blé, or Corn Market, a vast circular building, with a curious roof of iron and copper, which will hold thirty thousand sacks of grain. After a glance into this structure, the company visited the Church of St. Eustache, and were then conducted to a restaurant, of a kind peculiar to France. Long tables were spread, on which were placed only cups and saucers, with a little roll at each. The boys stood up around the table, and presently the waiters, each with two long-handled coffee-pots in his hands, filled the cups with equal parts of coffee and boiled milk — *café au lait*. The simple roll, without butter, and the coffee, form the early or first breakfast of the Frenchman. At eleven or twelve o'clock he takes his second breakfast, which, among the wealthy, is elaborate enough for an American dinner.

After this simple meal, the students proceeded to the Palais Royal, which is a continuous line of buildings around a central court, laid out as a garden, in which the boys were drawn up to hear the history of the palace. The lower part of the building is cut up into minute stores, occupied by jewellers, dealers in fancy goods, and similar wares, while at the north end are the celebrated restaurants, the Trois Frères, Véfour, and Véry.

"The Palais Royal was commenced by Cardinal Richelieu, in 1624, and was bequeathed by him to Louis XIII.," said Professor Mapps. "It was presented to the Duke of Orleans by Louis XIV., from whom it descended to *Philippe Egalité*, — so called because he opposed the government, and espoused the cause of the people, — who was the father of Louis Philippe. He was a reckless and profligate man, and to raise money converted the lower part of the palace into shops, as you now see it. In this garden Desmoulins and other mob-speakers addressed the revolutionary multitude in 1789, and here was given the signal for the destruction of the Bastille. On this occasion were blended the old French colors, white, and the red and blue of Paris, which form the 'tricolor,' so celebrated in the revolutionary history of France. Philippe Egalité was a member of th

Convention, and voted for the execution of his cousin, Louis XVI.; but he soon incurred the hostility of the lawless leaders, was tried on frivolous charges, and perished himself on the guillotine. After his death the Palais Royal was sold to different persons at auction, but was finally purchased by the Orleans family. When the allies occupied Paris, in 1814, it contained many gambling houses, where Marshal Blucher and others lost immense sums of money. In 1848 it was purchased by the people; but when the present emperor came into power, he gave it to his uncle Jerome, and at his death the state apartments, opposite the Louvre, were appropriated to his son, Prince Napoleon. One of the regimental bands of the army plays on certain afternoons in the garden. The vast number of chairs which you see are let at one sou for a common, and two sous for an arm chair on such occasions."

The party passed under the arches, in the front of the palace, to the Place du Palais Royal, crossed the street, and through an arch entered the Place du Carousel, the open space between the Louvre and the Tuileries, which have been connected by wings, called the New Louvre, by Napoleon III. The square, therefore, is enclosed by buildings. It contains a triumphal arch, erected by the first emperor. The Louvre is the older palace. It was a hunting seat in the time of the Merovingian kings, and its name is supposed to have been derived from the wolves (*louve*) in the vicinity. Francis I. commenced the edifice, which has been in process of enlargement and improvement down to the present time. It now con tains no less than fifteen different museums of painting, sculpture, antiquities, relics of the kings of France, and many other curiosities. The students passed through its long halls, whose oaken floors, polished as smooth as glass, render walking a tiresome and difficult labor. It must be confessed that they gazed with singular indifference upon the works of Raphael, Rubens, Leonardo da Vinci, Titian, and other old masters; and even the Ascension of the Virgin, by Murillo, which Marshal Soult brought from Spain, purchased for one hundred and twenty-three thousand dollars, — the largest sum ever paid for a painting, — hardly created an emotion, except at the price paid for it.

It was impossible to do anything more than glance at these pictures, for a week would not be too long a time to enable one to see them in detail. The great gallery is three hundred and twenty feet long, and forty-two feet wide; and persons not deeply imbued with a love of art find the journey through all these halls rather tiresome. The Museum of the Sovereigns occupies five halls, one of which is called the Salle de Napoléon I., and is exclusively devoted to articles connected with him, including his coronation robes, uniforms, swords, dressing-cases, the clothing he wore at St. Helena, the camp-bed and furniture used in his campaigns; the throne and the cradle of the King of Rome. His old hats, drab overcoats, and boots seemed to bring him back to the students, so that he was more real than ever before. In the Salle des Rois are the relics of the kings, such as the armor worn by the early sovereigns; Charlemagne's Book of Hours, written in 730, his sword, spears, and sceptre; the

Bible and Prayer-book of Charles the Bald; the Breviary of St. Louis, and the font in which he was baptized; the jewel-boxes of Anne of Austria and Marie Antoinette.

The Palace of the Tuileries is the city residence of Louis Napoleon, as it was of many of the preceding sovereigns of France. It was once a tile-yard, and derives its name from this circumstance. The entrance is under the triumphal arch in the Place du Carrousel. A couple of mounted dragoons, and the imperial standard flying on the clock tower, indicated that the emperor was at home, and visitors were not admitted; but the students had an opportunity afterwards to see Napoleon and Eugénie.

Having seen three palaces in one forenoon, — or rather glanced at them, — the party were ready for the "second breakfast," which had been prepared for them at the Café Voisin, a short distance from the palace.

"When you enter a café," said Dr. Winstock to those around him, "you will bow politely to the young lady who sits at the counter. She is sometimes called the 'daughter of the café,' and represents the dignity of the establishment. It is the universal custom to salute her on entering."

The students were polite enough to observe this injunction, and the lady smiled upon them as sweetly as a new-blown rose. They seated themselves at the little tables, and with capital appetites disposed of the second breakfast.

CHAPTER XV.

RIDES AND WALKS ABOUT PARIS.

MR. ARBUCKLE, as he was the host of the ship's company on the present occasion, was considerate enough to see that four hours' walking was quite enough for the students in one day, especially when a considerable portion of it was over the waxed floors of the Louvre, on which locomotion is about as difficult as on glare ice. His agent had procured over twenty *voitures de place*, and *voitures de remise*, as the two classes of public vehicles in Paris are termed. The former have stands about the streets, and are numbered with red figures. The fare for *voitures* with two places is one franc and seventy-five centimes an hour; with four places, two francs. The *voiture de remise* stands under cover, and is numbered with yellow figures. The fare is half a franc more an hour than the other class, and the vehicles are much better. By the course, or a drive not exceeding fifteen minutes, the fare is a franc and a half for the best class, and two francs for more than fifteen minutes within the fortifications. A small perquisite, or "*pour boire*," must be given to the driver.

The professors and students seated themselves in these carriages, each of which was drawn by one horse. Paul Kendall was honored with a place in the voiture with Mrs. Arbuckle and Grace, while Mr. Arbuckle rode with the principal. As the young captain was entering the vehicle, the driver handed him a little blue paper, on which were printed the tariff of prices for his class of carriages, and a blank form, which the traveller can fill out if he wishes to complain of his driver to the lieutenant of police. The number is printed upon it in very large figures, and the occupant is requested to preserve it, that he may be able to reclaim anything left in the vehicle.

"I wish we had the Paris police to take care of the New York hackmen," laughed Paul, as he read the paper.

"But even in Paris the drivers will cheat," added Mrs. Arbuckle. "A friend of mine paid about double fare once, simply because he was in a hurry."

"The carriages seem to be very well regulated, but I suppose it is impossible to prevent some frauds. If people will not complain of being cheated, they must suffer the consequences," added Paul, as the procession of carriages moved off.

"Captain Kendall, what do you understand by a *boulevard?*" asked Grace.

"Mr. Mapps says the word is derived from the fact that ball was formerly played upon them — *bouler sur vert*. I suppose the term is applied to a wide street, though some of the avenues are wider than some of the *boulevards;* but the latter, as a rule, are wider than the former; and the Rue de Turbigo is as wide as either."

The procession crossed the Champs Elysées to a

broad avenue called Cours la Reine, on the bank of the Seine. Between the street and the river was a continuous line of *quais*, as in all parts of the city bordering the stream. As different portions of the same *boulevard* may receive half a dozen different names, so the *quais* seem to have no arbitrary dividing line. In front of the Tuileries the space is called Quai des Tuileries; before the Louvre, the Quai du Louvre. In front of and below some of the *quais* are landing places, called ports. The *Chemin de Fer d'Amérique*, as it is called, is the only horse railroad in Paris; but the omnibuses which run upon it change from the track on the Cours la Reine, to the common street, before entering the more densely peopled portion of the city.

As the procession approached the fortifications, Paul, who had attentively studied the map of Paris, had an opportunity to explain the use of a high viaduct of the light yellow stone used in the city, beneath the arches of which the carriages passed. It is a railroad connecting the different lines that diverge from Paris. Passing through the Porte d'Anteuil, one of the gates of the city, the party entered the Bois de Boulogne, the most beautiful park in Paris. It contains two thousand five hundred acres, laid out with walks, drive-ways, groves, flower-beds, lawns, artificial lakes and rock-work, cascades, and a race-course. Central Park, in New York, contains about eight hundred and fifty acres, but what there is of it rather surpasses the Bois de Boulogne. Passing out of this park, at its northern end, the company proceeded to the Chapelle de St. Ferdinand. It is a beautiful little marble building in the form of a Greek cross, and commemorates the death of the Duke of Orleans, the oldest son of Louis Philippe, and heir to the throne, who was killed on this spot by a fall from his carriage, in 1842. The horses ran away; the duke, in attempting to get out, was thrown to the ground, and his skull fractured. He was carried into a house near the spot, and died in a few hours, surrounded by his family and friends. He was buried at Dreux, and the king, purchasing the house in which he died, erected this chapel upon its site. It contains several memorials of the duke, pictures and bass-reliefs, representing his death, and a canoe, brought from Canada by his brother, the Prince de Joinville, which the deceased used upon the Seine. The rooms now occupied by the keepers were formerly used by the royal family when they visited the chapel, and contain two clocks, one indicating the instant of the accident, and the other the time of the duke's death.

Leaving this mournful place, the cortége drove to the nearest gate. The drivers stopped to permit the officers of the *octroi* to examine the carriages in search of goods liable to the city duty. Following the broad Avenue de la Grande Armée, the party arrived at the Arc de Triomphe, or Arc de l'Etoile. It is an immense arch, the largest in the world, commenced in 1806 by Napoleon I., to commemorate the victories of the French armies. It is one hundred sixty-one feet high, one hundred forty-five wide, and one hundred and ten deep. The arch itself is nearly a hundred feet high. It has upon it bass-reliefs of various French battles, and allegorical representations of national subjects. It cost over two million dollars. A dark staircase leads to the top, where a beautiful view of the city is obtained. Admission, twenty-five centimes.

It was now about five o'clock in the afternoon, and the *ton* of Paris were on the Avenue des Champs Elysées — at the head of which, and on an elevation, stands the structure described. Many dashing equipages, with footmen and outriders, were to be seen. While the students were examining the *arc*, the lieutenant of police, in charge of the party, announced that the emperor was coming up the avenue. The word was given to form a line, where they could see his majesty, and they were instructed what to do and say. The approach of the emperor was indicated by the profound obeisances paid to him by the people. He was seated in a light cabriolet, drawn by two high-spirited horses, which he drove himself. At his side sat the prince imperial, while near them rode a small squad of dragoons, in helmets and long boots. His majesty was plainly dressed in black clothes, and wore nothing to distinguish him except the cross of the Legion of Honor. His look was hard and stolid, but it was full of imperial dignity.

"*Vive l'empereur!*" shouted the students, removing their caps, as the royal turnout approached.

His majesty bowed gracefully, but did not smile, though he seemed to wonder who and what the party were.

After a ride through the Parc de Monceaux, the excursionists returned to the hotel, and dined as on the preceding day. After this important duty had

been discharged, those of the students who could be trusted were permitted to take a stroll on their own account. Ben Duncan, the wag of the Josephine, and Captain Haven, of the Young America, happened to be together, and agreed to take a walk. Though many of the boys were what is called good French scholars in school, there was hardly one of them who could speak the language fluently. It was a notorious fact that the people of Paris could not understand their own tongue, as our tars spoke it. When they attempted to express themselves, the Parisians stared and looked blank.

Captain Haven and Ben strolled through the Palais Royal, and then into one of the curious by-streets, gazing about them at the strange little shops, so unlike in their petty proportions the fine stores of New York and Boston, but filled with rare and costly merchandise. They paused to examine the dim and grimy walls which enclosed the palatial residence of some French noble, who traced his ancestors back to the days of Charlemagne.

"Hold on a minute, Ben. I wonder whose shop this is," said Captain Haven, suddenly stopping.

"It isn't a shop at all," replied his companion.

"It has a sign over the door, but I can't make it out."

"Spell it out loud, then," added Ben, laughing, as he always did in school when he came to a "jaw-breaker."

"L-e-g —"

"Leg!" shouted Ben. "Any one in or out of France knows what that is, I should say."

"Nonsense! Don't interrupt me. L-e-g—*Léga tion des Etats Unis*. That means Young America, or I'm a Dutchman!"

"You are a Dutchman, then, for the sign means Legation of the United States. I'm surprised that the captain of a big ship should not know that."

"These marks over the letters bother me," laughed the commander.

"I suppose this is the residence of the American minister," continued Ben. "The moment an American sets his foot on that threshold he is on United States territory."

"Is he? Then let's set our feet on it immediately."

"Shall we call on the minister?"

"Why not?" asked the captain, who considered himself equal to the occasion.

"We have no one to introduce us. We are strangers. I can't say, 'Mr. Minister, allow me to introduce my friend Captain Haven,' because Mr. Minister might very naturally reply, 'Before you introduce your friend Captain Haven, perhaps you will be so good as to get some one to introduce *you*.'"

"He would be an unmannerly fellow to do that. Let's try, at all events," persisted the captain. "If we are going to be the Decaturs, and the Perrys, and all that sort of thing, of the next generation, we are not going to be frightened at the prospect of meeting an old gentleman. Come on."

Ben was never behind any one; and they entered the stone archway, and walked up the alley on the rough pavement; for, as people who live in these grand establishments never walk, there was no smooth sidewalk.

"*Qu'y a-t-il pour votre service?*" called an old woman, in the shrillest of tones.

"Ahem!" exclaimed Ben, clearing his throat; for, proficient as he was in the *langue française*, it was a choking operation for a beginner to speak it. "We — that is, *nous — désirons voir Monsieur le Ministre.*"

"*Bien, bien, messieurs,*" responded the woman, coming out of the dark hole where she sat, — and where, it may be added, she ate and drank, and cooked and slept, and lived with her husband and two children, though the visitors were not informed of the fact, — and clattered on the rough pavement with her wooden shoes, "*C'est au fond — au fond de la cour à gauche. Son Excellence est chez lui. Je ne l'ai pas vu sortir ce soir. Au fond, mes petits messieurs — tout au fond à gauche, mes jolis petits messieurs.*"

"Whew!" whistled Ben; "that's a big dose of French; but I caught enough of it to know where to go. 'His excellency is at home, and we are to turn to the left at the foot of the court.' We'll try it."

The old woman was a French institution. Her tongue went like a railroad train. She was an ugly-looking creature. She wore a yellow handkerchief tied around her head, and an immense blue apron, with one great pocket in the centre of it.

"They would have drowned her as a witch if they had caught her in Salem," whispered Captain Haven.

Up to the age of about thirty, French women of the

lower class are blooming, merry, and as pretty-looking as one would wish to see. After they pass that age, they dry up like withered apples. Their faces become yellow and wrinkled, their forms shrivelled and unshapely, their finger joints knotted and gnarled; and, taking them all together, they are very unsightly women. Give them the broomstick, and they seem to be ready for a flight in the air. After seeing a few of them, one is not greatly surprised to read that the women were worse than the men in the revolutions which have overturned Paris.

The ancient portress saw that the young gentlemen did not yet know where to go, and she gesticulated wildly towards the back of the court yard.

"*Là, là, là!*" cried she, pointing with her skinny fingers.

"La, si, do!" sang Ben, striking the notes of the scale.

At the end of the court yard stood quite a handsome house, on which was the same sign they had seen at the door. Duncan rang the bell, and a neat-looking man-servant, dressed in black, with a white neck-tie and gloves, opened the door.

"*Nous désirons voir Monsieur le Ministre,*" said Ben.

The man, who was polite, polished, good-looking, and attentive, — the very reverse of the frouzy old woman, — desired them to have the kindness to walk in, to take the trouble to sit down, and to be good enough to give him their cards, with which he disappeared within an inner room. The apartment in which the visitors sat was neatly, but not luxuriously, furnished.

On the wall hung an engraving of Washington, which reminded them of home, and called forth some patriotic remarks from Ben, who declared the original was ever so much more of a man than the trumpery kings and emperors of Europe. The minister made his appearance, and gave the young gentlemen a cordial welcome. The shoulder-straps and bands of Captain Haven did not escape his attention, and in a short time the story of the cruise of the squadron had been told, including the capture of the Josephine. His excellency had heard of the Academy squadron before, and was pleased to learn of the arrival of the students in Paris.

"Can I do anything to make your stay in the city more agreeable?" asked the minister. "You seem, however, to be in good hands, if you are attended by a lieutenant of police and the *sergents de ville*."

"Yes, sir; we are well cared for; but some of us would like to go to court, if you can manage it for us."

"To court!" exclaimed the minister. "Well, I have a great many applications; but perhaps I can arrange it."

Captain Haven was amazed at the audacity of his companion, but he did not object to putting his feet within the court of royalty. They took their leave, and strayed next into the Boulevard des Italiens.

"*Habits de cour*," said Captain Haven, reading a sign in the window of a fashionable tailor.

"Court clothes," added Ben, interpreting the sign. "Crackee! I never thought of that. I wonder if we mustn't get a monkey dress to go to court in."

"'*Ici on parle anglais,*'" added the captain, reading another sign in the window—"'English spoken here.' We will go in, and see about the court dresses."

They went in, and Captain Haven stated his business.

"*Je ne vous comprends pas, monsieur,*" interposed the shopkeeper, shrugging his shoulders and shaking his head.

"*Parlez-vous Anglais?*" demanded Ben.

"*Un peu.*"

"Why don't you speak it, then?" laughed Duncan.

"*Un peu.*"

"Do you keep court clothes?" asked the captain.

The shopkeeper shrugged his shoulders, and looked around him as if to find some hole by which he could escape the dilemma. At last he declared that the man who spoke English was out.

"*Avez-vous des habits de cour?*" added Ben.

"*Oui, oui — oui — oui — oui,*" replied the man, suddenly brightening up, as he discharged this volley of "ouis" after the manner of Frenchmen when they get at an idea which it has bothered them to obtain.

"Do we need them?" asked Ben, in French.

"O, yes; you must have them," replied the rogue, though he knew that the uniform of the ship would satisfy the demands of court etiquette. "It will be best for messieurs to order each a court suit. I will show you one made up for the Marquis de Potderoses."

The suit was duly paraded before them. It consisted of a fine blue cloth coat, with swallow-tail skirts, a standing black velvet collar, beautifully embroidered with gold. The sleeves and skirts were also ornamented in the same manner. The rest of the suit consisted of white satin knee-breeches, silk stockings, low shoes, with buckles, a sword, and cocked hat.

"Shouldn't I be a swell, rigged out in that tomfoolery?" laughed Ben Duncan, as he examined the finery with much interest. "I don't think my exchequer will warrant me in ordering such gear."

"It wouldn't pay if it would," replied the republican captain of the ship.

At this point Duncan took it into his head to speak nothing but English. He informed the shopkeeper that he should not order a court dress that night, and politely bade him good evening. The man was importunate, but Haven could not, and Duncan would not, speak French. The shopkeeper followed them to the door, but the young Americans made good their retreat. It is not very surprising that boys, like them, with inquiring minds, should desire to see royalty in its own quarters, and Duncan was rather disappointed when he found that a court dress was imperative. He decided to trouble the minister again, and, what was worse, to face the shrewish old woman. His excellency informed him that a uniform only was necessary for an American, whereat the young aspirants were disposed to give three cheers for the American Eagle.

The young tourists, having settled this important question, — though Duncan was not much better off than before, for, not being an officer, he did not wear a uniform, — took a stroll through the boulevards, and paid a visit to a café. On the broad sidewalk in front of it was a great number of little tables, at which ladies and gentlemen were seated, drinking coffee, wine, and lemonade, the men smoking. Within, little groups of two or more were engaged in the same way, while a score of billiard tables were in full operation, as well as some other games. The air was dense and redolent of tobacco smoke; but all the people seemed to be enjoying themselves. There was no boisterous noise, and no evidences of drunkenness.

The young tars called for *café au lait*, which was poured from the duplicate pots with long wooden handles. To each was placed a little silver saucer, on which were four cubes of white sugar. At an adjoining table, Duncan saw a gentleman roll up two of them he did not use in his coffee, in a paper, and put it in his pocket. The Frenchman takes what he pays for, whether he consumes it on the spot or not; and it is not an unusual thing for him to carry off the bread he does not eat, in his pocket. The price of the *demitasse*, or small cup of coffee, was forty centimes; and, according to the custom, they each gave the waiter two sous, which he dropped into a glass urn on the counter, for the perquisites are equally divided among all the servants.

Returning to the hotel, they found Captain Kendall and the Arbuckles in the reading-room, and Captain Haven related their adventures, insisting that the commander of the Josephine should make one of the party when they went to court.

"Will you go with me, Grace?" asked Paul, laughing.

"I should be delighted!" she replied, with enthusiasm.

"It is impossible," interposed Mr. Arbuckle, shaking his head. "None of my family are eligible to the honor, since we have not been presented at the court of our own sovereign."

"Then I will not go," exclaimed Paul, glancing at the fair young girl.

"You Americans, with your democratic institutions, are highly favored, and I advise you to go, by all means, Captain Kendall," added Mr. Arbuckle.

"I don't care a fig for it. I would rather stay here than toady to those crowned heads."

"Then lend me your uniform," whispered Duncan.

"I will, with the greatest pleasure."

"It will just fit me."

Mr. Arbuckle believed in crowned heads, and, perhaps, did not exactly approve of Paul's democratic tendencies; but the young gentleman was fully determined not to go to court, unless Grace could go with him.

After breakfast the next morning the business of sight-seeing was resumed, but not with as much zest as on the first day. The Arbuckles employed a *voiture de remise*, but a procession of carriages was so unwieldy to manage, that Mr. Lowington preferred to go on foot when the distance was not great. A short walk brought them to the church of St. Roch, near which Napoleon I. came into notice by firing upon the mob which had risen against the Directory. The building, which is large, and far from elegant, contains many old paintings and sculptures.

Following the Rue St. Honoré the tourists reached the Place Vendôme, a handsome square, in which is a column erected by Napoleon I. to commemorate his victories in Germany, the various incidents of which are represented by a spiral line of bass-reliefs, three feet wide, and containing two thousand figures. The column is one hundred and thirty-three feet high, and the outer shell is of bronze, cast from twelve hundred pieces of cannon taken from the Austrians and the Russians. It is surmounted by a statue of Napoleon in his cocked hat and great coat, cast from Algerian cannon, and placed there by Louis Philippe. On the railings of the fence the students saw many wreaths of immortelles, placed there by the old soldiers of Napoleon.

Passing through the Rue de la Paix, the party glanced at the Grand Hôtel, and the magnificent Opera House, then in process of erection, and next visited the Chapelle Expiatoire, which stands on part of the old Cemetery of the Madeleine, where Louis XVI. and Marie Antoinette were hurried, without ceremony, into their graves. The remains of the king and queen were exhumed and removed to St. Denis, the burial-place of the kings of France, and this chapel was erected as an expiatory memorial of their unhappy fate. The next object of interest was the Madeleine, a large and magnificent church, built in imitation of a Greek temple. It was commenced in 1764, but suspended during the revolution. Napoleon, in the midst of his splendid victories, decreed that it should be altered into a "Temple of Glory;" but, in 1816. its object was again changed, though it was not completed till 1842. It is surrounded with fluted columns, and on the pediment is an immense bass-relief of the Last Judgment, the central figure of which is the Magdalen interceding with Christ. The interior is very elaborately decorated.

The Madeleine stands at the head of the Rue Royal, a broad street, leading to the Place de la Concorde, from which its classic front may be seen. Passing through the square and over the bridge, called the Pont de la Concorde, the company reached the Palais du Corps Legislatif. It is a handsome old building, built by the Bourbons, whose name it once bore. Various legislative bodies have held their sessions here, from 1792 to the present time.

From this structure the party proceeded to the Hôtel des Invalides, an immense establishment for old soldiers. The façade of the front building is over six hundred feet long. The kitchens are on the left, in which provisions for six thousand men can be cooked every day, though the occupants of the institution are less than half that number.

Both officers and privates are residents at the Invalides, but the rank of the former is carefully respected, for they eat and sleep by themselves, while those above the rank of captain dine in their own rooms. The chambers each contain fifty single beds. The principal articles of food are soup, corned beef and cabbage, with a litre (a pint and three quarters) of wine a day. The students gazed with interest at the number and size of the soup kettles, and at the quantities of meat and vegetables they contained. They regarded with wonder the old, decrepit soldiers who had followed the great French captain in his mighty campaigns. They all wear a long blue frock coat and cocked hat, and when on guard around the building they carry a sabre. In the chapel hundreds of them were telling their beads and saying their prayers. This apartment, over two hundred feet long, is decorated with flags taken in battle. On Sundays the old soldiers attend a military mass at noon, after which there is a grand parade in the square, which contains a great number of captured cannon, that are fired on national occasions. The main building is surmounted by an immense dome, the summit of which is three hundred and twenty-four feet high.

The entrance to the church of the Invalides, or St. Louis, is at the south end of the building. All the treasures of art have been lavished upon the interior construction. The floor in the middle of the church has a circular opening, surrounded by a marble balustrade, in the middle of which, in the crypt below, is the sarcophagus of Napoleon I. Two marble staircases wind down to the vault, on each side of which are monuments to the emperor's faithful friends Duroc and Bertrand. Over the entrance is an extract from Napoleon's will: "I desire that my remains may repose on the banks of the Seine, in the midst of the French people, whom I have loved so much." The sepulchral urn of the emperor is of polished red sandstone, in one block, weighing thirteen tons, and was brought from Lake Onega, in Finland. Jerome Bonaparte is also buried in this church.

The boys were not a little moved by the solemn

grandeur of the place, which seemed to render real all they had read of the great captain. A hasty glance at the Archbishop's Palace, and the vast military school which fronts the Champ de Mars, completed their observations in that vicinity, and they returned to the hotel, ready for dinner.

CHAPTER XVI.

THE EXCHEQUER OF THE RUNAWAYS.

AFTER the choice of officers on board of the Josephine, a consultation was held to determine what course should be pursued. It was dark when the election was finished, and the vessel was still headed towards the broad Atlantic, steering west by compass. During the afternoon, the rough shores of the Channel Islands had been seen in the distance, and before the darkness settled down, the runaways were out of sight of land.

"Now, fellows, we must decide what to do, and where to go," said Perth, after supper had been disposed of.

"I thought it was decided already that we were to go up the Mediterranean," snarled Greenway, who had been an aspirant for the office of fourth lieutenant, as indeed seven eighths of those who now found themselves common seamen had been.

"That was the idea before we started. But I am satisfied that Lowington will send a lot of steamers out after us," added Perth, profiting by the suggestion of Shuffles.

"They can't catch us now," said Adler. "We have been out twenty hours, with a fresh breeze, and not many of those French steamers make more knots an hour than we do."

"We can easily keep out of the way of the steamers if we stick her right out to sea," continued Perth.

"I don't believe in that," protested the prudent Monroe. "It will be nothing but hard work, and no fun."

"That's so," chimed in Howe, who, as one of the foremost of the knights, was bitterly out of joint because he had failed to receive the suffrages of a majority of his companions for third lieutenant. "We know what hard work is, and we don't mean to do it for the fun of the thing. We want to go into port, and have a good time."

"We haven't anything on board to eat but salt junk and hard tack," interposed Herman. "The fellows were to be away for three weeks, and no fresh provisions were taken in."

"We are not going to live on fo'castle fare," growled Greenway.

"All this is very pretty," replied Perth, disgusted with the din of murmurs which came up from the crew, and even from the officers. "If we go into a French port, I have no doubt Lowington will have us nabbed. That's what's the matter. He has telegraphed before now to all the custom-house officers."

"Then don't go into a French port: there are enough others," suggested Howe.

"You know our plan was to put in at Cherbourg and Brest, and then follow the coast round," added Perth.

"I move you we leave it to the officers," said Lamb. "Let them decide where we go."

"I move you they don't take us out to sea," persisted Greenway. "I don't call it fun to bend your back over that fore-topsail yard in a gale of wind."

"We must take care of the vessel, even if we do have to work," added Wilton.

"It is easy enough for you to talk, Wilton. You are an officer, and have nothing to do but look on," snapped Greenway.

"Leave it to the officers," shouted Richards, one of the most sensible of the runaways, who was satisfied that this turbulent crowd could never settle the question.

"Second the motion," added Ibbotson.

"I'll vote for it on condition they don't take us to sea," said Greenway.

But the motion was carried without any conditions, and the officers gathered around the captain to settle the momentous question.

"What do you say, Little?" asked Perth.

"I say, go to sea. I would rather be in cold than in hot water," replied the little rascal.

"But we have no fresh provisions," suggested Adler.

"We can live on salt junk and hard tack for a few days, in order to make the thing a success," said Little. "I should head her to the south-west till we get into the latitude of Gibraltar, and then go east. In this manner we should keep clear of all steamers, and ports where Lowington's agents will be on the lookout for us."

"But where's the fun in doing that?" demanded Adler, impatiently. "We might as well ship before the mast, reef topsails in a gale, and live on seamen's grub. We are not all fools. While the rest of the fellows are seeing Paris, we are working hard on salt junk and hard tack. I tell you the fellows won't stand it."

"What would you do?" asked Captain Perth.

"Where are we now?"

"About forty miles west of the Channel Islands, and perhaps seventy miles from Eddystone Light."

"What is the nearest English port?"

"We will go down and look at the chart," replied the captain, as he led the way into the cabin.

The chart and the sailing directions were carefully examined by the officers, and it appeared that the most available port was Plymouth, which could easily be reached by daylight the next morning. Adler and Phillips were decidedly in favor of bearing away for this port, while Wilton and Little thought it was better to go to sea. Perth was undecided. He preferred to avoid the land, but he feared that the crew would rebel against hard work, hard tack, and salt junk. The latter consideration proved stronger than the former, and it was decided, by a majority of one, to go into Plymouth.

"There is no officer in charge of the deck," said the captain, suddenly, when the fact flashed upon his mind. "This will never do."

"You told us to come down," replied Wilton, who was displeased because his plan had been rejected.

"You and Little go on deck, and attend to your

duty," added the captain, rather sharply, for he felt that his officers were not altogether subordinate and respectful. "Give out the course north-west by west."

"North-west by west," replied Wilton, in a surly tone, as he went on deck, followed by Little.

"Every fellow seems to have a will and a way of his own," said Perth.

"Between you and me, Captain Perth, we need a few broken heads to put things to rights," replied Phillips. "I'm in favor of good discipline. If a fellow growls and is impudent, I go for giving him some."

Phillips did not say how it would have been with him if he had not been elected an officer; but it was a fact that those who had been chosen before him had electioneered for him, because they were afraid of him, and because they wanted his influence and his fists on their side, in case of trouble.

"I wish the fellows would stick together a little closer. Every one is mad if he can't have his own way," added Perth, mildly, and perhaps with the feeling that he had undertaken a big job.

"We mustn't stand any nonsense from any one. If the fellows won't mind and be respectful, we must lay them out."

"What can we do against five and twenty of them, if they choose to disobey us?"

Phillips doubled up his hard fist, and indicated precisely what he should do in such an emergency. He was an officer, and he should do his duty, and make others do theirs. Shuffles, who sat at another table in the cabin, with a book open before him, listened with interest to this conversation. These dissensions were what he had anticipated, and he hoped the time would soon come when he could commence upon the mission which had induced him to remain in the vessel.

"I dread this going into port," continued Perth, after he had gazed in silence at the chart for some time.

"Why?" asked Adler.

"I'm afraid the fellows will get into a row. There are a dozen ways in which we may make a slip of the whole thing. We must take a pilot to go into Plymouth. Suppose Shuffles, or one of the waiters, should tell him just what we are up to, and the vessel should be seized by the officers of the port?" said the anxious captain, in a whisper.

"The pilot must not see any of them. We can easily manage that."

"Perhaps we can," added Perth, dubiously; and he seemed to be already realizing the prophetic words which Shuffles had read to him from his Bible, that the way of the transgressor is hard. "All the fellows will want to go on shore. They are reckless, and may drink, or get into a row."

"Don't let them go on shore," suggested Phillips.

"We can't help it."

"I'll bet we can," added the bully, emphatically. "A single officer and four seamen shall go on shore and bring off a supply of provisions in one of the four-oar boats. Not another fellow shall leave the vessel."

Perth approved of this plan if it could be carried out; but he dreaded the insubordination of his reckless crew. The watch was changed, and Wilton and Little came below to hear what further arrangements had been made. Both of them approved the plan of permitting no one but an officer and a boat's crew to go on shore in Plymouth; and the cabin, for once, was a unit in opinion.

"Now, where's the money to come from?" asked the captain. "I have overhauled the iron box in Captain Kendall's state-room, but I can't find the key, and I should as soon think of breaking open the vaults of the Bank of England as that safe."

"We will open it by and by," added Little, confidently. "But I have plenty of rocks without that."

Shuffles opened his eyes and his ears. Little went to one of the pantries, between the cabin and the steerage, and pulling out a drawer, took from under it the bag of gold, which had excited so much interest on board of the ship. Returning to the cabin, he dropped it heavily upon the table at which Wilton and the captain were seated.

"There's the spondoolicks!" exclaimed he, triumphantly.

"Where did that come from?" asked Perth, amazed at the sight, for he had not heard its history.

"I'll tell you where it came from," replied Little; "and I suppose my friend Shuffles would like to know about it. When I was pitched into the water with that Dutchman on the spar, he gave me this bag, for he was too much used up to hold on to it any longer. I dropped it into the boat. The man was lost — it wasn't any body's fault but his own, for if he had dropped his gold, he would have been hauled into the barge the first time we tried to save him. I took it on board the ship, and hid it under Shuffles's berth, for that was the best place I could find."

" And then you told Ellis that I had it!" exclaimed Shuffles, rising indignantly, and approaching the table where the party were seated.

" Keep cool, friend Shuffles," added the little rascal, quietly. " It was not prudent for me to say that I had it myself. Before the search was made, I popped it into the fire engine, and that night stowed it away under the top-gallant forecastle."

" Why did you say I had it?" demanded Shuffles. who could not yet fathom the iniquity of Little.

" Never mind that, my dear fellow; what's the use of bothering your head about it now? I intended you should come with us on this cruise, and here you are," laughed the villain.

Little was not disposed to be very definite in his explanations; but at last the truth dawned upon Shuffles that the charge made against him was part of the plot to drag him into the conspiracy. More than ever he regretted that he had attempted to " fight the devil with his own weapons." Simple truth alone is the best sword to overcome the powers of evil. If he had avoided the counsels of the wretch before him altogether, the rebels would have been defeated, and their plan would have failed: nothing was plainer; but it was too late to retrace his steps.

" How much is there?" asked Perth, who was not interested in Shuffles's affair.

" Four hundred pounds," replied Little.

" Whew!" exclaimed Wilton. " We are in luck."

"I hand it over to you, Captain Perth," added Little. "It is to be used for the benefit of the crowd."

The captain took the bag, and carried it into his state-room.

"I am afraid the cook and the two waiters will give us some trouble," said Wilton, when the captain returned.

"Never mind them," added Little. "We must buy them up. I go for giving them five sovereigns apiece, to keep them quiet."

"Will that keep them still?" asked Perth.

"I will talk with them, and I think we can make it all right," continued Little, as he rose, and went forward to find the men.

Wilton and the captain left the cabin soon after, and Shuffles was alone. He was still thinking of the conspiracy. He feared that Little would be able to buy up the cook and stewards, and thus defeat his purpose to recapture the Josephine at the right time. He rose from the table, and looked into the captain's state-room. The stewards had done their duty precisely as though the vessel were still in the hands of her lawful owners, and the cabin and the rooms were all lighted. The bag of gold lay behind the safe, under the berth. No special pains had been taken to conceal it, Perth perhaps thinking that, as the runaways were equal owners of the gold, they would not attempt to steal it.

Shuffles had come on board after this treasure, and was anxious not only to secure it now, but to prevent the little villain from bribing the three men on board. He dropped it into the pocket of his pea-jacket, and returned to the cabin. But the bag was an elephant, in its way, under the circumstances, which could not easily be disposed of; for when the captain missed it, Shuffles would at once be charged with appropriating it. The success of the runaway cruise seemed to depend upon this gold; for supplies must be purchased, and no other money was available. By placing this treasure out of the reach of the conspirators, he might break up the trip, and compel them to return. If this consideration were not strong enough, he had the additional one that the gold rightfully belonged to the heirs of the German who had perished in the waves near the burning steamer.

His strongest motive was to defeat the plan of the runaways. There seemed to be no secure hiding-place in the cabin for the bag, and he was tempted to throw it overboard, so that by no possibility could his reckless companions find it; but this would be wronging the heirs of the deceased owner. It was folly to hide it in the cabin, and he turned his attention to the hold. He was not familiar with the interior of the Josephine, but he soon found a trap-door in the cabin floor, which opened into the run. He raised the door, and jumped down; but it was so dark he could not see anything, and he returned to the cabin for a lantern, which was kept there for the use of the officers. Lighting it, he went into the hold again, closing the trap after him.

The hold seemed to be as deficient in hiding-places for the treasure as the cabin. There were ballast, water-casks, beef-barrels, and boxes of ship stores, but none of them seemed to be proof against the keen scrutiny of the conspirators. After much careful consideration, he decided to pour the contents of the bag into one of the water-casks, choosing a full rather than an empty one, because if it was moved the coins would not rattle, and thus reveal their presence. With a stone from the ballast he removed the bung, by pounding on each side of it. Untying the bag-string, he poured the gold into the water. Driving in the bung, he returned to the cabin, which was fortunately still empty. He was pretty strongly assured that no one would find the money where he had deposited it, for the contents of the water-cask might even be drawn off without revealing the secret. He put the bag into the stove, where it was soon consumed.

Having accomplished his purpose, Shuffles turned in, not to sleep, but to consider still further how he might redeem the Josephine from the hands of the conspirators. In his wayward days he had been skilful enough in plotting against lawful authority, and he was now ready, in the interests of order and discipline, to put forth all his abilities. But it was hardly time to operate yet, for the runaways were still confident of a good time, and loyal, in their way, to their leaders and the enterprise.

Little found the cook and the stewards in the galley. They had no objection to receiving a present of five pounds apiece, but they were not forward to commit themselves to their new masters. Evidently they had discussed the subject among themselves; and while they were not disposed to quarrel with the runaway students, they did not mean to compromise themselves with the principal.

The wind was lighter during the night, but at daylight the vessel was off Plymouth Sound, with Eddystone Lighthouse on the weather-beam. A pilot boat was seen in the distance, and the fact was announced to Perth, who immediately turned out. He had not yet discovered the loss of the gold; but as he would have to pay the pilot, and purchase the provisions, his attention was directed to it as soon as he left his berth. He put his hand behind the safe. He felt a cold chill when he discovered that the treasure was not there. He searched carefully in the vicinity of the safe, and then overhauled everything in the room. Of cours· he did not find it, and he was both alarmed and vexed. Little's story had been told through both watches during the night, and every soul on board knew that funds were abundant in the cabin. He called Little, and stated the case to him.

"It's gone; that's all I know about it," said he, winding up his explanation.

"That isn't all Shuffles knows about it," suggested Little. "Where did you put the bag?"

"Behind the safe."

"Why didn't you leave it on the table in the cabin?" sneered Little.

"I had no better place to put it," pleaded the discomfited captain. "Do you think Shuffles has taken it?"

"Of course he has: he would have been a fool if he hadn't," answered Little, candidly, judging his victim by himself.

"Call him. If he has, he shall give it up, or we will throw him overboard," added Perth, angrily.

"Hallo, Shuffles! Plymouth, ahoy!" shouted Little, going to the sleeper's berth.

"As I have nothing to do with the vessel, it does not make much difference to me," replied Shuffles, who had heard part of the conversation between Little and the captain.

"Turn out — will you? We want to see you."

Shuffles was willing, since if there was to be a row, he preferred to be on his feet.

"Have you seen that bag of gold?" asked Little, as Shuffles was putting on his coat.

"I have."

"Where is it?"

"That you may not know," answered Shuffles, calmly, but decidedly.

"O, come! don't be waspish!"

"You brought me on board of the Josephine after that bag of gold. I have it now, and am satisfied."

"Do you mean to say you intend to keep it?"

"I haven't it about me, but I think it is where you will not get hold of it."

"Tell us where it is — won't you, Shuffles? That's a good fellow!"

"I shall not tell you."

"Do you mean to keep it?" demanded Perth, savagely.

"I have nothing more to say."

"We will make you say something," threatened Perth.

"I am prepared to defend myself," answered Shuffles, who, feeling that in this instance he was to fight in a good cause, if at all, was firm and decided, but without bluster or bullying.

Perth looked at him, and evidently did not like

the firm but quiet expression of his face. He went on deck, and ordered the vessel to come about, and stand close-hauled to the southward.

"What's that for?" demanded Wilton.

"It's no use to go into Plymouth without money," replied Perth, as he proceeded to detail the events which had just occurred in the cabin.

The situation was deemed sufficiently grave to justify the calling of all hands for counsel, if not for fight. Shuffles was the marplot of the enterprise, and deep and savage was the indignation the conspirators expressed. Some of them were in favor of throwing him overboard, if he did not give up the money; others insisted that he should be turned adrift in one of the boats.

"All this is very fine, but where is the money?" added Perth.

"It is somewhere on board," replied Wilton. "Shuffles had not been on deck since dark last night, and he could not have thrown it overboard."

"Of course he wouldn't throw it overboard," added Little. "If it is in the vessel, I know I can find it. But if we can't, there is plenty of money in the safe, in the captain's state-room."

"We'll put Shuffles on the rack," said Phillips, shaking his head as an indication of the big things he intended to do. "I'll make him tell what he has done with the money."

"Don't say a word to him yet," interposed Perth. "He will be an ugly customer."

"I guess not," replied Phillips. "I can handle him alone. If I can't, I'll eat him."

"Shuffles isn't a baby, I can tell you," said Little. "I move you we search for the money. If we don't find it, there will be time enough to have a row."

By this time it was sunrise. Probably those on board of the pilot boat, which was headed for the Josephine, were mystified by their singular movement in coming about so suddenly; but, as Perth declared, it was useless to go into Plymouth without the funds to purchase fresh provisions, and it was better to have the anticipated row at sea than in an English port. All hands, except those required on deck, immediately commenced a vigorous search for the missing treasure, upon which the runaways depended for the "good time coming." Every berth and locker was examined, and even the most impossible hiding-places were overhauled. The hold was not neglected, and every article there was turned over. The water-casks were rolled forward and back, the empty ones shaken, and the ballast dug up in every foot of its surface. They did not find the bag, and their wrath rose to fever heat under the disappointment. The search was abandoned, and the iron safe in the captain's state-room was rolled out into the cabin. Hammers, chisels, and bars were vainly applied to the lid. It could not be opened; not a shilling could be raised.

As soon as the runaways had finished the search in the hold, Shuffles was relieved of all anxiety. The water-cask which contained the gold had not yielded up its secret. While the excited conspirators were trying their skill upon the safe, Shuffles went forward to the galley, where the cook and the two waiters had assembled to discuss the strange movements of their new masters. He sat down by the side of the cook before the stove, on which the coppers, filled with corned beef, — the only provision, except ship-bread, on board, — were boiling.

"What is to be the end of this thing?" asked the cook. "The young villains are trying to break open the safe, the stewards tell me."

"It is about time to put a stop to it," replied Shuffles. "They have no money to buy anything to eat, or even to pay for a pilot into port. That's the reason they came about."

"But I'm not willing to risk my neck much longer in the hands of such fellows," continued the cook.

"Will you stand by me, if I attempt to take the vessel back to Havre?" asked Shuffles, earnestly.

"What do you mean by standing by you?" inquired the cook.

"Will you obey my orders, instead of Perth's?"

"I will," replied the man, inspired with confidence by the manly and earnest demeanor of Shuffles.

"Will you?" he continued, appealing to the two stewards.

They followed the lead of the cook, who was their oracle in all matters of doubt, and promptly consented to do as he did. They were disgusted with the disorder and confusion which prevailed on board. The season of heavy gales was approaching, and they were fearful that the vessel would be lost in the hands of her reckless crew. Though Shuffles had never served in the Josephine, they knew him as one of the most energetic and decided of the crew of the ship; and his gallant behavior in rescuing the sufferers from the burning steamer won their respect and regard.

"Where's Shuffles?" shouted some one in the waist, while he was still engaged in explaining his purpose.

"Here I am," replied he, stepping from the galley, as the crew, led on by Phillips, rushed out of the cabin, and moved forward.

Planting himself against the rail, with the three men near him, Shuffles waited the issue.

"Did you take that bag of money?" demanded the bully of the runaways, who had worked himself up to the highest pitch of excitement.

"I did," replied Shuffles, quietly.

"What have you done with it?" roared Phillips, savagely.

"I shall not tell you."

"Yes, you will."

"No, I will not."

"If you don't, I'll maul you within an inch of your life," roared the bully.

"I am prepared to defend myself."

"Then do so!" cried Phillips, as he rushed furiously upon Shuffles.

The latter had not forgotten how to use his fists, and now, in a good cause, he handled them even more skilfully than ever he had in a bad one. It was a sharp battle, and in a moment the faces of both the combatants were covered with blood. In another moment Phillips was down, and Perth, supported by Wilton and a few others, sprang forward to assist their fallen champion. But the cook and the two stewards leaped into the breach, and, regardless of the fact that the assailants were mere boys, struck

THE FATE OF THE JOSEPHINE DECIDED. — Page 286.

such heavy blows that half a dozen of the conspirators, including Perth and Wilton, soon lay stunned upon the deck. It was rough usage, but it was successful.

"Bring me a lanyard," said Shuffles, panting with his exertions, as he held the struggling bully beneath him.

One of the stewards gave him a rope, and assisted him to bind his fallen foe, who was then cast into the brig, the door locked, and the key put in Shuffles's pocket.

"Cook, take the helm," shouted Shuffles. "Keep her east; if any one disturbs you, knock him down!"

"Ay, ay!" replied the cook. "It won't be safe for any of the young rascals to meddle with me."

The runaways were completely overpowered and cowed down by the sudden onslaught of the men, and most of them had retreated to the steerage to avoid the belaying-pins with which the stewards had armed themselves. Shuffles wiped the blood from his face. He had fought the battle, and decided the fate of the Josephine.

CHAPTER XVII.

THE PRESENTATION AT COURT.

WHEN the students returned to the Hôtel du Louvre, a great square envelope was delivered to Captain Haven. It was nearly six inches square, and its size seemed to indicate its importance. It was from the American minister, presenting his compliments to the commander of the Young America, and expressing his pleasure that he should be able, on the following Wednesday evening, to present six of the officers of the Academy squadron to the emperor and empress. Cards for the court ball were enclosed in the same envelope.

The captain showed the note to Ben Duncan, who had been forward in obtaining the invitation, and both were as much astonished as delighted at their success. The matter was submitted to Mr. Lowington, who promptly consented that the boys should accept the invitation.

"The note says officers, but I am not an officer," said Ben.

"You are a petty officer, and that will answer just as well," laughed Mr. Lowington. "Captain Kendall has applied to me for permission to loan you his uniform, and you may go as his representative, since he does not desire to go himself. Who else are to go?"

"The invitation is extended to six of us," replied the captain.

"Since you have managed the affair yourself, Captain Haven, you shall select your own companions."

Commodore Gordon, Lieutenants Goodwin, Terrill, and Ellis, the highest in rank, were chosen, so as to avoid anything like favoritism.

The next morning, the party resumed the business of sight-seeing, commencing with a visit to St. Germain l'Auxerrois, an ancient church opposite the east end of the Louvre, where the members of the royal family were formerly baptized. The bell of this church, partly built before the twelfth century, gave the signal for the horrible massacre of St. Bartholomew, and within it Admiral Coligny was shot. Crossing the Pont Neuf, which is the longest bridge in Paris, the excursionists reached the Ile de la Cité, and proceeded to the Palais du Justice. They passed through its gloomy halls, and were more interested in the lawyers wearing silk gowns, bands, wigs, and caps than in the building itself. They paused a moment in one of the court-rooms, without seeing anything very different from similar places at home.

Adjoining it is the Concergerie, an ancient prison, in which Marie Antoinette was confined in a low and damp dungeon, and from which Danton, Robespierre, Madame Roland, and other victims were taken to the guillotine. Louis Napoleon was also imprisoned within its walls for a short time, after the failure of the rebellion at Boulogne. In the room now used as a chapel the Girondists held the famous banquet on the night before their execution. On the side of the Palais du Justice is Sainte Chapelle, said to be the most beautiful specimen of Gothic architecture, on a small scale, in France. The interior is magnificent in all its parts, proportions, and ornamentation. It was erected in the thirteenth century to receive " the thorns of our Lord's crown, and the wood of the true cross," which the king, St. Louis, purchased of Baldwin, Emperor of Constantinople, at a cost of two million francs. In the time of the revolution, it was used as a club-house, then as a store, and finally as a depository for law records. Louis Philippe restored it. On each side of the nave are recesses for the king and queen. On the south side is a square hole extending diagonally through the wall to a chamber within, where Louis XI. used to hear the mass without the peril of being assassinated.

Opposite the chapel is an immense *caserne*, or barracks for soldiers, of which there are forty in Paris. Following the Quai by the side of this building, the party came to the Cathedral of Notre Dame, the grandest church in Paris. It was begun in the twelfth century, and about three hundred years were employed in its erection. It is nearly four hundred feet long, and the interior, from the floor to the crown of the arching, is one hundred and four feet high. It is of Gothic architecture, highly ornamented outside, the finest effect of which is seen at the rear of the structure. In one of the towers is the Bourdon bell, weighing sixteen tons. In 1793 the church was transformed into the " Temple of Reason " by the impious mob

ists, and in it was celebrated the Feast of the Goddess, who, on this occasion, was personated by Madame Momoro, and who, seated on the high altar, returned the devotion of her adorers with a kiss! The high altar, dedicated to the Savior, occupies the centre of the interior; behind it is that of the Virgin; while around three sides of the building are nearly thirty chapels, each in a lofty arch, and each having its own altar, and dedicated to its own saint. As the students walked around the space, they saw a baptism in one, and a marriage in another, of these chapels. Most of those who enter the church dip their finger in the font of holy water, or moisten it from an implement held by an attendant, and cross themselves as they face the high altar. It is contrary to custom, and deemed an offence, for a lady and gentleman to walk arm in arm in a church in Catholic countries.

Leaving the edifice by the front door, the tourists walked around to the rear, to observe the architecture, and see the dragons' heads on the side. On the Quai Napoléon, a small building was pointed out to them as the Morgue. They were warned that the spectacle within would be disagreeable and loathsome, but with boy-like curiosity they crowded into it. The Morgue is a house where the dead bodies of those taken from the river, or other places, are exposed to the public gaze in order to be recognized by friends. The interior of the edifice is divided into two nearly equal portions by a glass partition, behind which the corpses are exhibited. They are placed on black marble slabs, somewhat inclined towards the spectator, with no covering but a piece of leather over the loins. Upon them trickle streams of cold water, to delay the process of decomposition. Near them, on the walls, are hung the clothing in which they were found, to assist in the recognition. When the students entered, the bodies of three men were lying on the slabs, two of them much discolored, and in such a condition that their nearest friends could hardly have identified them. The sight was repulsive and sickening, and they retreated as hastily as they had entered the charnel-house. Nearly three hundred corpses are thus exposed every year, of which one sixth are women, and about the same proportion of new-born children.

Crossing a bridge, the party visited the Hôtel de Ville, which is the official residence of the Prefect of the Seine, the chief magistrate of the city. It is a magnificent structure, and cost three millions of dollars. It is a palace, and several of the kings and other noted persons were married within its walls, among them Louis Napoleon and the empress. It contains vast state apartments, ball and banquet halls, as well as business rooms, wherein over four hundred clerks are employed.

In Paris there are sixteen hospitals, with more than seven thousand beds, and eleven establishments for the support of aged, infirm, and insane people. One of the largest and most ancient of these is the Hôtel Dieu, said to have been founded in the time of Clovis.

On the following day the tourists went out to Versailles. On the walk to the railroad station, they met a funeral, conducted on a grand scale, with mourning coaches. The business of the undertakers in Paris is a monopoly in the hands of a company styled the *Administration des Pompes Funèbres*. The charges, which are regulated by the city government, vary from four dollars up to fifteen hundred. About two thirds of the funerals are without charge to the friends, who have not the means to bury their dead, and the company receives about one dollar from the city for the service. It employs nearly six hundred persons, two hundred carriages and hearses, and keeps on hand six thousand coffins. Its annual receipts are four hundred thousand dollars.

The omnibuses and carriages are also owned by companies, and some of the regulations for each might be advantageously adopted in the cities of the United States. Omnibuses take no more passengers than can be seated. A person wishing to ride in one of these carriages may go to the station, and receive a number, which entitles him to a seat in the order of his coming. The fare is usually six sous inside, and three outside. Checks are issued without extra charge to those who pay full fare, which entitle them to a ride in any of the cross lines.

The ride to Versailles was through a beautiful country abounding in palaces and cottages. The *chateau* of Meudon, the summer residence of Prince Napoleon, was pointed out to them. The town of Versailles is seven miles from Paris, and its only attraction is the magnificent palace, so stupendous in its magnitude, so luxurious and splendid in its stately apartments, its wilderness of fountains, its extensive gardens, as to exceed in grandeur any ideal which a republican from the New World can form of regal glories. A volume would not suffice to describe it, for, besides being a royal residence, it is a palace of art, and there seems to be no end to the galleries of pictures and sculpture, and of state halls, filled with the trappings of royalty.

The Palace of Versailles was erected by Louis XIV., though his immediate predecessor had built a hunting-seat upon the spot. The land for sixty miles around was purchased in order to afford plenty of space for the improvements, and the face of the country was entirely changed by levelling hills, filling up valleys, and the digging out of immense artificial ponds, which were supplied with water brought from a great distance. Over two hundred millions of dollars were spent upon its construction. Louis XV. enlarged it by the addition of a theatre and another wing. Standing in the Cour d'Honneur, the continuous piles of buildings look more like a city than a single palace. Louis XVI. and Marie Antoinette occupied it until compelled by the Parisians to remove to Paris, and it has not been used as a residence since, though Queen Victoria was entertained there in 1855. Louis Philippe spent nearly five millions of dollars upon it, and it now contains four thousand paintings and one thousand pieces of sculpture.

The students first visited the stables where the state carriages are kept. They look like the golden vehicles of the fairy tales, for they seem to be literally of gold. The carriage used by Napoleon as first consul is a gaudy affair; that in which Charles X. rode to his coronation has been repaired and newly decorated for the present sovereign. The party then walked to the Grand Trianon, and the Petit Trianon, the former built by Louis XIV. for Madame de Maintenon, and the latter by Louis XV. for Madame du Barri. The Little Trianon was presented to Marie Antoinette by her husband, who had the gardens laid out in English style, with Swiss cottages, lakes, and groves. Returning through the gardens of the Grand Trianon, the tourists entered the magnificent grounds of the Palace of Versailles. On the grand canal — a vast artificial body of water in the form of a cross — floated a beautiful barge, similar to the gondola of Venice. The Tapis Vert is a broad avenue, bounded on each side by trees, whose dense foliage was trimmed as square and even as if it had been solid wood, with a walk on each side bordered by marble statues, the space between them laid out as a lawn. At the head of this avenue is the Bassin de Latone, and the entrance of the palace. The Bassin de Neptune is a multitude of fountains in a mass. These fountains, of which there are a score, are played only on occasional Sundays and *fête* days.

Within the palace the halls and galleries appear to be interminable, and one may walk seven miles in-doors. The Galerie des Glaces, or hall of mirrors, is nearly two hundred and fifty feet long, is profusely gilded and painted in brilliant colors, and was the ballroom of the monarchs. The bedroom in which Louis XIV. died, and the apartments of other members of royal families, are shown, all of them containing curious articles of furniture used by them. The picture halls are classed according to the subjects found in them. The Galerie des Batailles is four hundred feet long, and is filled with representations of the historic conflicts in which France has been engaged. The Galerie de l'Empire is devoted to the time of Napoleon I., and several of David's pictures are here exhibited. The floors of all these apartments are waxed as smooth as glass; and before the students had seen half of them, they were tired out, and begged for mercy. It requires at least a week to comprehend fully the glories, the wonders, and the beauties of Versailles; and nowhere else can one obtain so clear an idea of regal grandeur. It is impossible even to mention more than a tithe of the attractions of the place; and if we are astonished at its present grandeur, we cannot but wonder what it must have been when it was fresh and new, in the prevailing style, and in the occupancy of its royal owner.

Seats in the railway carriages were never so agreeable to the party as when they returned to the station. The Arbuckles had abandoned the chase long before the course was run, worn out with fatigue. But the boys were amply compensated for the weariness of the day by the wonders they had seen.

The next day they visited St. Cloud (pronounced *Sang Cloo*), another palace, with grand gardens, on the Seine, five miles from the city. It was the favorite residence of Napoleon I., and is occasionally occupied by the present emperor. Its grounds are laid out in a style similar to those of Versailles, but on a smaller scale. St. Denis, six miles north of Paris, was the burial-place of the kings of France from 580 to the time of Louis XVIII. At St. Germaine, fifteen miles from Paris, Francis I. built a splendid palace, and it was a royal residence till Louis XIV. built the palace of Versailles.

The students devoted Saturday to sights within the city, and first visited the palace and gardens of the Luxembourg, built by Marie de Medicis. It is now the Senate House, and the Salle du Trône is a magnificent apartment, where the emperor delivers his speech to the senators. Near the palace is the Hôtel de Cluny, formerly inhabited by various members of the royal family, but now occupied as a museum, for the exhibition of specimens of ancient carving, glass, pottery, metal work, dresses, furniture, guns, and other curious articles: among them are a richly wrought night-cap of Charles V., emperor of Germany, the lower jaw of Molière, and a collection of gold crowns, of the seventh century, found at Toledo. Leaving this interesting collection, the excursionists went to the Church of St. Genevieve, commonly called the *Panthéon*, one of the largest and finest churches in Paris. In the days of the revolution it was converted into a "Pantheon," to perpetuate the memory of illustrious citizens. It is surmounted by a grand dome. Beneath it is a crypt, containing a labyrinth of arcades, full of tombs, among them those of Rousseau, Voltaire, and Marshal Lannes. Mirabeau and Marat were buried here, but their remains have been removed.

Near this church is that of St. Etienne du Mont, which contains the tomb and shrine of St. Genevieve, the patron saint of Paris, and a singular bridge or gallery, extending across the body of the interior. The celebrated Polytechnic School was passed on the way to the Halle au Vins, or wine market, which covers one hundred and ten acres. The wines are stored in eight ranges of low buildings, with five hundred and forty stores, which hold half a million barrels. About twenty-five gallons of wine are consumed annually in Paris for every person, women and children included. The next object of interest was the Jardin des Plants, which includes vast botanical and zoölogical gardens. All sorts of plants and all sorts of animals are to be seen there.

Crossing the Pont d'Austerlitz, the company proceeded to the Place de la Bastille, where the state prison with that name formerly stood. On the 14th of July, 1789, the mob attacked and captured it, murdering the governor, and carrying his head on a bayonet through the streets. The prison was afterwards demolished, and the materal used in building the Pont de la Concorde. In 1831 Louis Philippe laid the foundation of the present Colonne de Juillet, in memory of those who fell in the three days' revolution of 1830, whose remains were interred beneath it. In 1848 the throne of the "citizen king" was brought to this square and burned by another mob. In the same year, the insurgents built an enormous barricade, on which the Archbishop of Paris was shot, in attempting to parley with the rebels.

On the return to the hotel, the party stopped at the Tour de St. Jacques, a fine Gothic tower, in the Rue Rivoli. The church, of which it originally formed a part, was removed to make room for improvements. A beautiful garden lies behind it. In the afternoon carriages were provided, and the excursionists visited the Imperial Carpet Manufactory, where the Gobelin tapestries are made, admission to which may be obtained by exhibiting the traveller's passport. The fabric is a worsted carpet, wrought with the most beautiful pictures, so delicately shaded as to vie with the richest paintings. The boys gazed with wonder at an immense piece, which contained full-length portraits of the emperor and empress. The work is done by hand, the threads being woven in, according to the pattern, with the fingers. A single carpet had kept a dozen men busy for six years. They are not sold, but are sometimes presented to great personages by the emperor.

The ride was continued to several places not before visited, and convents, colleges, palaces, public offices, orphan asylums, and other buildings were pointed out by the drivers to those who knew French enough to understand them. On Sunday the visitors attended church at the American chapel, and on Monday went to Père Lachaise, the oldest and largest cemetery in Paris; but it is not worthy to be compared with Greenwood, Mount Auburn, Laurel Hill, and other noted American burial-places. It received its name from Pére Lachaise, the confessor of Louis XIV. The students gazed with interest at the monument of Abélard and Héloïse, whose genius and whose affection seem to speak from the cold marble, and upon the quaint and curious memorials to the dead. The French are as extravagant in their grief as in their mirth. On many of the tombs were miniature chapels, in which *immortelles* were placed; and where a child was buried, its playthings were sometimes deposited. It contains some splendid monuments to the great.

Père Lachaise encloses two hundred acres of land. There are three classes of graves. For four dollars an "open grave" is purchased, in which forty or fifty coffins are deposited, three deep, in a trench; but in five years they are removed. For ten dollars a separate grave and ten years of occupancy are purchased. For one hundred dollars about six feet of ground are bought, to be retained forever. On these the monuments are usually built, and the stone is labelled "*Concession à perpétuité.*" Montmartre and Mont Parnasse are the two other principal cemeteries.

About one tenth part of Paris is undermined by quarries, from which the stone for building purposes was formerly taken. These subterranean galleries are now used as repositories for the remains taken from the cemeteries above. They are called the catacombs, and the bones of over three million human beings are fantastically piled up in them. The public are not admitted. That night Shuffles arrived in Paris, and told the story of the recapture of the Josephine; which, however, we will not anticipate.

On Tuesday the students went to Fontainebleau, another magnificent palace of the sovereigns, where Napoleon signed his abdication. On Wednesday the Palais de l'Elysée Napoléon, the School of Fine Arts, the Bourse, and Sevres, where the government porcelain manufactory is established, whose products, like those of the Gobelins, are only used or given away by the emperor, were visited. Although there was much more to be seen in Paris, this day closed up the sight-seeing. Mr. Lowington had delayed the departure for Switzerland one day to enable those provided with invitations to be presented at court.

The time appointed for this great event had arrived, and the half dozen young gentlemen who were to be the recipients of the distinguished honor prepared themselves with the nicest care for the ceremony. Paul Kendall appeared about the hotel dressed as a common sailor, which was a new guise for him, and Ben Duncan, in the captain's uniform, looked just as odd, though the garments fitted him splendidly, and became him perfectly. Mrs. Arbuckle had furnished them with little bunches of roses for the button-holes of their coats, and Grace had lavished the treasures of her perfume-bottles upon their handkerchiefs. They were as guiltless of the odor of tar and pitch as though they had never seen a ship in their lives. They were provided with spotless white kids, and, when ready for the carriage, any American, not soured by a bilious stomach, would have been proud of these juvenile representatives of his country.

The carriage which contained them entered the Place du Carrousel, and the gates opened wide to admit them. There were three carriage loads in charge of the American minister. Mrs. Wall Streete, of New York, with her diamonds and her bad grammar, was there, attended by her niece, with die-away manners, escorted by a young southerner, who was deeply in love with her because the cotton crop had failed. A distinguished military officer talked technically and professionally of Napoleon Bonaparte, and declared that he intended to discuss his tactics with the emperor, and doubtless would have attempted to do so if the minister had not told him he must say nothing unless he was spoken to by the royal personages, according to the rules of etiquette which obtain at court.

The party, most of them in a flutter of excitement, passed through the magnificent rooms of the palace, which were thronged with innumerable servants in green and gold, the livery of the emperor. The party were conducted to the Salle des Maréchaux, and our students declared it was the most elegantly decorated room they had ever seen. The guests were formed in lines, according to their nationalities, the Americans being in one section, the English in another, the Austrians in a third, and so on, each headed by the minister. The Russian ambassador was a count, the Austrian a prince, and the English an earl; so that the boys saw sundry great men who were not down on the programme for the show. Ben whispered that the whole thing was decidedly " nobby."

At length — for " great bodies move slow " — there were indications of the approach of the imperial couple, and the lines of guests, sighing for a royal nod, straightened the files, and their breathing was heavy with anxiety. The emperor and empress entered the room, and passed along the lines. The ministers called off the name of each person presented, who bowed or courtesied low, and retired. Her majesty wore a high diamond crown, and a dress of thin, white fabric, raised here and there with loops of diamonds. Ben Duncan took particular notice of her dress, in order to give his sister a minute account of it in his next letter.

"*Est-il assez gentil, ce petit marin?*" (Is he pretty enough, this little marine?) said the empress, in a low voice to the emperor, as they glanced at Ben, who, as Paul was not present, was really the best looking fellow in the party.

Ben's quick ear caught the compliment, and, though he objected to being called a marine, which is a sailor's especial aversion, his cheeks glowed with pleasure, for it is not everybody whose good looks are praised by an empress. The presentation did not occupy five minutes; and, when the royal couple had retired, the guests were invited to pass into other rooms, where the company were assembled for the grand ball, which was to take place in the Salle du Trône. Directly over the two throne-chairs, to be occupied by the imperial couple, was a band of musicians, who discoursed the sweetest strains from behind a perfect embankment of flowers, which nearly concealed the performers, and filled the vast apartment with delicious odors.

"That's Strauss's band," said the minister, "and that is Strauss himself leading."

"Who is Strauss?" asked Ellis, who had no music in his soul.

"Don't you know Strauss, the man who writes the waltzes, and polkas, and things the girls strum on the pianos?" replied Ben.

He was a stout, short man, with a red face, dressed in a court suit, such as the boys had seen at the tailor's, and on his breast hung several orders and crosses. He held in his hand a *baton*, richly decorated with precious stones, with which he beat the time for the musicians.

"Isn't he a swell?" exclaimed Ben, as he surveyed the celebrated composer of waltzes and polkas. "I wonder what he is worth, just as he stands, *baton* and all!"

The young officers kept close together, for, in spite of Ben's irreverent remarks about the "nobs" present, they felt like cats in a strange garret. The minister had left them, and was now talking with the emperor.

"I wish he would come back and introduce me to some of the girls," said Ben, irreverently again. "For my part, I want some fun, and would like to dance."

"It's perfectly splendid here, as my sister says," added Captain Haven, as he surveyed the brilliant colors, the diamonds, the flowers, and the ladies, and bestowed a bewildered glance at the court dresses of the Marquis de Port-de-roses and others, the servants, in green and gold, and the guards, with steel cuirasses and helmets.

"As a picture, it is the most brilliant thing I ever saw, and I shall long remember it," replied Commodore Gordon.

By and by the minister returned to them, and Ben Duncan eagerly seized his arm.

"Won't you introduce us to some of the ladies?" asked he. "We don't often see such a ball as this, and we want to dance just enough to say we have done so."

"Ask any lady you like to dance with you," returned the minister; "she will not refuse unless she is previously engaged, or is not inclined to dance."

"Whew! Ask these swellish ladies to dance, without the ghost of an introduction!" exclaimed Ben.

"Yes, that is the custom in France, and a very sensible one it is, too. You are not dependent upon the accident of finding friends to introduce you for the enjoyment of the evening."

"I like that; they are forming a set for the Lancers, and I shall profit by your suggestion," said Ben, glancing at a lovely young lady, who had attracted his attention as soon as he entered the hall.

She was not more than sixteen, and was dressed in pure white, with no other ornament than a necklace of tiny pink natural roses around her throat, with a few of the same buds in her golden hair. Ben felt no little trepidation as he approached her, in spite of what the minister had said. Suppose she should be indignant at being asked to dance by a stranger, and snub him! But the sets were nearly filled, and his chances were passing away. Bringing his courage up to the sticking point, he darted boldly forward, and "made his manners" to the golden-haired creature.

"*Mademoiselle veut-elle m'accorder l'honneur de danser* — ahem — *danser la danse avec elle — avec moi?*" stumbled he, the perspiration breaking out on his forehead, for it was awful to have his French desert him at such a trying moment.

"*Mais avec plaisir, monsieur*," replied she, lifting a pair of glorious eyes upon him.

She rose gracefully, and took the arm which Ben offered. As they were moving off to take places in the nearest set, a young fellow, dressed in a scarlet coat, with the Victoria cross "*For Valor*" on his left breast, presented himself before her.

"I beg your pardon, Lady Feodora," said he, "but you promised this dance to me."

"O, no, indeed!" replied she. "It was the first quadrille I promised you, Sir William, and this is the first Lancers."

"*Sir*" William! "*Lady*" Feodora! Ben could not help feeling that he was in high company. His fair companion smiled as he led her off in triumph from the juvenile baronet.

"*C'est un ami qui trouve bien extraordinaire*," added she.

"Would you mind speaking English?" asked Ben. "I understand it better."

"Do you? So do I! I'm so glad! It's so stupid, talking so much French!" laughed she.

Was it possible this enchanting being, after all his blunders, took him for a Frenchman? Ben had a higher opinion than ever before of his proficiency in "*la langue Française*." The young couple soon became well acquainted, and got along nicely together. She was the daughter of an English earl, and Ben soon learned to say Lady Feodora without choking. In a couple of hours he was as easy and self-possessed as though he had been born and brought up in a royal court. Later in the evening, after they had danced together again, they heard a chamberlain calling out to make room for the emperor and empress. The royal pair passed through the brilliant throng, bowing to the guests, and Ben felt very proud to have the Lady Feodora leaning on his arm. Eugénie bowed sweetly to him in return for his bow, and when she saw his golden-haired companion, she stopped.

"Good evening *miladi*," said the empress. "Is madame the countess, your mother, here?"

"*Non, majesté*," answered Lady Feodora. "The Duchess de Lourmel brought me here this evening."

"Ah! I have not perceived her yet. *Mes compliments à cette bonne Madame de Lourmel, n'est-ce pas*," added the empress, as Lady Feodora made her obeisance, and the imperial couple passed on.

It was a big thing to Ben to hear "*l'impératrice* Eugénie" talk, and Ben realized that he had a brilliant story to tell the next day, if not every day for a year to come. Commodore Gordon and the other officers danced occasionally, and explained their "quality" to inquiring ladies and gentlemen. The dancing continued till supper time, and then the young republicans were again astonished at the quantity and richness of the viands. At five o'clock in the morning Ben Duncan bade adieu to Lady Feodora, and his companions to the new acquaintances they had made. The servants in green and gold brought their overcoats, and assisted them as tenderly as though they had been babies.

They returned to the hotel, but had hardly gone to sleep, with the glitter and the gold, and the fair forms lingering in their minds, before they were called to take the train for Lyons.

CHAPTER XVIII.

THE WAY OF THE TRANSGRESSORS.

THERE was a very sudden change in the affairs of the runaway crew of the Josephine. The bold movements of Shuffles, first in taking possession of the exchequer of the runaways, and then in fighting the battle with the bully of the conspirators, had checkmated the knights and utterly demoralized them. The three men with belaying-pins in their hands, which they seemed to have no scruples about using, were a guarantee of peace for the present. As Little and others had suggested, Shuffles was not a baby; and it was evident enough now that he had come with the runaways for the sole purpose of accomplishing the work which he had now so expeditiously executed. After the overwhelming defeat of Phillips, who had been supposed to be a match for any two on board, no others were disposed to resist the will of Shuffles, backed as he was by three men.

Perth, Wilton, and others, who had been stunned by the heavy blows of the cook and stewards, were picked up, and were soon restored to a realizing sense of the altered condition of affairs. They were not seriously injured, though the hard fist of the cook had given them something to remember him by for a few days.

The men had given the boys credit for more fight and more opposition than they had offered, and had really expended more force than was necessary upon their assailants. Neither at home, nor at school, nor even in the Academy Ship, had these boys ever been subjected to corporal punishment, and they seemed to have an idea that under no circumstances would the arbitration of force be applied to them. It never would have been on board of the ship, except to quell actual mutiny. They talked of using force themselves to carry out their purposes, but they appeared to have had no suspicion that the men on board had hard muscles and big fists.

For the present the victory was complete and overwhelming. The runaways looked at each other with blank astonishment. The conquest had been achieved so suddenly that they hardly realized their misfortune, or comprehended that the enterprise was a total failure. They had seen nothing of the good time they had anticipated: they had only kept watch a couple of nights, and lived on corned beef and hard bread. The beautiful vision of a cruise along the sunny shores of Spain had vanished into thin air.

"Our game is up," said Perth, who had been sitting for some time in the cabin, with both hands pressed to his aching head.

"That's so," replied Little.

"And it's all your fault," growled the commander.

"I suppose it is," sneered Little. "I left the money where Shuffles could put his pious paws upon it — didn't I?"

"It was you who wanted to keep Shuffles on board.

If I had had my way, he would have gone into the barge with Ellis," retorted Perth.

"He promised to join us; and he is a smarter fellow than any other one on board of this craft. If he had had the management of the thing, we should have put it through straight."

"O, my head!" groaned Wilton.

"What's the matter with it?" asked Little.

"I believe that fellow meant to knock my brains out," replied Wilton, with a long sigh.

"He would have done so if you had had any brains to knock out," snapped Little, as ill-natured as it was possible for so small a fellow to be.

"Can't we take the vessel again?" asked Perth, suddenly.

"Those three men, to say nothing of Shuffles, can lick the whole of us," replied Little.

"They hit you over the head with a belaying-pin," said Adler. "I didn't think that of them."

"If Shuffles hadn't taken the money, I could have fixed them all right," added Little. "Perth might as well have asked the lamb to keep the money for us, as to put it where he did."

"I didn't try to make the lamb captain!" growled Perth.

"What's that?" demanded Adler, springing to his feet from the force of habit, as the shrill pipe of the boatswain's whistle was heard on deck.

"Let them pipe! I don't go, for one," said Little.

"Nor I," added Perth.

So they all said, and set their teeth firmly together to resist the new authority on board, declaring that if

Shuffles intended to take the vessel back to Havre, he must do it alone: they would not lift a finger, or touch a rope or a sail, even if the Josephine foundered in a gale.

Shuffles was full of energy and determination. He had been thoroughly aroused by the sharp battle he had fought, and, assured that he was engaged in a good cause, he was resolved to be master of the situation. He had called up the boatswain appointed by the new officers, and ordered him to pipe to muster. The fellow looked at the stalwart cook, who stood at the wheel, and then obeyed. About one half of the runaways heeded the summons; the rest paid no attention to it.

"Jones, take the helm!" said Shuffles to one of the conspirators who was competent to perform the duty.

"I won't do it!" replied Jones.

He had hardly spoken the rebellious words before one of the stewards had him by the collar. Shuffles had conferred with the three men, and it was decided that discipline must be enforced at once, for if bad weather came on, the vessel might be lost for the want of obedience. But the new captain had cautioned the men not to use the belaying-pins unless attacked by a dozen of the rebels. The steward dragged Jones to the wheel.

"If you don't obey orders, Jones, it will be the worse for you," interposed Shuffles.

"I won't take the wheel!" replied the rebel.

Without waiting to be prompted, the steward shook him till poor Jones thought the life was to be knocked out of him.

"Let me alone!" yelled he. "You'll kill me!"

"Will you obey orders?" asked the excited steward, as he cast the rebel heavily upon the deck.

"Will you take the wheel?" demanded Shuffles.

Jones made no reply; but, getting up, he went to the wheel, and took hold of the spokes. Crying with anger, and shaking his head in the fury he dared not express in any other manner, he yielded to the stern mandate which had been so vigorously enforced. Those who had answered the summons of the boatswain's whistle were not the most daring of the party, or an attempt might have been made to support Jones in his resistance: as it was, those in the waist only looked on, more in terror than in indignation.

"Boatswain, pipe again, and call all hands," said Shuffles, as the cook, giving up the wheel to the unwilling Jones, took his place near the companion way.

The call was not heeded, and Shuffles directed the cook and one of the stewards to go into the cabin and steerage, and enforce the summons. Perth, Wilton, and Adler positively refused to obey. But the cook exhibited his bludgeon, which convinced Wilton, and he went on deck.

"I can't go; you have almost killed me now," whined Perth.

"I'll finish you if you don't mind," replied the cook, as savagely as a West Indian pirate.

"I'm not able to go on deck!" groaned Perth.

The cook took him by the collar, dragged him off the locker, where he was seated, ud pitched him upon the floor at the foot of the ladder.

"This is mutiny, and if some of you get killed, it won't be my fault," added the cook.

Perth crawled up the ladder, followed by Adler. It looked like a matter of life and death, and the poor fellows were actually afraid the cook would murder them. Little had sneaked into the steerage, but the steward there drove him on deck at the point of his bludgeon. This was the end of all open resistance, for disobedience seemed to insure a blow on the head with the belaying-pin. Never before had any of the conspirators seen such sharp practice. The cook and stewards had suddenly, from quiet, orderly men, been transformed into savages, who appeared to be as ready to murder them as they were to eat.

The knights were all mustered in the waist. Perth was mad with himself for yielding, and something was said by him and Wilton about arming the runaways with such weapons as they could lay their hands on, and making a sudden rush upon their conquerors; but facing that awful cook was as terrible as marching up to a twenty-four pounder loaded with grape-shot. They growled and howled, but they did nothing more.

"Fellows," said Shuffles, when the party were assembled, "I have no long stories to tell; but I want you to understand how things are between us. I came with you in the Josephine, when I had a chance to leave her, in order to bring the vessel back; and I'm going to do it. This is all I have to say on that point. As you are already divided into watches, you will perform your duty on deck as before. Those who were officers will take berths in the steerage, but will serve in the watches to which they were appointed. Those who perform their duty faithfully from this time I will report to Mr. Lowington. Those who are not willing to obey orders shall be compelled to do so. The port watch is dismissed; the starboard will remain on deck."

About two thirds of the conspirators came to the conclusion that it would be better to fall in with the new order of things, while the others obeyed only with growls and threats; but they dared not refuse to do as they were required. Phillips, in the brig, had howled and sworn, and beaten against the hard wood pales of his prison till he had worn himself out in stupid resistance to his fate. He was informed by some of the port watch of what had transpired on deck. He called the runaways cowards, and declared if he had been among them there would have been a bigger fight than the first one. The restless Little planned half a dozen schemes to retake the Josephine, but he could find none who were willing to face the terrible cook. He had yet another project, which was to be executed at night, when some of their tyrants would be asleep. Several were willing to take part in this plot. Three of the actors were each to throw a handful of black pepper, taken from the castors, into the faces of the cook and Shuffles, or whoever might be in charge on deck, while others knocked them down with handspikes. In this vicious scheme there was hope, and the runaways kept very quiet and orderly during the day, animated by the prospect of its success.

Instead of heading the Josephine directly for Havre,

Shuffles, as the weather looked threatening, had directed her towards the Isle of Wight, so that he could readily make a port in a storm, for he had not much confidence in his crew. At four o'clock in the afternoon, a steamer, flying the French flag, was discovered making for the schooner. It was one of the two sent out, with Mr. Fluxion on board, in quest of the runaways. She had gone to Dieppe on Sunday, to Brighton during the night, and to Cowes on Monday morning. She had obtained intelligence of the Josephine, from the captain of a steamer who had seen a vessel answering to her description, off Alderney, bound to the north-westward. Mr. Fluxion left Cowes, and sailed for Plymouth, but had made out the Josephine in the afternoon, headed to the eastward.

The steamer ran up under the stern of the Josephine, and Mr. Fluxion hailed her from the paddle-box. Shuffles promptly recognized his voice, and hove to. Among the conspirators all was consternation. The vice-principal was a sharp disciplinarian, and the game was now certainly up. The scheme for that night was indefinitely postponed. A crew, in charge of Lincoln as coxswain, was sent to the steamer. The rebels were disposed to resist; but there stood the cook and his backers, with the belaying-pins in their hands, and it was impossible to escape their manifest destiny.

While the boat was pulling to the steamer, Mr. Fluxion wrote a letter to the principal, in Paris, informing him of the discovery of the Josephine, which the French captain was to mail on his return to Havre. He added, that he should take the vessel to Brest, where she could lie in safety, without docking, during the absence of the tourists. The vice-principal and Gage, the carpenter, went over the side into the boat, as the steamer started on her return.

Mr. Fluxion obtained the leading facts of the runaway cruise from Lincoln. He learned that Shuffles had recaptured the vessel, and was now returning to Havre in her. If he had ever had any doubts in regard to the reformed student, they were now removed. As he went on deck, he took the acting captain by the hand, and generously complimented him upon his gallant and faithful conduct. After he had heard a detailed account of the proceedings on board, all hands were piped to muster, and the vice-principal laid down the law so forcibly that it could not be misunderstood. He gave Shuffles the command for the rest of the voyage.

"Young gentlemen," said the vice-principal, in conclusion, " by this silly enterprise, which could not possibly have been a success under any circumstances, you have deprived yourselves of all privileges for the rest of this season's cruise. I am directed by the principal to allow you no liberty, and to keep you busy at ship's duty and your studies, till the return of the rest of the students from their travels. You have made a great blunder. It is always a blunder to depart from the plain path of duty. I shall take the vessel to Brest, where we can lie at anchor, and you can pursue your studies without interruption."

The students were dismissed, and Mr. Fluxion went into the cabin with Shuffles, leaving Gage in charge of the deck. A long conversation ensued, in which Shuffles explained more minutely what he had done.

"After being outwitted by Little, I felt that I ought to do something to redeem myself," said he. "I knew these fellows would soon quarrel, and afford me an opportunity to do something; but I could not resist the temptation to check them by taking possession of the gold. That brought things to a head, and we soon had the battle."

"You say you hid the gold. Where did you put it?" asked Mr. Fluxion.

"In a cask of water."

"You have done very well, with the odds all against you. When we get to Brest, you shall join the students in Paris."

Mr. Fluxion wished to satisfy himself in regard to the safety of the gold. The cook was directed to draw off the water in the cask, and one of the heads was taken out. Every coin was found, and the whole was placed in the iron safe, of which the vice-principal had an extra key. The Josephine was now headed to the south-west. The storm which Shuffles had feared came the next morning, and it was five days before the vessel could reach her destined port. All hands were frequently called, and the runaways had to work hard night and day. As there were no provisions on board but hard bread, salt beef and pork, the fare was no better than seamen have in ordinary merchant vessels. It was a hard time for all hands, and the runaways did not enjoy it. When, after this rough cruise, the Josephine went into port, even review lessons were a luxury, compared with night watches in the cold, the rain, and the gale.

The vessel came to anchor, on Saturday night, in

the harbor of Brest, and Sunday was a day of grateful rest to the worn-out Knights of the Golden Fleece. Roast beef was a treat, and even a plentiful supply of cold water to drink was a luxury, for they had been on short allowance for three days. On Monday morning Shuffles started for Paris, and on his arrival was warmly welcomed by the principal, to whom Mr. Fluxion had written full particulars of the runaway cruise of the Josephine on Sunday morning. Not less warmly was he greeted by Grace Arbuckle and the rest of the party.

CHAPTER XIX.

A VISIT TO CHAMOUNI AND MONT BLANC.

AS Grace Arbuckle had predicted, Shuffles was more of a hero than he had been before; and he was obliged to tell the story of the runaways till he was thoroughly wearied with the subject. When the train started for Lyons, he was invited to take a seat in the compartment with the Arbuckles, from which, however, Paul Kendall was not excluded.

The country through which the train passed was certainly beautiful, and the students had seen so many palaces in Paris and its vicinity, that the sight of the cottages which dotted the landscape was really a luxury. They were generally very pretty, and in the fields adjoining was occasionally seen a patch of Indian corn, which made the scene more like home. Many exceedingly wiry and ghost-like poplars grew near them, for which the people seem to have a singular partiality.

At Dijon the train stopped for half an hour, and the *buffet* was all that could be desired. Having ten minutes to spare, — for we are sorry to say they bolted their dinner after the American fashion, — some of the students took a hasty run into the place, which is an old city, and presented some interesting relics of the ancient time when it was the capital of the Duchy of Burgundy. The train moved on through a region abounding in vineyards, which produce vast quantities of wine every year, the principal wealth of the country. After leaving Châlons, the road ran along the bank of the Saône. From the window of the carriage could be seen the lofty peaks of the Jura Mountains, and it was said that Mont Blanc, a hundred miles distant, could be discerned in very clear weather.

"Between the Huguenots and the revolutionists, this part of France has suffered severely," said Dr. Winstock, as the train dashed through Mâcon. "Dijon was ruined by the revolutionists, and in Mâcon nearly all the religious edifices were destroyed by them and the Huguenots. By the way, Lamartine was born in Mâcon. Much of the red wine used in Paris comes from this district."

At five o'clock the train arrived at Lyons, and the excursionists hastened to the Grand Hôtel de Lyon, where Mr. Arbuckle's agent had secured accommodations. The boys had been sitting in the carriages for ten hours, and were anxious to stretch their limbs among the sights of Lyons. The city is principally located on a tongue of land between the Rhône and the Saône, though its limits extend beyond both these rivers. It is the second city in population and commercial importance in France, and the first in the extent of its manufactures — silk being the most important fabric.

The students walked down the quais on the Rhône, quite as much interested in the strange-looking boats, which floated on the broad river, as in the stately buildings that adorn the city; crossed the tongue of land, less than half a mile wide at this point, through the Cours Napoléon, a magnificent avenue, bordered with double rows of trees. Returning on the quasi of the Saône, they visited the Place Bellecour, a square which covers fifteen acres. The next morning, attended by the professors, the boys crossed the bridge over the Saône called the Pont du Palais de Justice, visited the Cathedral, and then ascended the height behind it, on which stands the church of Notre Dame de Fourvières. It has a lofty dome crowned by a gilded figure of the Virgin. Over the entrance is an inscription to the lady whose name the church bears, stating that by her saintly intercession Lyons was miraculously saved from the ravages of the cholera. The walls within are literally covered with pictures, four thousand in number, offered to the saint for her kindness.

Near the church is an observatory, six hundred and thirty feet above the river, which many of the students ascended. It commands a fine view of the city and its suburbs. The attendant, pointing to an object which looked like a white cloud in the distance, declared that it was Mont Blanc. The Alps of Dauphiné, and other mountains, were also pointed out to them there. All around them was a vast system of fortifications, which extends in a circle of twelve miles around Lyons, erected as much to put down insurrections within the city, as to repel invasion from without, for the manufacturing population have proved to be exceedingly turbulent in times of revolution or of scarcity. The Faubourg of La Croix Rousse is almost wholly inhabited by silk weavers, crowded into very high houses, on narrow streets, ten to twenty families in each. The guns of Fort Montessay command this quarter, and could level it to the ground in a few minutes; for this is the section where violence and sedition usually break out.

Beneath the observatory Mr. Mapps gathered his pupils together, to give them a lecture on the history of Lyons, only a brief sketch of which can be repeated here. It is said to have been founded by the Greeks, six hundred years before Christ. It was an important Roman city, and various remains of their occupancy, including an amphitheatre, and the ruins of an aqueduct, are still seen. It was held by the archbishops in virtue of a grant from the Emperor of Germany, in the twelfth century, but was restored to France in the reign of Philip the Fair, in the thirteenth. In the sixteenth century it was ravaged by both Catholics and Protestants, as each came into power; and in the French Revolution it suffered terribly. Though the people at first embraced revolutionary principles, they were disgusted with the terrorism of their leaders, and the tyranny of the municipal officers, and tried and executed the president of one of the clubs.

In consequence of this rebellion against its authority, the National Convention collected sixty thousand troops to subdue the place. Thirty thousand of the citizens manned the walls, and resisted the attack for two months. Thirty thousand persons perished within the walls; eleven thousand red-hot shot and more than twice as many shells had been thrown into the place; but the citizens yielded only when famine compelled them to do so. In order to humble the pride of the Lyonnais, the Convention decreed the total destruction of the city. The command was obeyed to the letter, and the place was reduced to a pile of ruins, at a cost of three and a half millions of dollars for merely pulling down the buildings.

The work of the guillotine was commenced, but it was too slow, and the citizens were tied together in groups of sixty, and shot down with grape-shot from cannon. Over two thousand were massacred to satisfy the fury of the Terrorists. A reaction ensued, and seventy or eighty of the butchers fell victims to the indignation of the people. In 1834 the silk-weavers of Croix Rousse "struck," drove out the military, and held the city till an army could be sent to retake it, which cost a thousand lives. It requires thirty thousand troops to keep Lyons in order. The city has suffered several times from floods, that of 1856 driving thousands of people to encamp for the want of houses, and destroying a vast amount of property.

At one o'clock the party took the train for Geneva. The route for some distance lay on the bank of the River Rhône, which in places had broken from its bed, and covered the plain with sheets of sand. After a ride of twenty-eight miles, the train rattled in among the Jura Mountains, through the picturesque valley of the Rhône. At Bellegarde, the last town in France where the train stopped for refreshments, most of the students, instead of wasting the time in eating, ran down to the Perte du Rhône, which Mr. Mapps had mentioned in his lecture. The river was not more than sixteen feet wide at this point; but the wonderful phenomenon had been partially destroyed by the blasting of the rocks in order to permit timber to float freely down to a market. The cars started again, and crossing a high viaduct, and plunging through a tunnel two miles long, passed the very strong and picturesque Fort de l'Eluse, which is perched high up in the mountain. Its batteries have been cut out of the solid rock, and a staircase, one hundred feet high, has been hewn out within the mountain. It is a French fortress, which commands the valley and protects France from invasion by this pass.

On the arrival of the train at Geneva, — or *Genève*, as the French call it, — the party went to the Hôtel Beau Rivage, a new house on the Quai du Mont Blanc. It was too late to see anything of the city that night, and after supper Mr. Mapps gave his lecture on Switzerland in the dining-room.

"Switzerland," said he, pointing to the map which he had borrowed for the occasion, "lies in the latitude of Upper Canada and New Brunswick. It is bounded on the north and east by Germany, on the south by Italy and France, and on the west by France. Its greatest length from east to west is two hundred and sixteen miles. Its greatest breadth from north to south is one hundred and fifty-six. Its area is fifteen thousand two hundred and thirty-three miles. Equal in area to what state, young gentlemen?"

"Half the size of Maine," replied one.

"Twice as large as Massachusetts," added another.

"Right; we have no state of similar size. It has a population of two and a half millions, or one hundred and fifty-seven to a square mile — about the same as Massachusetts. I need not tell you that the greater part of its surface is covered with mountains, and that it presents the finest scenery in the world. The country is covered by the Alps and their branches. The principal chains are the Pennine, which begins in France, is continued by the Helvetian on the southern border, and the Rhætian Alps, which completes the chain in Switzerland. North of the Pennine are the Bernese Alps. The highest peak is Monte Rosa, over fifteen thousand feet, in the canton of Valois. Six others are between fourteen and fifteen thousand feet high; eight are between thirteen and fourteen, and eight between ten and thirteen thousand feet high.

"The highest of these mountains are covered with perpetual snow. Through the Pass of St. Gothard, seven thousand feet high, diligences travel regularly; and the Simplon Road, built by Napoleon, is sixty-six hundred feet high in its loftiest part. The Pass of St. Bernard, eight thousand feet high, was traversed by Napoleon and his army on the way to Italy. The hospice, on the summit, is the highest permanent habitation in Europe, and is occupied by some Benedictine monks, for the entertainment of travellers stopped by the wintry storms; and such there are even in summer. You know all about the great tawny dogs which go to the relief of the unfortunate passengers. Connected with the hospice is a dead house, where the bodies of those found in the snow are kept for a long time, preserved from decay by the icy cold. The monks are young men, who serve for a term of years in this frigid locality, and then are sent to more genial climes.

"The Rhine and the Rhône both rise in Switzerland, but the rivers are generally mountain torrents fed by the glaciers in the icy regions of the upper air. Of course, in this rough country are numerous cascades and waterfalls. It contains many large and deep lakes, most of which are navigated by steamboats. Lake Geneva, the largest, is fifty-five miles long and six broad. Lake Constance, the next in size, is forty-four miles long and nine miles wide.

"Of the history of Switzerland I need say but little. The original people were Celts from the North, called Helvetians, from whence the country was named Helvetia. For centuries it was a Roman province; in the sixth century it was subjugated by the Franks, and Christianity was established within its borders. Under Charles the Fat it was wrested from France, and divided among the Germans and Burgundians. The three ancient cantons of Schwytz, Uri, and Unterwalden, from the first of which the country obtained its modern name, laid the foundation of Swiss independence. Most of the country was subject to Austria, the house of Hapsburg having obtained the imperial throne of Germany, whose princes sought to make Switzerland a part of their domain. Berne and Zurich maintained their independence, but the three old cantons were conquered and held for a time. A league was formed by the citizens of the three cantons, which resulted in the expulsion of the Austrians. William Tell figures in this eventful period.

"The league of the three cantons was joined by others, and for hundreds of years the Swiss were at war with the Austrians and others, but they maintained their independence. The reformation in the sixteenth century distracted the country, and civil war ensued ; but the difficulty was finally settled by allowing each canton to choose its own religion, though frequent wars have since resulted from the same cause. Even in the same canton, the two religious sects have been arrayed against each other, and three of them have been divided into half cantons, each having its own government.

"Switzerland is a federal republic, like the United States, each canton making its own laws, except in certain matters expressly delegated to the general government. The constitution vests the legislative and executive authority in a kind of congress, composed of two chambers, the 'Ständrath,' or State Council, corresponding to our Senate, and the 'Nationalrath,' or Federal Council, corresponding to our House of Representatives. The first consists of forty-four members, or two from each canton, and the other of one hundred and twenty-eight members, or one for every twenty thousand of the population. They are elected for three years, and every citizen who has reached the age of twenty, may vote, and any voter, not a clergyman, is eligible to office. The supreme executive authority is vested in a federal council of seven members, elected by the two houses, which together are called the Federal Assembly. The president and vice-president of the Federal Council are the chief magistrates of the republic. The first receives a salary of two thousand dollars, and the second, and the other members of the council, seventeen hundred. This congress has the power to make war, conclude peace, and negotiate treaties with other nations. There is also a Federal Tribunal, to settle matters in dispute between the cantons.

"The people of Switzerland are about equally divided between the Protestants and Catholics, with a small majority in favor of the former. All Christian sects are tolerated, though the Jesuits are excluded from the country. Education is compulsory between the ages of five and eight, and the people are intelligent and well taught. No standing army is maintained in Switzerland, but every citizen is liable to serve as a soldier, and instruction is given by the government in tactics, gunnery, and other branches of military art. Nearly three hundred and fifty thousand men are available for service, and are in actual readiness to take the field.

"Three fourths of the population are wholly or partly supported by agriculture. Silk goods, watches, jewelry, embroidery, are largely manufactured. The currency of Switzerland is the same as that of France. In different parts the people use the French, German, and Italian languages. Four times as many speak German as French. The western cantons speak French, the northern German, and the southern Italian, or the language of the great nationality nearest to them."

The professor closed his lecture, and the party were treated to some music, given in honor of a bridal party in the house. Early the next morning, the students hastened in scores to the border of the lake, which Byron has immortalized in his famous poem, Childe Harold — "Clear, placid Leman!" Its waters have a greenish-blue tint, like the ocean, the cause of which has not been clearly explained. Near the shore were moored several flat-boats, with roofs over them, in which women were washing clothes. The boats are picturesque, having lateen sails. Just above the hotel is a breakwater, to prevent the waves, which are sometimes heavy in east winds, from washing the bridges and *quais*. It forms a fine promenade on a warm day.

After breakfast the party went in omnibuses to visit the magnificent country-seat of Baron Adolph Rothschild, at Pregny, the hotel-keeper furnishing tickets for the purpose. The estate is extensive, and is laid out in groves, flower-gardens, and lawns. A hill afforded a splendid view of the lake and surrounding scenery, as well as of the distant mountains. The country in this part is only moderately uneven, and the panorama is beautiful. In the grounds is an artificial grotto, with stalactites hanging from the roof, and a stream of water trickling into a pool in the centre. The mansion-house is not a palace; but it is an elegant residence, and, as the students passed the front door, they saw some of the liveried servants, who were dressed in bob-tailed blue coats with a profusion of gilt buttons, knee-breeches of yellow, with white stockings. In the gardens is quite a collection of deer — some cream-colored — and of rare fowls.

Leaving this fine place, the omnibuses drove through some of the principal streets of the city; but there is nothing of special interest to the traveller to be seen. A horse railroad, in one of the streets, had a familiar look to the Americans. The party returned over one of the bridges which cross the lower end of the lake and connect the two parts of the town. Leading from one of these bridges is a causeway to the "Ile de J. J. Rousseau," which contains a statue to this philosopher, who was born in Geneva. The city contains a large number of hotels, most of which advertise "Pension in the winter months," which signifies that they take boarders at reduced rates, and many strangers reside here the whole year. In the Jardin Anglais is a fine model of Mont Blanc, upon which the artist was engaged for ten years. The staple articles of manufacture are watches, jewelry, and music-boxes. One hundred thousand watches a year are made here.

John Calvin, the reformer, lived and preached in Geneva; and so great was his influence, though he entered the place as a fugitive, that he banished Roman Catholicism, and established the reformed church. He was a politician as well as an orator and theologian, and, as president of the consistory, assisted in enacting some severe sumptuary laws; as, a dinner for ten persons was limited to five dishes; plush breeches were interdicted; those who violated the Sabbath were publicly admonished from the pulpit, and the gambler was placed in the pillory with a pack of cards tied around his neck. He was a great and powerful man. At his death he forbade the Genevese to build a monument over his grave, and his burial-place is not now known.

At two o'clock the excursionists took the steamer Helvétie for the trip up the lake. The boat was quite ordinary, and a little American enterprise is needed to increase the pleasure of travelling in this beautiful region. The scenery, tame, but pretty, near Geneva, becomes grand and sublime at the upper end. The steamer makes several stops on her trip, and the description of each place was eagerly sought in the guide books. Coppet was the residence of Necker, the unfortunate minister of finance of Louis XVI., and of his daughter, Madame de Staël, the author. At Lausanne, the capital of the canton Vaud, the boat stopped for some time, and the students went ashore and had a glance at its Gothic cathedral and its castle or château. Gibbon, the historian, lived here, and the garden of his house is now attached to the hotel which bears his name.

It was dark on Saturday evening when the party reached Montreux, and on Sunday they attended the English church service in the place. The village is said to be the healthiest in Europe. The hills are covered with *pensions*, or boarding-houses, and the Hotel Byron, in the vicinity, is one of the best establishments in Switzerland. On Monday morning the tourists visited the Castle of Chillon, which Byron's poem has made an object of interest to all who read the English language. It is situated on an isolated rock within a stone's throw of the shore, from which it is reached by a wooden bridge. It was built by the Duke of Savoy, and used as a state prison in the thirteenth century. Byron's story in the poem is a fiction; but Bonnivard, a monk, having offended his royal master in his efforts to free the Genevese, was confined in this castle six years, in its deepest dungeon, and the poet's story was more real than he supposed. The prison looks like the crypt of a church. Byron's name is written on one of the pillars, which are covered with the autographs of visitors, some of them distinguished persons. The castle is now used as a depository for military stores. The scenery of the lake and mountains is very attractive, and the students enjoyed it, for they had all read in the school-books the extracts from Byron which celebrate its glories.

Taking the train at Villeneuve, at the head of the lake, the excursionists arrived in an hour at Vernayaz, and visited the famous waterfall of the Sallenche, one of the grandest in Switzerland. The river falls two hundred and eighty feet in its descent to the valley of the Rhône, making one hundred and twenty feet of this distance at one leap. The region was almost as much infested with beggars and importunate guides as Killarney, in Ireland. The party were now in the midst of the mountains, which towered to a vast height all around them. The rest of the day was spent in exploring the wild region in the neighborhood.

After an early breakfast on Tuesday, the company started to walk to Mont Blanc over the Col de Balme, a distance of twenty miles. It was a long and weary journey, but it was full of exciting interest. The path was steep and rugged. On the crest of the Col de Balme, the view surpassed anything they had ever seen before. Mont Blanc, from its summit to its base, in the vale of Chamouni, was before them. The immense glaciers were, indeed, seas of ice, and many were the exclamations of wonder and delight which burst from the travellers.

A lunch was obtained at the house of refuge built for those overtaken on the mountains by storms, and the descent, following the Arve, was commenced.

Early in the afternoon, the excursionists arrived at Chamouni, where accommodations had been secured at the Hôtel de Londres. The village is a large place, deriving its importance from the crowd of people who visit it to see the scenery. Its hotels are on the grandest scale, and no better ones are to be found in the world. The principal business of the inhabitants is attending to the wants of tourists. The state regulates all affairs pertaining to guides and mules for excursions. There are two hundred of the former under the management of a *guide-en-chef*, who controls the others. Men and mules are subjected to an examination, to ascertain their qualifications for the work. For a guide and mule the charge is six francs a day each, though particular excursions are made at fixed prices. The students remained at Chamouni three days, making trips to the Cascade du Dard; to the Montanvert, which includes a visit to the Mer de Glace, and a short walk across its rough, icy surface, to the Chapeau; to the Jardin, a rock among the glaciers, seven acres in area, and nine thousand feet above the sea level, covered with green and flowers — an oasis in the desert of ice; and the ascent of the Brevent Mountains, on the side of the river opposite the Mont Blanc range, which commands a splendid view of the towering heights, the seas of ice, and the rushing torrents. In this lofty position, Professor Modelle read Coleridge's sublime Address to Mont Blanc.

On Saturday the tourists returned to Martigny, by the Tête Noir, taking the valley of the Trient, instead of crossing the mountain, and, by the last train, at dark, reached Sion, where they were to spend Sunday.

CHAPTER XX.

A RUN THROUGH SWITZERLAND.

SION contains three old castles, on the heights, to one of which some of the students climbed. At this point in the journey railroads were no longer available; but the zealous agent of Mr. Arbuckle had provided six diligences for the exclusive use of the guests, in which they were to proceed to Brieg, on the Simplon Road, built by Napoleon. These vehicles differ from any seen in the United States. They contain four compartments for passengers — a *banquette*, or covered seat on the top; the *coupé*, or front place in the body, with windows looking out under the driver's seat; the *intérieur*, with cross seats, in the middle; and the *rotonde*, opening, like an omnibus, from the rear. It accommodates eighteen passengers, their baggage being stowed upon the top. The distance to Brieg is thirty-three miles, and it was accomplished in about five hours. The route is among the high Alps, twelve or thirteen thousand feet high.

After a dinner at the Hôtel d'Angleterre, a miscellaneous procession of *char* wagons, voitures, and mules was formed, and moved up the valley of the Rhône, though a portion of the party were to go on foot, changing occasionally with those in the vehicles.

They seemed to be travelling in the clouds, though far above them were the Simplon, Aeggischhorn, St. Gothard, and the Grimsel. There was everything to see, but little to be described. Dr. Winstock pointed out to Grace, Paul, and Shuffles, who were his special care, the objects of interest on the route. It was quite dark when the tourists arrived at the village of Ober-Gestelen, which is forty-four hundred feet above the sea level.

Travelling in this lofty region was different from anything the party had ever before seen. Often the road was a mere shelf, not more than four feet wide, cut out of the rocks, with an abyss thousands of feet deep below it. Mountain steeps, which looked impassable in the distance, were overcome by the mules. Vast crevices yawned in the rocks, and unsteady bridges spanned stupendous chasms. Torrents leaped down dizzy heights, snow-clad peaks towered above, and even the most thoughtless of the boys were sublimated by the grandeur of the scene.

As the days were short, the excursionists left Ober-Gestelen at daylight in the morning, for Andermatt, visiting the Rhône glacier, one of the grandest in Switzerland, on the way. The source of the river is in a cavern of ice, and its waters fall over a precipice one hundred and fifty feet high, into an ice-bound cavern beneath. The water forces itself under the glacier, and issues from another cavern at its foot. Crossing the Furca at the pass between two peaks, over eight thousand feet above the level of the sea, the tourists descended to Andermatt, where they dined on red trout, and hastened on, in the vehicles provided by Mr. Arbuckle's agent, to Altorf.

"Three cheers for Billy Tell!" shouted Ben Duncan, as he leaped from the *char-à-banc*, which is a kind of sofa on four wheels.

In the open square in the centre of the town, tradition says that William Tell shot the apple from his son's head, and the place where he stood is marked by a plaster statue. The town contains nothing else of interest, being in the smallest and poorest canton in Switzerland, where poverty and pauperism are an eyesore to the traveller. Two miles beyond is Flüelen on the Lake of Luzerne, where the party embarked for the city at the other end of it, twenty-six miles distant. The lake consists of a series of inlets or bays, and has a bad reputation for stormy weather; but it behaved very well while the students were crossing it. Vast mountains rise in places from the surface of the water, high promontories and lofty precipices frown upon the voyager, and it would be hard to conceive of anything more wild and sublime than these rugged shores. On a little shelf, at the east shore of the lake, stands Tell's Chapel. According to the story, Gesler, the Austrian governor, was conveying the Swiss hero, bound, in a boat to the dungeon of Küssnacht; but a sudden storm coming up, the tyrant removed his fetters in order to enable him to steer the boat. Taking advantage of this circumstance, Tell leaped ashore upon the shelf where the chapel stands, made his escape, and afterwards killed Gesler. Mass is said, and a sermon preached, in this chapel on the Friday after Ascension Day. The inhabitants on the shores attend, and form an aquatic procession in their boats.

The tourists landed at the broad quay, and walked across the street to the Englischer Hof — one of the principal hotels. In the evening they visited the arsenal, which contains a sword of William Tell, and many other historical trophies. The most interesting sight in Luzerne is the monument to the memory of the Swiss guards who fell while defending Louis XVI. and Marie Antoinette in the Tuileries, in the first French revolution, which the tourists visited the next morning. It is the figure of a wounded lion, of colossal proportions, hewn out of the sandstone ledge, the recess forming a kind of cavern, in which it rests. It was designed by Thorwaldsen, the famous Danish sculptor, and is twenty-eight feet long and eighteen high. The lion, with a broken spear in his side, is dying, but is striving with his last gasp to protect a shield on which is represented the *fleur-de-lis* of the Bourbons.

Over the River Reuss, which divides the town, are several bridges of picturesque architecture, which are adorned with paintings. The students walked through some of the principal streets of the town, and then through one of the gates to the suburbs. They had regarded with peculiar interest the cottages of Switzerland — for there are no palaces. They are peculiar to the country, and rather belie the name, as it is understood in other countries, for they are often large enough to accommodate not only the farmer's family, but also his oxen, cows, and sheep. Some of them suggest a hotel, rather than a dwelling-house. They are often elaborately adorned in a rude way. The rear is frequently used as a stable, and sometimes there is a road from the hill-side into the second story, where a cart, laden with produce, may be driven in.

On a hill they obtained a fine view of the two noted mountains of this vicinity, Mount Pilatus, on one side of the lake, and Mount Rhigi on the other. The former is said to derive its name from Pontius Pilate, the wicked governor of Judea, who permitted the Savior to be crucified. Having been banished to Gaul by Tiberius Cæsar, he wandered about this mountain, conscience-stricken, and finally drowned himself in the lake. The mountain is, therefore, in bad odor, and formerly the government of Luzerne forbade its ascent.

The company left Luzerne in the steamer for Alpnach. On the way, Dr. Winstock pointed out Stanz, where Arnold Winkelried's statue stands in the market-place. He was a devoted patriot, and sacrificed himself to his country. Near Alpnach was the great slide, by which timber was formerly shot down from the mountains, to be floated nearly a thousand miles down the Rhine, into which the Reuss flows. From Alpnach the diligences conveyed the tourists to Brienz, where a steamer is taken to Interlaken. From the lake could be seen in the distance the Foulhorn, behind which are the glaciers of Grindelwald, the Wengern Alp, the Jungfrau, the Scheideggs, among which Byron wrote Manfred. Spending the night at Interlaken, a very pretty village of hotels and boarding-houses, in the midst of the grandest scenery in the world, which our party were forced to see as they travelled, they proceeded by steamer through the Lake of Thun to the beautiful village of that name, one of the most beautiful residences in Switzerland. The lake is bordered with splendid villas. But only a short stay was made there, and the tourists hastened to Berne by railroad.

The capital of Switzerland is an odd-looking place to an American. Most of the houses project over the sidewalks in the streets, like those in the Rue de Rivoli in Paris, and the buildings are antique and quaint. In this continuous arcade, exceedingly comfortable in rainy weather, the shopkeepers expose their goods for sale. The city is built on a kind of promontory, formed by the River Aar, which surrounds it on three sides. The stream is a rushing torrent, and flows at the bottom of a deep gully, over which a bridge, nearly a thousand feet in length, has been extended. The streets and squares are adorned with fountains, and wooden bears, stone bears, and iron bears confront the tourist wherever he goes; for this emblem is the device and "trade-mark" of the town. In old German, the word "bern" means "bear." The tradition is, that when the original founder of the city commenced the erection of the walls, a huge bear came out of the woods and attacked him, as an apparent protest against this invasion of his dominions. All hands turned out, and killed the monster. Glorying in the exploit, they kept the trophies of their victory, and adopted the bear as the emblem of the town. The bear was then painted on their battle standards, stamped on their coins, and carved in wood and stone to adorn their houses and public buildings. Not contented with these inanimate symbols of their favorite animals, the Bernese have, for hundreds of years, kept a number of living bears in the pits on the outskirts of the town, which are maintained at the public expense. When the French army captured Berne, in 1798, these bears were sent to the Jardin des Plantes in Paris; but as soon as the city was restored, the citizens were careful to procure another supply.

The clock tower, in the middle of the town, was a curious object, and attracted the attention of the boys. Just before the clock strikes, a wooden cock appears, crows twice, and flaps his wings. A figure strikes the hour on the bell with a hammer, and a procession of bears comes out, and marches round a throne, on which sits a king, who gapes and lowers his sceptre as the bell is struck.

A walk through the streets, a visit to the minster and the bear pits, satisfied the students; and, taking the express train, in the evening they reached Basle before midnight. The Hôtel Trois Rois, in which rooms were provided for them, is on the bank of the Rhône, which here flows with great rapidity. Its waters are of a light-green color. The first thing that attracted the attention of Paul Kendall, as he looked from his chamber window in the morning, was a singular ferry-boat, just above the bridge. A rope was stretched across the river, about twenty feet above the water, and hauled taut. A line, with a block on one end, whose sheaf ran freely on the tight rope, was attached to a flat-boat at the other end. In crossing, the helmsman headed the craft diagonally against the current, which, striking its side, as the wind does the sails of a ship when close-hauled, drives it at a rapid rate across the river.

The city is situated on both sides of the river, which divides it into Great and Little Basle. On the long bridge which connects them are a couple of picturesque little towers, in which the statistical history of the structure is inscribed. The Cathedral, in which Zwingle and other noted reformers preached, is a red sandstone edifice, built in the eleventh century, contains the tomb of Erasmus, some memorials of him, and the remaining frescoes of " The Dance of Death." In the museum of the town are some paintings by Holbein, who lived for many years in Basle. The *Rathhaus* is a Gothic building, with the exterior painted in fanciful pictures and devices. The streets are crooked, and most of them narrow. The houses are of the olden time, in the centre of the place, and old watch towers, some with clocks indicating the time with a single hand, are to be seen.

"Dr. Winstock, what is the Dance of Death? I see it mentioned in pictures and poems all over this place," said Paul, as he rode with the Arbuckles through Basle. "It seems to be a great institution here, whatever it means."

"It was a religious dance of the middle ages, which is a popular theme for poet and painter, especially in Basle. Holbein is said to have painted fifty-three scenes to represent it, in which Death is seen dancing with people of all ranks and conditions, and thus leading them to the grave. As you have observed, the subject is a mingling of the serious and grotesque. Five hundred years ago, a masquerade of this nature used to be performed in the churches, in which persons dressed to exhibit all the grades of society marched before a skeleton figure, talked with him, and then disappeared. Its object was to remind the people of their final departure."

By the fast train the excursionists reached Strasbourg in four hours, bidding adieu to Switzerland and its cottages. Sleeping at the Hôtel de Paris, the students spent the morning in visiting the citadel and forts of the place; but the Cathedral is the principal and almost the only object of interest in the place. Its spire is the highest in the world — four hundred and sixty-eight feet. The church was begun in the thirteenth century, and over four hundred years were occupied in its erection. It is one of the most celebrated cathedrals of the world, and the party gazed with deep interest upon its grand proportions and delicate architecture. In the north transept is the wonderful clock, which had even more interest to the boys than the ancient structure itself. It was made in 1571, and, after standing still for fifty years, was repaired, and now performs its curious mechanical evolutions. It shows the day of the week and of the month, the name of the month and the year, as well as the hours and quarter hours, when there is small display of figures. At noon the clock exhibits its grand pantomime. The twelve apostles march out with stately step, bow humbly to the Savior, who lifts his hand to bless each as he passes. An angel strikes the hour. Time repeats the stroke; a second angel turns an hourglass; and a gayly-painted cock flaps his wings and crows three times. The show over, the party hastened to the hotel for dinner, and then took the train for Paris, where, at midnight, they bade adieu to the

Arbuckles, and then dashed on to Havre, arriving there at six o'clock on Sunday morning.

The ship had been hauled out of the dock, and was lying in the roadstead, in readiness to receive her weary crew. Near her lay the Josephine, in which the vice-principal, with the runaways, had arrived the day before. The day was literally one of rest; and though the chaplain held an afternoon service, most of the students slept all the forenoon and a portion of the afternoon. The excursion had been extended one week beyond the time at first intended, and Mr. Arbuckle had treated the travellers in their long journey in the most princely style.

On Monday morning, all hands, including the runaways, were assembled on the deck of the Young America. The conspirators appeared to be rather disconcerted and chop-fallen when they met their companions. For four weeks they had been confined to the vessel, hardly stepping foot on shore; and it is no exaggeration to say that they were heartily sick of the game of running away.

"How are you, Sir Thomas Perth?" said Lynch, when the leader of the runaways came over the rail.

"Shut up!" growled the commander of the Knights of the Golden Fleece, who was disgusted with his title. "You haven't seen the end of it yet."

"What next?" laughed Lynch.

"That's telling; but if you think our fellows are going to stand it to be imposed upon as we have been, you mistake us."

"Who has imposed upon you?"

"Who? Haven't we been shut up on board of

the Josephine for four weeks, while you were seeing the country? Haven't we been compelled to study up back lessons every day?"

"It was your own fault. You might have gone with us, if you hadn't run away," laughed Lynch.

"No matter; Lowington will find out what is what in a few days," added Perth, shaking his head; and it appeared to be almost certain that another conspiracy had been formed, in which the runaways were to revenge themselves for their defeat.

"What's up, Perth?" asked Lynch.

"We have been insulted, trodden under foot, tyrannized over by Fluxion. We won't stand it! That's all!"

"What's the use, Perth? Don't be a fool. I have tried it on, and I have made up my mind that a fellow has the best time when he minds the rules," continued Lynch; and such language from him was certainly rather remarkable.

"Are we to go back without seeing Paris or Switzerland," replied Perth, indignantly. "What did our folks send us over here for, if it wasn't to see the country?"

"You might have seen it, if you had done your duty. I suppose you know we are going off again for two or three weeks."

"Fluxion said we were to be deprived of all privileges for the rest of the season," snarled Perth.

"Perhaps Lowington will let you up, if you behave well."

"I don't care whether he lets us up or not."

"We are going to Germany and down the Rhine

in a few days. Perhaps you will be allowed to go with us," suggested Lynch.

"I want to see Paris and Switzerland; all our fellows do, and we are going to see them."

The voice of Mr. Lowington interrupted the conversation. He congratulated the students upon their safe return, and praised them for their excellent conduct on the trip, declaring that not a single instance of decidedly bad behavior had occurred during the journey. The students had conducted themselves in a manner highly creditable to their country and the squadron. He then referred to the case of Shuffles and the bag of gold, giving the whole truth in regard to the mysterious subject, as it had been derived from Mr. Fluxion and others. Of course the reformed student was not only acquitted of all blame, but was warmly commended for his conduct on board of the Josephine.

During the tour in Switzerland, Ellis and Shuffles had compared notes; and though the second lieutenant could not quite forgive the coxswain for knowing more than he did himself, they were reconciled, and became tolerably good friends.

"Young gentlemen, with this month commenced a new quarter; and I will now proceed to read the list of officers for the ensuing term," continued Mr. Lowington, as he took the book handed to him by one of the professors. "Agreeably to the rule adopted three months ago, those who have served as captain of either vessel are not again eligible to office. Therefore Captain Haven and Captain Kendall must retire; but the highest in rank of the past officers is entitled to the position of flag-officer."

These announcements created a strong sensation among the ship's companies, and many of them had their hearts in their throats from sheer anxiety. Many glanced at Shuffles, for all were confident that he had won a high rank.

"Of the three past officers now on board, Captain Paul Kendall has attained the highest rank, and for the next term he will be the commodore."

"Commodore Kendall, I greet you," said Gordon, grasping his hand.

"I congratulate you, Paul," added Captain Haven, taking the other hand of the commodore.

If these distinguished young officers were disturbed by a feeling of envy and jealousy, they were but human, and it was more creditable to subdue and overcome such an unworthy sentiment, than it was not to have it. Paul was one of the most popular among the students, and his elevation was greeted by three cheers, in which all but the runaways heartily joined. The shouts ceased, and a dead silence ensued; for the anxiety to know who was to command the ship for the next term was intense.

"The highest in rank — higher than either of the past officers — is Robert Shuffles, who is the captain of the ship for the next three months," added the principal.

The cheers which followed this announcement were tremendous; but it must also be added that a volley of hisses was mingled with them. Of course they came from the runaways, whom Captain Shuffles had so signally defeated in their stolen cruise.

"The second in rank is George W. Terrill, who succeeds to the command of the Josephine.

This name was also warmly cheered, and the list was continued to the end. Goodwin retained his place as first lieutenant of the ship, while Pelham rose to the corresponding rank in the consort. Perth, in spite of the black marks set against him for the runaway cruise, and other things, came out second master of the ship. His name, read in this connection, was like a bombshell thrown into the midst of the runaways; and while the changes incident to the new order of things were in progress, they were observed to be anxiously whispering among themselves. Their leader's promotion seemed to defeat their plan; but Perth soon found an opportunity to inform his brother knights that he was still with them.

"Young gentlemen," said Mr. Lowington, when he had completed the list, "we shall sail for home during the first week in November. In the spring we shall probably return, and go up the Baltic, spending the fall and winter in the Mediterranean. In order to complete my programme for the present season, I shall be obliged to give you two or three weeks more of vacation. The unexampled liberality of Mr. Arbuckle enables me to do this, and you will spend the most of this month on the Rhine and in Germany."

This announcement was heartily applauded, and the principal stated his arrangements. Everybody was satisfied except the runaways, and with them the main question was, whether or not they were to be left behind.

The new crew of the Josephine went on board of the consort, and the changes of positions and berths were made. Many were happy, and many were bitterly disappointed. Some, who had never worn a uniform before, appeared in one now; and some who were thus distinguished during the last term appeared in the garb of seamen. It was a day of excitement, but finally it subsided into the ordinary quiet of the vessels.

Before the return of the students from their tour, Mr. Fluxion had written to Harwich in regard to the bag of gold. By the aid of the list of passengers on the burnt steamer, the name and residence of the unfortunate German were discovered, and the money was forwarded to his heirs.

The runaways were fearfully demoralized, disconcerted, and angry, not only at the failure of their plan, but because they had been deprived of the pleasure of seeing Paris and Switzerland. The question of all questions with them was, whether they were to join their shipmates in the excursion into Germany, or be cooped up on board the ship for the next three weeks. Whether they went or not, and what those who did go saw and did on the journey, shall be told in DOWN THE RHINE, OR YOUNG AMERICA IN GERMANY.

NEW AND ATTRACTIVE PUBLICATIONS

OF

LEE & SHEPARD,

PUBLISHERS AND BOOKSELLERS,

BOSTON.

LEE, SHEPARD & DILLINGHAM, New York.

"A Grand Success."

THE AMERICAN GIRL ABROAD. By Miss ADELINE TRAFTON. Illustrated. $1.75.

"A bright, merry-hearted girl, 'off on a good time,' and she and her readers are decidedly of the opinion that the journey was a great success." — *Liberal Christian.*

"A delightful Book, original and enjoyable."

THE DOCTOR'S DAUGHTER. By SOPHIE MAY. Illustrated. 1.50.

"So lovable and so genuine that she takes one's heart by storm." — *New York Republican.*

"A Book every Girl will be delighted with."

SALLY WILLIAMS, THE MOUNTAIN GIRL. By MRS. EDNA D. CHENEY. Illustrated. $1.50.

"Mrs. Cheney's stories have all the charm of romance, and better than that, a power to do good by their wholesome unobtrusive teachings."

"Another of the Girlhood Series."

ONLY GIRLS. By MISS VIRGINIA F. TOWNSEND, Author of "Deering Farm," "Daryll's Gap," &c. Illustrated. $1.50.

Miss Townsend is a charming writer, and this one of her very best productions.

"One hundred and twenty Selections."
MISCELLANEOUS READINGS IN PROSE AND VERSE.
By Prof. L. B. Monroe. $1.50.

"Some of the best things of current literature may be found gathered here." — *Boston Advertiser.*

"For Social Amusements."
SOCIAL CHARADES AND PARLOR OPERAS. By M. T.
Calder, Author of "College Ned," &c. 16mo. Cloth, 75c; fancy bound, 60c.

"These charades and operas, prepared for private representation, have been received with great favor by those requiring exhibition pieces."

Underwood's American Authors.
HAND-BOOK OF ENGLISH LITERATURE.
Intended for the use of High Schools, as well as a Companion and Guide for Private Students, and for General Readers. (American Authors.) By F. H. Underwood, A. M. Crown 8vo. Cloth. $2.50.

It is confined to American authors, and includes the most prominent writers in the three periods which cover our entire national history.

Underwood's British Authors.
HAND-BOOK OF ENGLISH LITERATURE.
Intended for the use of High Schools, as well as a Companion and Guide for Private Students, and for General Readers. (British Authors.) By Francis H. Underwood, A. M. Crown 8vo. Cloth. $2.50.

Mr. Underwood's Biographical Notices, which precede the selections from prominent authors, are admirable in construction, gems of literary work, attractive and valuable.

The Young Voyagers again.
YOUNG AMERICA ABROAD.
By Oliver Optic. To be completed in 6 volumes. Illustrated. Per vol., $1.50.

1. UP THE BALTIC.
2. NORTHERN LANDS.
3. CROSS AND CRESCENT.

A library of romantic travel and adventure.

Illustration to
AMERICAN GIRL ABROAD.

By Oliver Optic.

THE YACHT CLUB SERIES. By OLIVER OPTIC. To be completed in 6 volumes. Illustrated. Per vol., $1.50.

    1. LITTLE BOBTAIL.
    2. THE YACHT CLUB. (In press.)

Each story complete in itself, and all in Oliver Optic's best vein.

By B. P. Shillaber.

PARTINGTONIAN PATCHWORK.

BLIFKINS THE MARTYR; OR, THE DOMESTIC TRIALS OF A MODEL HUSBAND.

THE MODERN SYNTAX: DR. SPOONER'S EXPERIENCE IN SEARCH OF THE DELECTABLE.

PARTINGTON PAPERS; STRIPPINGS OF THE WARM MILK OF HUMAN KINDNESS.

NEW AND OLD THINGS FROM AN UNPRETENDING INK-STAND. Humorous, Sentimental, Rhythmical. By B. P. SHILLABER (*Mrs. Partington*). 12mo. Cloth. Illustrated. $1.75.

The genial author of this volume has packed it full of bright and witty things.

By Elijah Kellogg.

THE WHISPERING PINE SERIES. By ELIJAH KELLOGG. To be completed in 6 volumes. Illustrated. Per vol., $1.25.

    1. THE SPARK OF GENIUS.
    2. THE SOPHOMORES OF RADCLIFFE.
    3. WINNING HIS SPURS.
    4. THE TURNING OF THE TIDE. (In press.)

Mr. Kellogg presents some admirable characters among his college boys, and every volume of this series is brimful of fun and adventure.

"Nothing better ever written."

THE PLEASANT COVE SERIES. By ELIJAH KELLOGG. To be completed in 6 volumes. Per vol., $1.25.

    1. ARTHUR BROWN, THE YOUNG CAPTAIN.
    2. THE YOUNG DELIVERERS.
    3. THE CRUISE OF THE CASCO.
    4. THE CHILD OF THE ISLAND GLEN.

"The Elm Island Stories," by this author, are deservedly popular. "The Pleasant Cove Series" deals with many of the same characters.

www.ingramcontent.com/pod-product-compliance
Lightning Source LLC
Chambersburg PA
CBHW031427230426
43668CB00007B/462